Alt Mo...

Bellevue

Siegessäule
(Victory Column)

Tiergarte

U-bahn

Strasse des 17. Juni

Tiergartenstrasse

Academy **Zoological**
of Arts **Garden**

Zoo

Kurfürsten

Kurfürsten

Käthe Kollwitz
Museum

Tauentzienstrasse

Nürnberger

Wittenberg

Musical Theatre
Berlin

Augsturger

Nollendorf

Bülow-
strasse

Spichern

Spichern-
strasse

Viktoria-
Luise

Hohenstaufenstrasse

Bundesallee

Potsdamer Strasse

All inquiries should be addressed to:
Barron's Educational Series, Inc.
250 Wireless Boulevard
Hauppauge, New York 11788
http://www.barronseduc.com

Library of Congress Catalog Card No. 99-80143

International Standard Book No. 0-7641-1255-4

Cover and Book Design Milton Glaser, Inc.
Illustrations Juan Suarez

PRINTED IN HONG KONG
9 8 7 6 5 4 3

GERMAN

AT A GLANCE

PHRASE BOOK & DICTIONARY FOR TRAVELERS

BY HENRY STRUTZ, M.A.
Formerly Associate Professor of Languages
State University of New York,
Alfred State College of Technology

Third Edition

BARRON'S

PREFACE

So you're taking a trip to one of the many fascinating countries of the world. That's exciting! This phrase book, part of Barron's popular *At a Glance* series, will prove an invaluable companion.

In these books we present the phrases and words that a traveler most often needs for a brief visit to a foreign country, where the customs and language are often different. Each phrase book highlights the terms particular to that country, in situations that the tourist is most likely to encounter. This new edition includes dialogues using words and expressions for each situation. Travel tips found throughout the book have been updated. With a specially developed key to pronunciation, this book will enable you to communicate quickly and confidently in colloquial terms. It is intended not only for beginners with no knowledge of the language, but also for those who have already studied it and have some familiarity with it.

Some of the unique features and highlights of the Barron's series are:

- Easy-to-follow *pronunciation keys* and complete phonetic transcriptions for all words and phrases in the book.
- Compact *dictionary* of commonly used words and phrases—built right into this phrase book so there's no need to carry a separate dictionary.
- Useful phrases for the *tourist*, grouped together by subject matter in a logical way so that the appropriate phrase is easy to locate when you need it.
- Special phrases for the *business traveler*, including banking terms, trade and contract negotiations, and secretarial services.
- Thorough section on *food and drink*, with comprehensive food terms you will find on menus.
- *Emergency phrases* and terms you hope you won't need: legal complications, medical problems, theft or loss of valuables, replacement or repair of watches, camera, etc.
- *Sightseeing itineraries*, with shopping tips, practical travel tips, and regional food specialties to help you get off the beaten path and into the countryside, to the small towns and cities, and to the neighboring areas.
- A *reference section* providing: important signs, conversion tables, holidays, abbreviations, telling time, days of the week, and months of the year.
- A brief *grammar section*, with the basic elements of the language quickly explained.

Enjoy your vacation and travel with confidence. You have a friend by your side.

CONTENTS

QUICK PRONUNCIATION GUIDE

German pronunciation is not difficult to learn because in German spelling letters consistently represent the same sounds. The phonetic transcriptions in this book are English approximations of the German sounds and should be read as you would normally read them in English. Capitalized syllables indicate stress and should be pronounced with more emphasis than lower-case letters in the same word.

VOWELS

Vowels may be long or short. A vowel is long when:

1. doubled (B<u>ee</u>thoven, B<u>oo</u>t, W<u>aa</u>ge)
2. followed by an <u>h</u> (Br<u>ah</u>ms, <u>Oh</u>m, F<u>eh</u>ler)
3. followed by a single consonant (Sch<u>u</u>bert, M<u>o</u>zart, T<u>o</u>n)

When followed by two or more consonants, a vowel is usually short, as in B<u>a</u>ch.

VOWELS	SOUND IN ENGLISH	EXAMPLE
a	aa (**long:** f<u>ar</u>)	**haben** (*H<u>AA</u>-ben*)
	ah (**short:** h<u>o</u>t)	**hatte** (*H<u>AH</u>-teh*)
ä	ay (**long:** w<u>ay</u>)	**Bäder** (*B<u>AY</u>-duh*)
	eh (**short:** m<u>e</u>t)	**Gepäck** (*geh-P<u>EH</u>K*)
e	ay (**long:** h<u>ay</u>)	**leben** (*L<u>AY</u>-ben*)
	eh (**short:** <u>e</u>nd)	**helfen** (*H<u>EH</u>L-fen*)
	e (**unstressed syllables** ending in -<u>n</u>, -<u>l</u>, and -<u>t</u>, like -<u>en</u> in hidden)	**lieben** (*LEE-b<u>en</u>*)
	uh (**unstressed syllables** ending in –<u>er</u>: mother)	**Ritter** (*RIT-<u>uh</u>*)
i	ee (**long:** fl<u>ee</u>t)	**Ihnen** (*<u>EE</u>-nen*)
	i (**short:** w<u>i</u>t)	**wissen** (*V<u>I</u>-ssen*)
ie	ee (always **long:** mart<u>i</u>ni)	**Liebe** (*L<u>EE</u>-beh*)
o	oh (**long:** r<u>o</u>se)	**Rose** (*R<u>OH</u>-zeh*)
	o (**short:** l<u>o</u>ve)	**komm** (*k<u>o</u>m*)

VOWELS	SOUND IN ENGLISH	EXAMPLE
ö	er (like h<u>er</u>, but sounded with the lips forward and rounded)	**hören** (*HER-en*)
u	oo (**long:** bl<u>oo</u>m)	**Schuh** (*shoo*)
	u (**short:** b<u>u</u>ll)	**Bulle** (*BUL-eh*)
ü	ew (like dr<u>ea</u>m, but with lips forward and rounded)	**Brüder** (*BREW-duh*)
y	ew (like the German <u>ü</u>)	**lyrisch** (*LEW-rish*)

DIPHTHONGS

LETTERS	SOUND IN ENGLISH	EXAMPLE
ai, ay	eye (<u>eye</u>)	**schreiben**
ei, ey		(*SHREYE-ben*)
au	ow (br<u>ow</u>n)	**braun** (*br<u>ow</u>n*)
äu, eu	oy (j<u>oy</u>)	**treu** (*tr<u>oy</u>*)

NOTE: German vowels are often described as "tense" or "pure." This means that they are more distinct and do not "glide" or fall into another sound. German is pronounced more vigorously and with sharper vowels than in English.

CONSONANTS

LETTERS	SOUND IN ENGLISH	EXAMPLE
f, h, k, l, m, n, p, t, x	usually pronounced as in English	
b	p (between vowel and consonant or at end of word: ma<u>p</u>)	**Lei<u>b</u>** (*leye<u>p</u>*)
	b (elsewhere as in English)	**<u>b</u>in** (*<u>b</u>in*)
c	ts (before <u>e</u>, <u>i</u>, <u>ö</u>, and <u>ä</u>: wi<u>ts</u>)	**Cäsar** (*<u>TS</u>AY-zahr*)
	k (elsewhere: <u>c</u>old)	**<u>C</u>oburg** (*<u>K</u>OH-boork*)

LETTERS	SOUND IN ENGLISH	EXAMPLE
ch	kh (strongly aspirated (breathy) sound: "<u>H</u>awaiian <u>h</u>ula-hula," or "<u>H</u>ugh")	**dur<u>ch</u>** (*door<u>kh</u>*)
chs	k (sometimes: <u>k</u>ind)	**La<u>chs</u>** (*lah<u>k</u>s*)
d	t (between vowel and consonant and at end of word: ca<u>t</u>)	**Hun<u>d</u>** (*hun<u>t</u>*)
	d (otherwise: <u>d</u>ollar)	**<u>D</u>ank** (*<u>d</u>ank*)
g	g (**hard**: <u>g</u>ods)	**<u>G</u>eist** (*<u>g</u>eyest*)
	k (at end of word: ba<u>ck</u>pack)	**Ta<u>g</u>** (*taa<u>k</u>*)
	kh (words ending in ig: <u>h</u>appy or whis<u>k</u>y)	**windi<u>g</u>** (*VIN-di<u>kh</u>*)
j	y (<u>y</u>ear)	**<u>J</u>ahr** (*<u>y</u>aar*)
qu	kv (<u>k</u>, followed by <u>v</u> as in <u>v</u>eal)	**<u>Qu</u>ell** (*<u>kv</u>ehl*)
r	r (preferably rolled in the throat, as in French, or trilled with the tip of the tongue, as in Spanish or Irish or Scottish brogues)	**<u>R</u>eise** (*<u>R</u>EYE-zeh*)
s	z (preceding vowels or between them: <u>z</u>ap)	**<u>S</u>ee** (*<u>z</u>ay*)
	sh (at beginning of syllable, before <u>p</u> and <u>t</u>: <u>sh</u>ell)	**<u>s</u>pielen** (*<u>SH</u>PEE-len*)
	s, ss (elsewhere: <u>s</u>ing)	**Wa<u>s</u> i<u>s</u>t da<u>s</u>?** (*vah<u>s</u> ist dah<u>s</u>*)
ß, ss	s, ss (always: <u>s</u>ell)	**wie<u>ß</u>** (*veye<u>s</u>*) **wi<u>ss</u>en** (*VI-<u>ss</u>en*)
sch	sh (<u>sh</u>ow)	**<u>sch</u>lau** (*<u>sh</u>low*)
tsch	ch (<u>ch</u>eer)	**Ki<u>tsch</u>** (*ki<u>ch</u>*)
tz	ts (wi<u>ts</u>)	**Ka<u>tz</u>e** (*KAH-<u>ts</u>eh*)
v	f (<u>f</u>ather)	**<u>V</u>ater** (*<u>F</u>AA-tuh*)
	v (words of non-Germanic origin: <u>v</u>iolin)	**<u>V</u>ioline** (*<u>v</u>ee-o-LEE-neh*)
w	v (<u>v</u>est)	**<u>W</u>asser** (*<u>V</u>ah-suh*)
z	ts (gri<u>ts</u>)	**<u>Z</u>eit** (*<u>ts</u>eyet*)

Travel Tips Most airlines allow passengers to select a seat location and the type of meal preferred at the time reservations are made. Especially on overseas flights, good choices mean the difference between a pleasant or a miserable trip. To get some sleep, choose a window seat well away from the galley (kitchen area). If you like to walk around, request an aisle seat. The reservations agent will know the type of aircraft being used and can help you pick the best location. Among the meal options are vegetarian, kosher, and low-fat, low-salt menus. If you have other special dietary needs, ask the reservations agent if those can be met. Be sure to confirm your seat assignment and meal choice when checking in for the flight.

THE BASICS FOR GETTING BY

MOST FREQUENTLY USED EXPRESSIONS

These are the phrases you'll use again and again, the fundamentals of conversation and social interaction. They will help you express what you want or need, and give you some simple formulas for making all kinds of requests and questions from just a few elements. Practice these until they become automatic.

Yes.	**Ja.**	*yaa*
No.	**Nein.**	*neyen*
Maybe.	**Vielleicht.**	*fee-LEYEKHT*
Never again!	**Nie wieder!**	*nee VEED-uh*
Please.	**Bitte.**	*BIT-eh*
Thank you.	**Danke.**	*DAHNK-eh*
Thank you very much.	**Vielen Dank.**	*FEEL-en dahnk*

NOTE: You will also hear variations like **besten Dank, schönen Dank,** and **danke vielmals**.

You're (very) welcome.	**Bitte (sehr).**	*BIT-eh (zayr)*
Don't mention it.	**Gern geschehen.**	*gehrn ge-SHAY-en*
That'll be fine.	**Schon gut.**	*shon goot*

Excuse me.	**Verziehung!**	*fehr-TSEYE-ung*
I'm sorry.	**Es tut mir leid.**	*ehs toot meer leyet*
Just a second.	**Augenblick mal!**	*OW-gen-blik maal*
That is (not) ___.	**Das ist (nicht) ___.**	*dahs ist (nikht) ___.*
■ right	**richtig**	*RIKHT-ikh*
■ important	**wichtig**	*VIKHT-ikh*
■ good	**gut**	*goot*
■ true	**wahr**	*vaar*
■ beautiful	**schön**	*shern*
■ necessary	**nötig**	*NERT-ikh*
It doesn't matter.	**Das macht nichts.**	*dahs mahkht nikhts*
It's all the same to me.	**Das ist mir gleich.**	*dahs ist meer gleyekh*
(The) gentleman, Mr.	**(Der) Herr.**	*(dehr) hehrr*
(The) lady, Mrs.	**(Die) Frau.**	*(dee) frow*
(The) girl, Miss.	**(Das) Fräulein.**	*(dahs) FROY-leyen*
Good morning.	**Guten Morgen.**	*GOOT-en MORG-en*
Good afternoon.	**Guten Tag.**	*GOOT-en taak*
Good evening.	**Guten Abend.**	*GOOT-en AAB-ent*
Good night.	**Gute Nacht.**	*GOOT-eh nahkht*
Good-bye.	**Auf Wiedersehen!**	*owf VEED-uh-zayen*

	Auf Wiederschauen!	*owf VEED-uh-show-en*
	Uf Wiederluege! (Swiss)	*uf VEED-uh-lueh-geh*
See you soon.	**Bis bald.**	*bis bahlt*
See you later.	**Bis später.**	*bis SHPAYT-uh*
Till tomorrow.	**Bis morgen.**	*bis MOR-gen*
I speak little German.	**Ich spreche wenig Deutsch.**	*ikh SHPREHKH-eh VAYN-ikh doytch*
Do you speak English?	**Sprechen Sie Englisch?**	*SHPREHKH-eh zee EHNG-lish*
You're speaking too fast.	**Sie sprechen zu schnell.**	*zee SHPREKH-en tsoo shnell*
Please speak more slowly.	**Bitte sprechen Sie langsamer!**	*BIT-eh SHPREKH-en zee LAHNG-zaam-uh*
Please repeat.	**Wiederholen Sie bitte!**	*VEED-uh-hoh-len zee BIT-eh*
Do you understand?	**Verstehen Sie?**	*fehr-SHTAY-en zee*
I (don't) understand.	**Ich verstehe (nicht).**	*ikh fehr-SHTAY-eh (nikht)*
What was that you said?	**Wie bitte?**	*vee BIT-eh*
What does that mean?	**Was bedeutet das?**	*vahss be-DOYT-et dahs*
How do you say that in German?	**Wie heißt das auf deutsch?**	*Vee heyest dahs owf doytch*

Do you know ____?	**Wissen Sie ____?**	*VISS-en zee*
I don't know.	**Ich weiß nicht.**	*ikh veyess nikht*
What is that?	**Was ist das?**	*vahs ist dahs*
Is that possible?	**Ist das möglich?**	*ist dahs MERG-likh*
That is (im)possible.	**Das ist (un)möglich.**	*dahs ist (un)-MERG-likh*
I am an American. (-*in* for women)	**Ich bin Amerikaner (Amerikanerin).**	*ikh bin aa-meh-ri-KAAN-uh (aa-meh-ri-KAAN-uh-rin)*
I am English.	**Ich bin Engländer (Engländerin).**	*ikh bin EHNG-lehnd-uh (EHNG-lehnd-uh-rin)*
I am Canadian.	**Ich bin Kanadier (Kanadierin).**	*ikh bin kah-NAA-diuh (kah-NAA-diuh-rin)*
I am Australian.	**Ich bin Australier (Australierin).**	*ikh bin ow-STRAA-liuh (ow-STRAA-liuh-rin)*
My name is ____.	**Ich heiße ____.**	*ikh HEYESS-eh*
What's your name?	**Wie heißen Sie?**	*vee HEYESS-en zee*
How are you? (How do you do?)	**Wie geht es Ihnen?**	*vee gayt ehs EEN-en*
How are things?	**Wie geht's?**	*vee gayts*
Fine, thank you. And you?	**Gut, danke. Und Ihnen?**	*goot DAHNK-eh unt EEN-en*

How much does that cost?	**Wieviel kostet das?**	*VEE-feel KOST-et dahs*
I'm ____.	**Ich bin ____.**	*ikh bin*
■ hungry	**hungrig**	*HUNG-rikh*
■ thirsty	**durstig**	*DOORST-ikh*
■ tired	**müde**	*MEWD-eh*
■ sick	**krank**	*krahnk*
Please bring me ____.	**Bitte bringen Sie mir ____.**	*BIT-eh BRING-en zee meer*
■ a glass of water (beer, hard liquor)	**ein Glas Wasser (Bier, Schnaps)**	*eyen glaass VAHSS-uh (beer, shnahps)*
Please show me the room.	**Bitte zeigen Sie mir das Zimmer.**	*BIT-eh TSEYEG-en zee meer dahs TSIM-uh*
I don't want that.	**Das will ich nicht.**	*dahs vill ikh nikht*
Think it over.	**Überlegen Sie sich's mal.**	*EW-behr-lay-gen zee zikhs maal*

QUESTIONS

Why?	**Warum?**	*vah-RUM*
When?	**Wann?**	*vahn*
Where?	**Wo?**	*voh*
What?	**Was?**	*vahs*
How?	**Wie?**	*vee*
Who?	**Wer?**	*vayr*

PROBLEMS, PROBLEMS, PROBLEMS (EMERGENCIES)

I'm looking for ____.	**Ich suche ____.**	*ikh ZOOKH-eh*
■ my hotel	**mein Hotel**	*meyen ho-TEL*
■ my friends	**meine Freunde**	*MEYEN-eh FROYND-eh*
■ my suitcase	**meinen Koffer**	*MEYEN-en KOF-uh*
■ the railroad station	**den Bahnhof**	*dayn BAAN-hohf*
■ my husband	**meinen Mann**	*MEYEN-en mahn*
■ my wife	**meine Frau**	*MEYEN-eh frow*
■ my child	**mein Kind**	*meyen kint*
■ my bus	**meinen Bus**	*MEYEN-en bus*
I'm lost. (on foot)	**Ich habe mich verlaufen.**	*ikh HAAB-en mikh fehr-LOWF-en*
I'm lost. (driving)	**Ich habe mich verfahren.**	*ikh HAAB-eh mikh fehr-FAAR-en*
Can you help me please?	**Können Sie mir bitte helfen?**	*KERN-en zee meer BIT-eh HELF-en*
Does anyone here speak English?	**Spricht hier jemand Englisch?**	*shprikht heer YAY-mahnt EHNG-lish*
Where is the American (British, Canadian, Australian) Consulate?	**Wo ist das amerikanische (britische, kanadische, australische) Konsulat?**	*voh ist dahs aa-meh-ri-KAAN-ish-eh (BRIT-ish-eh, kah-NAA-dish-eh, ow-STRAA-lish-eh) kon-zoo-LAAT*
Which way do I go?	**In welche Richtung soll ich gehen?**	*in VELKH-eh RIKHT-ung zol ikh GAY-en*

■ to the left	**links**	*links*
■ to the right	**rechts**	*rehkhts*
■ straight ahead	**geradeaus**	*ge-RAAD-eh-OWS*

____ is stolen.	**____ ist gestohlen.**	*ist ge-SHTOHL-en*
■ My car	**mein Wagen**	*meyen VAAG-en*
■ My briefcase	**meine Aktentasche**	*MEYEN-eh AHKT-en-tahsh-eh*
■ My jewels	**mein Schmuck**	*meyen shmuk*
■ My money	**mein Geld**	*meyen gelt*
■ My purse	**meine Handtasche**	*MEYEN-eh HAHNT-tahsh-eh*
■ My suitcase	**mein Koffer**	*meyen KOF-uh*
■ My ticket	**meine Fahrkarte**	*MEYEN-eh FAAR-kahrt-eh*
■ My wallet	**meine Geldbörse**	*MEYEN-eh GELT-berz-eh*
■ My watch	**meine Uhr**	*MEYEN-eh oor*

| Call the police! | **Rufen Sie die Polizei!** | *ROOF-en zee dee pol-its-EYE* |

Where is ____?	**Wo ist ____?**	*voh ist*
■ the dining room	**das Esszimmer**	*dahs ESS-tsim-uh*
■ the elevator	**der Aufzug**	*dehr OWF-tsug*
■ the entrance	**der Eingang**	*dehr EYEN-gahng*
■ the highway entrance	**die Einfahrt**	*dee EYEN-faart*
■ the exit	**der Ausgang**	*dehr OWS-gahng*
■ the highway exit	**die Ausfahrt**	*dee OWS-faart*
■ the toilet	**die Toilette**	*dee toy-LET-eh*
■ the men's room	**die Herrentoilette**	*dee HEHR-en-toy-let-eh*
■ the ladies' room	**die Damentoilette**	*dee DAAM-en-toy-let-eh*

| I want to go to the American (British, Australian, Canadian) Consulate. | **Ich will zum amerikanischen (britischen, australischen, kanadischen) Konsulat.** | *ikh vil tsoom aa-mehr-i-KAAN-ish-en (BRIT-ish-en, ows-TRAAL-ish-en, kah-NAAD-ish-en) kon-zoo-LAAT* |

EXCLAMATIONS, IDIOMS, AND EXPLETIVES

I would like ____.	**Ich möchte ____.**	*ikh MERKH-teh*
I need ____ .	**Ich brauche ____.**	*ikh BROWKH-eh*
■ information	**Auskunft**	*OWSS-kunft*
■ help	**Hilfe**	*HILF-eh*
■ time	**Zeit**	*tseyet*
■ money	**Geld**	*gehlt*
That is ____.	**Das ist ____.**	*dahs ist*
■ wonderful	**wunderbar**	*VUND-uh-baar*
■ excellent	**ausgezeichnet**	*OWSS-ge-tseyekh-net*
■ beautiful	**schön**	*shern*
■ splendid	**herrlich**	*HEHR-likh*
■ disgusting	**ekelhaft**	*AYK-el-hahft*
■ terrible	**schrecklich**	*SHREK-likh*
■ awful	**scheußlich**	*SHOYSS-likh*
Hurry up!	**Machen Sie schnell!**	*MAHKH-en zee shnel*
Good Heavens!	**Ach du lieber!**	*akh doo LEEB-uh*
What's the matter?	**Was ist los?**	*vahs ist lohs*
Watch out! Be	**Passen Sie auf!**	*PAHSS-en-zee*

careful!	**Vorsicht!**	*owf FOR-zikht*
Danger!	**Lebensgefahr!**	*LAYB-ens-ge-faar*
Attention!	**Achtung!**	*AKHT-ung*
That's enough!	**Das ist genug!**	*dahs ist ge-NUK*
Of course!	**Selbstverständlich!**	*ZEHLPST-fehr-shtehnd-likh*
That isn't so.	**Das stimmt nicht.**	*dahs shtimt nikht*
You don't say!	**Was Sie nicht sagen!**	*vahs zee nikht ZAAG-en*
Fire!	**Feuer!**	*FOY-uh*
Quiet!	**Ruhe!**	*ROO-eh*
Good luck!	**Viel Glück!**	*feel glewk*
Have a good trip!	**Gute Reise!**	*GOOT-eh REYEZ-eh*

NUMBERS

You will use numbers as soon as you get to Germany, either to change money at the airport, tell the customs official how long you're staying, or pay for your taxi into town. The following lists supply the cardinal and ordinal numbers and some other helpful quantities.

CARDINAL NUMBERS

0	**null**	*nul*
1	**eins**	*eyenss*

2	**zwei, zwo** (over the telephone)	*tsveye, tsvoh*
3	**drei**	*dreye*
4	**vier**	*feer*
5	**fünf**	*fewnf*
6	**sechs**	*zehks*
7	**sieben**	*ZEEB-en*
8	**acht**	*ahkht*
9	**neun**	*noyn*
10	**zehn**	*tsayn*
11	**elf**	*elf*
12	**zwölf**	*tsverlf*
13	**dreizehn**	*DREYE-tsayn*
14	**vierzehn**	*FEER-tsayn*
15	**fünfzehn**	*FEWNF-tsayn*
16	**sechzehn**	*ZEHKH-tsayn*
17	**siebzehn**	*ZEEP-tsayn*
18	**achtzehn**	*AHKHT-tsayn*
19	**neunzehn**	*NOYN-tsayn*
20	**zwanzig**	*TSVAHN-tsikh*
21	**einundzwanzig**	*EYEN-unt-tsvahn-tsikh*
22	**zweiundzwanzig**	*TSVEYE-unt-tsvahn-tsikh*
23	**dreiundzwanzig**	*DREYE-unt-tsvahn-tsikh*
24	**vierundzwanzig**	*FEER-unt-tsvahn-tsikh*

25	**fünfundzwanzig**	*FEWNF-unt-tsvahn-tsikh*
26	**sechsundzwanzig**	*ZEHKS-unt-tsvahn-tsikh*
27	**siebenundzwanzig**	*ZEEB-en-unt-tsvahn-tsikh*
28	**achtundzwanzig**	*AHKHT-unt-tsvahn-tsikh*
29	**neunundzwanzig**	*NOYN-unt-tsvahn-tsikh*
30	**dreißig**	*DREYESS-ikh*
31	**einunddreißig**	*EYEN-unt-dreyess-ikh*
40	**vierzig**	*FEER-tsikh*
41	**einundvierzig**	*EYEN-unt-feer-tsikh*
50	**fünfzig**	*FEWNF-tsikh*
60	**sechzig**	*ZEHKH-tsikh*
70	**siebzig**	*ZEEP-tsikh*
80	**achtzig**	*AHKH-tsikh*
90	**neunzig**	*NOYN-tsikh*
100	**(ein)hundert**	*(eyen)HUN-dehrt*
101	**hunderteins**	*HUN-dehrt-eyenss*
102	**hundertzwei**	*HUN-dehrt-tsveye*
200	**zweihundert**	*TSVEYE-hun-dehrt*
300	**dreihundert**	*DREYE-hun-dehrt*
400	**vierhundert**	*FEER-hun-dehrt*
500	**fünfhundert**	*FEWNF-hun-derht*
600	**sechshundert**	*ZEHKS-hun-derht*

700	**siebenhundert**	*ZEEB-en-hun-derht*
800	**achthundert**	*AHKHT-hun-derht*
900	**neunhundert**	*NOYN-hun-derht*
1000	**(ein)tausend**	*(eyen)TOW-zehnt*
2000	**zweitausend**	*TSVEYE-tow-zehnt*
1,000,000	**eine Million**	*EYEN-eh mil-YOHN*
1,000,000,000	**eine Milliarde**	*EYEN-eh mil-YAHRD-eh*

ORDINAL NUMBERS

first	**erst-**	*ayrst*
second	**zweit-**	*tsveyet*
third	**dritt-**	*drit*
fourth	**viert-**	*feert*
fifth	**fünft-**	*fewnft*
sixth	**sechst-**	*zehkst*
seventh	**siebt-**	*zeept*
eighth	**acht-**	*ahkht*
ninth	**neunt-**	*noynt*
tenth	**zehnt-**	*tsaynt*

In writing, ordinals are abbreviated by placing a period after the number.

| the first day | **der erste Tag (der 1. Tag)** | *dehr AYRST-eh taak* |
| for the second time | **zum zweiten Mal (zum 2. Mal)** | *tsoom TSVEYET-en maal* |

| once | **einmal** | *EYEN-maal* |
| twice | **zweimal** | *TSVEYE-maal* |

IDIOMS, PROVERBS, SAYINGS

Idioms, proverbs, and sayings express the essence of a language, giving it its own special character. As a traveler in a German-speaking country, you probably will not need or want to use these expressions often yourself, but it can add to the pleasure of your trip if you can recognize them if you see them or hear them. You will find a number of them scattered through this book, each group of them relating to the particular section it is in. Here are a few for you to reflect on as you set out on your trip.

Everything's hard at first.	**Aller Anfang ist schwer.**	*AH-luh AHN-fahng ist shvayuh*
All's well that ends well.	**Ende gut, alles gut.**	*EHND-eh goot AH-les goot*
Whoever takes a trip will have stories to tell.	**Wenn einer eine Reise macht, so kann er 'was erzählen.**	*vehn EYEN-uh EYEN-eh REYEZ-eh mahkht zoh kahn ehr vahs ehr-TSAY-len*

Travel Tips

Packing for a trip abroad is an art. Porters may sometimes be hard to find, so never take more luggage than you can handle alone. Wrap shampoo, mouthwash, or anything that can leak in recycled plastic bags or put them in small plastic bottles. To prevent wrinkling, pack suits, dresses, etc. in dry cleaning bags. To make room for new purchases, discard well-worn underwear, pajamas, etc. before heading home. Before closing your bag, mentally dress and groom yourself and take all your medications, as a checklist that nothing is forgotten.

WHEN YOU ARRIVE

PASSPORT AND CUSTOMS

Germany's borders have changed dramatically many times in the twentieth century. In 1990 the German Democratic Republic (East Germany), created in 1949, ceased to exist. Despite attempts to diminish the flow of immigrants, tourists will have little difficulty entering Germany for stays of less than three months. For longer stays, or if you plan to seek employment, a visa is required. Some years ago a survey of major airports said of Frankfurt's international airport, "You could bring in an elephant." But we don't recommend it! In recent years, security has been tightened at airports everywhere. Don't rule out the possibility of a spot check of your luggage. In general, however, border formalities in Germany, Austria, and Switzerland can be so informal that you will have to ask for a souvenir stamp in your passport if you want one.

Here is my passport.	**Hier ist mein Pass.** *heer ist meyen pahss*
Would you please stamp my passport?	**Würden Sie mir bitte meinen Pass stempeln?** *VEWRD-en zee meer BIT-eh MEYEN-ehn pahss SHTEMP-eln*
I will not be working in Europe.	**In Europa werde ich nicht arbeiten.** *In OY-roh-paa VEHRD-eh ikh nikht AHR-beye-ten*
I'm traveling on vacation.	**Ich mache eine Ferienreise.** *ikh MAHKH-eh EYEN-eh FAIR-yen-reye-zeh*
I'm on a business trip.	**Ich bin auf Geschäfts reise hier.** *ikh bin owf geh-SHEHFTS reye-zeh heer*

| I'm visiting my relatives. | **Ich besuche meine Verwandten.** *ikh be-ZOOKH-eh MEYEN-eh fehr-VAHNT-en* |
| I'm just passing through. | **Ich bin nur auf der Durchreise.** *ikh bin noor owf dehr DOORKH-reye-zeh* |

I'll be staying ____. **Ich bleibe ____.** *ikh BLEYEB-eh*

- a few days **einige Tage** *EYEN-ig-eh TAAG-eh*
- a few weeks **einige Wochen** *EYEN-ig-eh VOKH-ehn*
- sixty days **sechzig Tage** *ZEKH-tsikh TAAG-eh*
- a month **einen Monat** *EYEN-en MOHN-aat*

I'm traveling ____. **Ich reise ____.** *ikh REYE-zeh*

- alone **allein** *ah-LEYEN*
- with my family **mit meiner Familie** *mit MEYEN-uh fah-MEEL-yeh*
- with my wife **mit meiner Frau** *mit MEYEN-uh frow*
- with my husband **mit meinem Mann** *mit MEYEN-em mahn*

The following items can be brought duty-free:

DUTY-FREE ITEMS	INTO GERMANY OR AUSTRIA	INTO SWITZERLAND
cigarettes	200 *or*	400 *or*
cigars	50 *or*	100 *or*
smoking tobacco	250 grams	500 grams
alcohol (spirits)	1 liter	1 liter
wine	2 liters	2 liters
perfume	50 grams	
other products	total value of DM 250	total value of 100 Sw.Fr.

There are two sections for customs clearance on entering Germany. One, indicated by a green arrow, is for those with nothing to declare (**Anmeldefreie Waren**); a red arrow is for those with goods to declare (**Anmeldepflichtige Waren**).

ANMELDEFREIE WAREN	ANMELDEPFLICHTIGE WAREN

Oscar Wilde is said to have told American customs officials, "I have nothing to declare but my genius." You probably will want to say simply:

I have nothing to declare.	**Ich habe nichts zu verzollen.** *ikh HAAB-eh nikhts tsoo fehr-TSOL-en*
Here is my luggage.	**Hier ist mein Gepäck.** *heer ist meyen geh-PEHK*
Do I have to pay duty on this?	**Ist dies zollpflichtig?** *ist dees TSOL-pflikh-tikh*
These are gifts.	**Das sind Geschenke.** *dahs zint ge-SHENK-eh*

This is for my personal use.	**Das ist für meinen persönlichen Gebrauch.** *dahs ist fewr MEYEN-en pehr-ZERN-likh-en ge-BROWKH*
I only have two cartons of cigarettes.	**Ich habe nur zwei Stangen Zigaretten.** *ikh HAAB-eh noor tsveye SHTAHNG-en tsee-gahr-EHT-en*
And a few bottles of alcohol.	**Und einige Flaschen Schnaps.** *unt EYEN-ig-eh FLAHSH-en shnaps*
May I close the bag now?	**Darf ich den Koffer (die Tasche) jetzt zumachen?** *dahrf ikh dayn KOF-uh (dee TASH-eh) yetst TSOO-mahkh-en*

BAGGAGE AND PORTERS

With porters scarce at European airports, you'll probably do better using the baggage carts provided in the baggage claim area. You can usually wheel them through customs right to the street.

I'm looking for the luggage carts.	**Ich suche die Kofferkulis.** *ikh ZOOKH-eh dee KOF-uh-koo-lees*
I need a porter.	**Ich brauche einen Gepäckträger.** *ikh BROWKH-eh EYEN-en geh-PEHK-trayg-uh*
That's my (our) luggage.	**Das ist mein (unser) Gepäck.** *dahs ist meyen (UNZ-uh) geh-PEHK*
Accompany us to the taxi (the bus, the railroad entrance).	**Begleiten Sie uns zum Taxi (Bus, Eisenbahneingang).** *beh-GLEYET-en zee uns tsoom TAHKS-ee (bus, EYEZ-en-baan-eyen-gahng)*

Be careful with that one!	**Vorsicht damit!** *FOR-zikht dah-MIT*
A suitcase is missing.	**Ein Koffer fehlt.** *eyen KOF-uh faylt*
Where is the lost and found?	**Wo ist das Fundbüro?** *voh ist dahs FUNT-bew-roh*
I'll carry this one myself.	**Diesen trag ich selber.** *DEEZ-en traag ikh ZELB-uh*
How much do I owe you?	**Wieviel macht das?** *VEE-feel mahkht dahs*
Here's a little something for you.	**Hier haben Sie ein kleines Trink-geld.** *heer HAAB-en zee eyen KLEYEN-es TRINK-gelt*
Thank you. Goodbye.	**Danke. Auf Wiedersehen.** *DAHNK-eh owf VEED-uh-zayen*

If you wish to rent a car upon arrival, see page 75. For taxi travel phrases, see page 50. All major terminals have English-speaking tourist information and hotel reservation services. But if for any reason they should be closed, the following phrases may be useful:

Can you recommend a good (inexpensive) hotel to me?	**Können Sie mir ein gutes (preiswertes) Hotel empfehlen?** *KERN-en zee meer eyen GOOT-es (PREYESS-vayr-tes) hoh-TEL emp-FAYL-en*
Take me to the main railroad station.	**Fahren Sie mich zum Hauptbahn-hof!** *FAAR-en zee mikh tsoom HOWPT-baan-hohf*

In both large and small towns, a hotel or many hotels are almost invariably located near the railroad station. Once there, you can make your choice from several.

All commercial airports have airport–railway terminal connections (either by train or bus). You can go directly downtown from the airport and even make connections with the entire railway system.

Travel Tips Leave some space in your suitcase for small souvenirs that you buy on your trip. Otherwise, pack a fold-up tote bag to be filled and carried separately on your return. For large items, especially those bought early on a long journey, consider letting the merchant ship the packages home. Of course, be sure to get a receipt and try to insure the item.

BANKING AND MONEY MATTERS

The exchange rate will probably be less favorable at your hotel than at a bank. Since banks often have branches at major airports and stations, you may wish to change money there. Besides banks, you will also find small currency exchange offices called **Wechselstuben**. These and banks that provide the exchange services post a sign, **Geldwechsel** (money exchange). Banking hours are generally from 8:30 A.M. to 12:30 P.M. and 1:30 to 4 P.M., Monday through Friday (until 5:30 P.M. on Thursday). **Wechselstuben** are sometimes open outside regular banking hours. You may want to comparison shop, since exchange rates can vary from bank to bank.

Euro coins and bills will be in general circulation in Germany and Austria as of January 1, 2002. The Deutsche Mark (D-Mark) will still be legal tender for two months thereafter, till March 1, 2002, when the mark and the Austrian schilling will be history and of interest only to collectors.

There are 100 **Pfennig** *(PFEHN-ikh)* to a mark and a proverb proclaims:

Whoever doesn't honor the penny isn't worthy of the dollar.	**Wer den Pfennig nicht ehrt ist des Thalers nicht wert.** *vayr dayn PFEHN-ikh nikht ayrt ist dehs TAA-lehrs nikht vayrt*

Despite the proverb, Germans are not much interested in the infrequently seen 1- and 2-penny coins. Other coins of 5, 10, and 50 pfennigs exist. German banknotes come in denominations of 5, 10, 20, 50, 100, 500, and 1,000 marks.

Austrian schillings (abbreviated *S*) are divided into 100 **Groschen** *(GRO-shen)*. There are coins of 2, 5, 10, and 50 **Groschen**. The **Schilling** *(SHIL-ing)* comes in coins of 1, 5, 10, and 25 schillings and banknotes of 20, 50, 100, 500, and 1,000 schillings.

Swiss francs, abbreviated *Fr.*, are divided into 100 **Rappen** *(RAHP-en)*, abbreviated *Rp*. Look carefully at coins of 5, 10, 20, and 50 Rappen, and of 1, 2, and 5 francs. Anyone used to

American coins will find their sizes confusing. Present your passport with the travelers' checks you wish to cash.

Euro banknotes are printed in denominations of 5, 10, 20, 50, 100, 200, and 500 euros. One euro is divided into 100 Cent *(tsehnt)* and there are coins of 1, 2, 5, 10, 20, and 50 cents. There are also 1 and 2 euro coins.

Banks will supply the current rate of exchange, and the daily fluctuations are recorded in the newspapers. The following charts are for your use to record foreign currency values in relation to your own currency.

GERMAN DM	YOUR CURRENCY	AUSTRIAN S	YOUR CURRENCY	SWISS FR	YOUR CURRENCY
1	____	1	____	1	____
5	____	5	____	5	____
10	____	10	____	10	____
20	____	20	____	20	____
50	____	50	____	50	____
100	____	100	____	100	____

EXCHANGING MONEY

I want to change ____. | **Ich möchte ____ wechseln.** *ikh MERKH-teh ____ VEHK-seln*

■ money | **Geld** *gehlt*

■ dollars (pounds) | **Dollar (Pfund)** *DO-lahr (pfunt)*

■ travelers' checks | **Reiseschecks** *REYEZ-eh-shehks*

What is the exchange rate for dollars (pounds, euros)? | **Wie ist der Wechselkurs für Dollar (Pfund, Euro)?** *vee ist dehr VEHK-sel-koors fewr DO-lahr (pfunt, OY-roh)*

What commission do you charge? | **Welche Gebühr erheben Sie?** *VEHL-kheh geh-BEWR ehr-HAY-ben zee?*

Give me large (small) bills. | **Geben Sie mir große (kleine) Scheine.** *GAYB-en zee meer GROHSS-eh (KLEYEN-eh) SHEYEN-eh*

I also need some change.	**Ich brauche auch etwas Kleingeld.** *ikh BROWKH-eh owkh ET-vahs KLEYEN-gelt*
I think you made a mistake.	**Ich glaube, Sie haben sich verrechnet.** *ikh GLOWB-eh zee HAAB-en zikh fehr-REKH-net*
I want to cash a personal check.	**Ich möchte einen Barscheck einlösen.** *ikh MERKHT-eh EYEN-eh BAAR-shehk EYEN-ler-zen*
How long will it take to clear?	**Wie lange wird es für die Überprüfung dauern?** *vee LAHNG-eh veert ehs fewr dee EWB-uh-prew-fung DOW-ern*
Shall I sign (endorse) now?	**Soll ich jetzt unterschreiben (indossieren)?** *zol ikh yetst UNT-uh-shreye-ben (indoss-EER-en)*
Is it possible for foreigners to have an account here?	**Ist es Ausländern möglich, hier ein Konto zu haben?** *ist ehs OWSS-lehn-dehrn MERG-likh heer eyen KONT-oh tsoo HAAB-en*

CREDIT CARDS

Credit cards are not very popular in Germany. Germans usually carry large amounts of cash. Large stores, hotels, and restaurants, however, do accept credit cards or travelers' checks.

I want to use my credit card.	**Ich möchte meine Kreditkarte benutzen.** *ikh MERKHT-eh MEYEN-eh kray-DIT-kaar-teh beh-NUTS-en*
Has my letter of credit arrived?	**Ist mein Kreditbrief schon angekommen?** *ist meyen kray-DIT-breef shon AHN-ge-ko-men*

Will you accept this credit card?	**Nehmen Sie diese Kreditkarte an?** *NAYM-en zee DEEZ-eh kray-DIT-kaar-teh ahn*	
I don't have another credit card.	**Ich habe keine andere Kredit-karte.** *ikh HAAB-eh KEYEN-eh AHND-eh-reh kray-DIT-kaar-teh*	
This is the only one.	**Diese ist die einzige.** *DEEZ-eh ist dee EYENTS-ig-eh*	
I don't have a credit card.	**Ich habe keine Kreditkarte.** *ikh HAAB-eh KEYEN-eh kray-DIT-kaar-teh*	

BUSINESS AND BANKING TERMS

amount	**Betrag**	*beh-TRAAK*
bad	**ungedeckt**	*UN-geh-dehkt*
banker	**Bankier**	*bahng-KYAY*
bill	**Geldschein**	*GEHLT-sheyen*
borrow (to)	**leihen**	*LEYE-en*
cashier	**Kassierer**	*kah-SEER-uh*
capital	**Kapital**	*kah-pi-TAAL*
cashier's office	**Kasse**	*KAHS-eh*
checkbook	**Scheckbuch**	*SHEHK-bookh*
endorse (to)	**indossieren**	*in-do-SEER-en*
income	**Einkommen**	*EYEN-kom-en*
interest rate	**Zinsen**	*TSIN-zen*
investment	**Anlage**	*AHN-laag-en*
lend (to)	**leihen**	*LEYE-en*

letter of credit	**Kreditbrief**	*kray-DIT-breef*
loss	**Verlust**	*fehr-LUST*
make change (to)	**wechseln**	*VEHKS-ehln*
mortgage	**Hypothek**	*hew-poh-TAYK*
open an account (to)	**ein Konto eröffnen**	*eyen KONT-oh ehr-ERF-nen*
poster	**Plakat**	*PLAH-kat*
premium	**Prämie**	*PRAYM-yeh*
profit	**Gewinn**	*geh-VIN*
secretary	**Sekretärin**	*zeh-kreh-TEHR-in*
safe	**Geldschrank**	*GEHLT-shrahnk*
signature	**Unterschrift**	*UNT-uh-shrift*
window	**Schalter**	*SHAHLT-uh*

TIPPING

In ultraexpensive, overstaffed hotels and restaurants where your glass will immediately be refilled after the smallest sip, many a hand will be out looking for a gratuity. In the other 95% of establishments, practice varies. Since service charges are usually included, tipping is largely a matter of personal preference. Many Europeans leave small change (rounding off the bill). Others leave nothing.

Restaurant	In Germany and Austria a service charge of 10–15% is usually included. In Switzerland the service charge is invariably included.
Waiter	Leave small change—more if you wish.
Checkroom/ Washroom Attendants	50 pfennigs in Germany, 5–10 schillings in Austria, 1 Swiss franc in Switzerland.
Taxi Drivers	8–15% (usually included in Switzerland).
Hairdressers/ Barbers	About 10% (included in Switzerland).
Tour Guides	1 German mark.
Hotels	A service charge of 10–15% is usually included in Germany and Austria, and always in Switzerland.
Porters/Bellboys/ Doormen	1–5 German marks or Swiss francs and 5–20 Austrian schillings, depending on frequency of services performed.
Room Service	1 German mark.

Maids	About 10 German marks or Swiss francs, or 50 Austrian schillings per week.
Restroom Attendant	30–50 pfennigs in Germany.

Coffeehouses in Austria often do not include the service charge. Leave 10% of the bill there and anyplace else where the service charge is not included.

AT THE HOTEL

If you are unfamiliar with the city to which you are going, you'll probably find it best to make a hotel reservation in advance from home. You'll also find that some terminals have reservation desks, at which you may be able to reserve a room. Lastly, if you are unable to locate a hotel once you arrive, go to the tourist information office; someone there will be able to speak English and will help you in locating a suitable hotel.

GETTING TO YOUR HOTEL

I'm looking for the ____ hotel.	**Ich suche das ____ Hotel.** *ikh ZOOKH-eh dahs____ hoh-TEL*
Is it near (far)?	**Ist es in der Nähe (weit)?** *ist ehs in dehr NAY-eh (veyet)*
Do I have to take a taxi?	**Muss ich mit einem Taxi fahren?** *muss ikh mit EYEN-em TAHKS-ee FAAR-en*
Or can I take a bus?	**Oder kann ich einen Bus nehmen?** *OHD-uh kahn ikh EYEN-en bus NAYM-en*
What is the best way for me to get there?	**Wie fahre ich am besten dorthin?** *vee FAAR-eh ikh am BEST-en DORT-hin*
Do I have to take a bus at the railroad station?	**Muss ich einen Bus am Bahnhof nehmen?** *muss ikh EYEN-en bus ahm BAAN-hohf NAYM-en*
Or can I walk?	**Oder kann ich zu Fuß gehen?** *OHD-uh kahn ikh tsoo foos GAY-en*

| Where is the bus stop (taxi stand)? | **Wo ist die Bushaltestelle (der Taxistand)?** *voh ist dee BUS-hahlteh-shtehl-eh (dehr TAHK-see-shtahnt)* |
| How much is the fare? | **Was kostet die Fahrt?** *vahs KOST-et dee faart* |

TYPES OF HOTELS

As Empress Dowager of Germany, Viktoria Adelaide (eldest daughter of England's Queen Victoria and mother of the Kaiser) resided at Kronberg Castle, site of a much-publicized post–World War II robbery of royal jewels. You can stay there today—for a price. Other castle hotels are much less expensive and offer a wide range of accommodations.

Germany has numerous castle hotels. Several are on the **Märchenstraße** (Fairy Tale Road), and one even claims to be the one where Sleeping Beauty and her court fell asleep.

You will be able to find clean and comfortable accommodations in a variety of hotels, inns, boarding houses, youth hostels, etc.

RESERVATIONS AND RECEPTION

Most large hotels will have personnel who speak English. At the smaller ones, these phrases may come in handy.

| I'd like a single (double) room for tonight. | **Ich möchte ein Einzelzimmer (Doppelzimmer) für heute nacht.** *ikh MERKHT-eh eyen EYEN-tsel-tsim-uh (DOP-el-tsim-uh) fewr HOYT-eh nahkht* |
| I want a room with a private bath. | **Ich möchte ein Zimmer mit Privatbad.** *ikh MERKHT-eh eyen TSIM-uh mit pri-VAAT-baat* |

I want a room with ____.	**Ich möchte ein Zimmer mit ____.** *ikh MERKHT-eh eyen TSIM-uh mit*
■ air conditioning	**Klimaanlage** *KLEEM-ah-ahn-laa-geh*
■ a balcony	**Balkon** *bahl-KOHN*
■ a bathtub	**einer Badewanne** *EYEN-uh BAAD-eh-vahn-eh*
■ television	**Fernsehen** *FEHRN-zayen*
■ cable TV	**Kabelfernsehen** *KAAB-el-fehrn-zayen*
■ a nice view	**schöner Aussicht** *SHERN-uh OWS-zikht*
■ private toilet	**eigenem WC** *EYEG-enem VAY-tsay*
■ radio	**Radio** *RAAD-ee-oh*
■ shower	**Dusche** *DOOSH-eh*
■ a telephone in the room	**Telefonanschluss** *TAYL-e-fohn-ahn-shluss*
■ twin beds	**zwei Betten** *tsveye BEHT-en*
■ a view of the sea	**Blick aufs Meer** *blik owfs mayr*
Do you have a courtyard with a quiet room?	**Haben Sie einen Hof mit einem ruhigen Zimmer?** *HAAB-en zee EYEN-en hohf mit EYEN-em ROO-i-gen TSIM-uh*
I don't want to hear the noise of the street.	**Ich will den Straßenlärm nicht hören.** *ikh vill dayn SHTRAASS-en-lehrm nikht HER-en*
May I see the room?	**Darf ich mir das Zimmer ansehen?** *dahrf ikh meer dahs TSIM-uh AHN-zay-en*
I (don't) like it.	**Es gefällt mir (nicht).** *ehs ge-FEHLT meer (nikht)*

I'll take it.	**Ich nehm's.** *ikh naymss*
I will not take it.	**Ich nehm's nicht.** *ikh naymss (nikht)*
Do you have another room?	**Haben Sie ein anderes Zimmer?** *HAAB-en zee eyen AHND-eh-res TSIM-uh*
I (don't) have a reservation.	**Ich habe (nicht) reservieren lassen.** *ikh HAAB-eh (nikht) reh-zehr-VEER-en LASS-en*
May I leave this in your safe?	**Darf ich dies in Ihrem Tresor lassen?** *dahrf ikh dees in EE-rem treh-ZOHR LASS-en*
Would you have something ____.	**Hätten Sie etwas ____.** *HEHT-en zee ET-vahs*
■ in front	**vorne** *FORN-eh*
■ in back	**hinten** *HINT-en*

■ lower down	**weiter unten**	*VEYET-uh UNT-en*
■ higher up	**weiter oben**	*VEYET-uh OHB-en*
■ facing the lake	**auf der Seeseite**	*owf dehr ZAY-zeyet-eh*
■ overlooking the Rhine	**auf der Rheinseite**	*owf dehr REYEN-zeyet-eh*

I want something ____.
Ich will etwas ____. *ikh vill ET-vahs*

■ quieter	**Ruhigeres**	*ROOH-i-geh-res*
■ bigger	**Größeres**	*GRERSS-eh-res*
■ cheaper	**Billigeres**	*BILL-i-geh-res*
■ better	**Besseres**	*BESS-eh-res*
■ more elegant	**Eleganteres**	*eh-lay-GAHNT-eh-res*
■ more modest	**Bescheideneres**	*beh-SHEYED-e-neh-res*

If you have nothing more, could you call another hotel for me?
Wenn Sie nichts mehr haben, könnten Sie ein anderes Hotel für mich anrufen? *vehn zee nikhts mayr HAAB-en KERNT-en zee eyen AHND-eh-res ho-TEL fewr mikh AHN-roo-fen*

I want something with a view of the ____.
Ich möchte etwas mit Blick auf die ____. *ikh MERKHT-eh ET-vahs mit blik owf dee*

■ ramparts	**Stadtmauer**	*SHTAHT-mow-uh*
■ vineyards	**Weinberge**	*VEYEN-behr-geh*
■ roofs	**Dächer**	*DEH-khuh*

How much does it cost?
Wieviel kostet es? *VEE-feel KOST-et ehs*

Is breakfast (service, everything) included?
Ist das Frühstück (Bedienung, alles) mit einbegriffen? *ist dahs FREW-shtewk (beh-DEEN-ung, AH-les) mit EYEN-beh-gri-fen*

HOTEL SERVICES

If you need an extra blanket, pillow, or other things, say:

I need ____.	**Ich brauche ____.** *ikh BROWKH-eh*
We need ____.	**Wir brauchen ____.** *veer BROWKH-en*
■ an ashtray	**einen Aschenbecher** *EYEN-en AHSH-en-bekh-uh*
■ a blanket	**eine Decke** *EYEN-eh DEHK-eh*
■ matches	**Streichhölzer** *SHTREYEKH-herl-tsuh*
■ envelopes	**Briefumschläge** *BREEF-um-shlay-geh*
■ writing paper	**Schreibpapier** *SHREYEP-paa-peer*
■ postcards	**Postkarten** *POST-kaar-ten*
■ soap	**Seife** *ZEYEF-eh*
■ toilet paper	**Toilettenpapier** *toy-LET-en-paa-peer*
■ towels	**Tücher** *TEWKH-uh*
■ an extra bed	**ein zusätzliches Bett** *eyen TSOO-zehts-li-khes beht*
■ an extra pillow	**ein extra Kopfkissen** *eyen EHKS-traa KOPF-kiss-en*
■ a wastepaper basket	**einen Papierkorb** *EYEN-en paa-PEER-korp*
■ ice cubes	**Eiswürfel** *EYESS-vewr-fel*
■ more hangers	**mehr Kleiderbügel** *mayr KLEYED-uh-bew-gel*
What's the voltage here?	**Welche Stromspannung haben Sie hier?** *VEHLKH-eh SHTROHM-shpahn-ung HAAB-en zee heer*

Where is ____?	**Wo ist ____?** *voh ist*
■ the elevator	**der Aufzug** *dehr OWF-tsook*
■ the bathroom	**das Bad** *dahs baat*
■ the shower	**die Dusche** *dee DOOSH-eh*
■ the breakfast room	**das Frühstückszimmer** *dahs FREW-shtewks-tsim-uh*
■ the dining room	**der Speisesaal** *dehr SHPEYEZ-eh-zaal*
■ the checkroom	**die Garderobe** *dee gahrd-eh-ROHB-eh*
■ the pool	**das Schwimmbad** *dahs SHVIM-baat*
■ the children's playroom	**der Aufenthaltsraum für Kinder** *dehr OWF-ent-hahlts-rowm fewr KIND-uh*
■ the telephone (book)	**das Telefon (buch)** *dahs TAY-leh-fohn (bookh)*
What's my room number?	**Welche Zimmernummer habe ich?** *VELKH-eh TSIM-uh-num-uh HAAB-eh ikh*
Shall I register now or later?	**Soll ich mich jetzt oder später eintragen?** *zol ikh mikh yehtst OHD-uh SHPAYT-uh EYEN-traa-gen*
Do I need a key if I come back after midnight?	**Brauche ich einen Schlüssel, wenn ich nach Mitternacht zurückkomme?** *BROW-kheh ikh EYEN-en SHLEWSS-el vehn ikh nakh MIT-ehr-nahkht tsoo-REWK-kom-eh*
Or is somebody here?	**Oder ist jemand da?** *OHD-uh ist YAY-mahnt daa*
I'll leave the key here.	**Ich lasse den Schlüssel hier.** *ikh LAHSS-eh dayn SHLEWSS-el heer*

Please wake me tomorrow at ____ o'clock.	**Bitte wecken sie mich morgen um ____ Uhr.** *BIT-eh VEHK-en zee mikh MORG-en um ____ oor*
Please don't forget.	**Bitte vergessen Sie es nicht.** *BIT-eh fehr-GESS-en zee ehs nikht*
I don't wish to be disturbed.	**Ich will nicht gestört werden.** *ikh vil nikht geh-SHTERT VAYRD-en*

Travel Tips Even if you are fluent in the language of the country you are visiting, you may crave news from home in English. Large hotels often subscribe to the television service, Cable News Network (CNN). *The International Herald Tribune*, which is assembled jointly by *The New York Times* and *The Washington Post*, is distributed in more than 150 countries. *The Japan Times* and *The European Wall Street Journal* are excellent choices in the Far East.

COMPLAINTS

Where is ____?	**Wo ist ____?** *voh ist*
■ the bellboy	**der Hotelpage** *dehr ho-TEL-paa-zheh*
■ the elevator operator	**der Liftjunge** *dehr LIFT-yun-geh*
■ the porter	**der Hausdiener** *dehr HOWS-dee-nuh*
■ the chambermaid	**das Zimmermädchen** *dahs TSIM-uh-mayd-khen*
■ the manager	**der Geschäftsführer** *dehr geh-SHEHFTS-few-ruh*
■ the switchboard operator	**die Telefonistin** *dee tay-leh-foh-NIST-in*

There is ____.	**Es gibt ____.** *ehs gipt*
■ no hot water	**kein heißes Wasser** *keyen HEYESS-es VAHSS-uh*
■ no heat	**keine Heizung** *KEYEN-eh HEYETS-ung*
The room is cold.	**Das Zimmer ist kalt.** *dahs TSIM-uh ist kahlt*
When are you going to turn the heat on?	**Wann wird geheizt?** *vahn veert geh-HEYETST*
The room is dirty.	**Das Zimmer ist schmutzig.** *dahs TSIM-uh ist SHMUTS-ikh*
The window (door, blind) is stuck.	**Das Fenster (die Tür, die Jalousie) klemmt.** *dahs FENST-uh (dee tewr, dee zhah-loo-ZEE) klemt*
The ____ is defective.	**____ ist defekt.** *ist deh-FEHKT*
■ air conditioning	**die Klimaanlage** *dee KLEE-mah-ahn-laa-geh*
■ fan	**der Ventilator** *dehr ven-tee-LAAT-or*
■ ventilator	**der Lüfter** *dehr LEWFT-uh*
■ the radio	**das Radio** *dahs RAAD-ee-oh*
■ the television set	**der Fernseher** *dehr FEHRN-zay-uh*
■ the lamp	**die Lampe** *dee LAHMP-eh*
■ the plug	**die Steckdose** *dee SHTEK-doh-zeh*
■ the switch	**der Schalter** *dehr SHAHLT-uh*
■ the toilet	**die Toilette** *dee toy-LET-eh*
The bathtub (the shower, the wash basin) is clogged.	**Die Badewanne (die Dusche, das Waschbecken) ist verstopft.** *dee BAAD-eh-vahn-eh (dee DOOSH-eh, dahs VAHSH-behk-en) ist fehr-SHTOPFT*

BREAKFAST AND ROOM SERVICE

Hotels often have their own restaurants. Some (Vienna's Sacher, Berlin's Kempinski, Munich's Vier Jahreszeiten) are renowned. If it offers only breakfast, the establishment may call itself a **Hotel Garni.** Breakfast is usually included in the room rate. If you're not sure, ask:

Is breakfast included in the price of the room?	**Ist der Zimmerpreis mit Frühstück?** *ist dehr TSIM-uh-preyes mit FREW-shtewk*

In many hotels breakfast is a very carefully premeasured quantity. Waiting for you, often at a numbered table, will be a precise number of little plastic or foil containers of butter, jam, or **wurst.** Sometimes one slice of cheese or an egg will be included. Or you may have to pay extra for these things.

I want a soft-boiled egg.	**Ich möchte ein weichgekochtes Ei.** *ikh MERKHT-eh eyen VEYEKH-geh-kokh-tes eye*
■ a medium-boiled egg	**ein wachsweichgekochtes Ei** *eyen VAHKS-veyekh-geh-kokh-tes eye*
■ a hard-boiled egg	**ein hartgekochtes Ei** *eyen HAHRT-geh-kokh-tes eye*
I'd like ____.	**Ich möchte gerne ____.** *ikh MERKH-teh GEHRN-eh*
■ coffee	**Kaffee** *KAHF-fay*
■ tea	**Tee** *tay*
■ chocolate	**Schokolade** *shoko-LAAD-eh*
■ milk	**Milch** *milkh*
■ orange juice	**Apfelsinensaft** *AHP-fehl-zeen-en-zahft*
■ yogurt	**Joghurt** *YOH-goort*
■ an omelette	**eine Omelette** *EYEN-eh omeh-LET-eh*

■ fried eggs	**Spiegeleier** *SHPEEG-ehl-eye-uh*
■ scrambled eggs	**Rühreier** *REWR-eye-uh*
■ eggs and bacon (ham)	**Eier mit Speck (Schinken)** *EYE-uh mit shpek (SHINK-en)*

I'd like more ____. **Ich möchte mehr ____.** *ikh MERKHT-eh mayr*

■ butter	**Butter** *BUT-uh*
■ jam	**Marmelade** *mahr-meh-LAAD-eh*
■ sugar	**Zucker** *TSUK-uh*
■ cream	**Sahne** *ZAAN-eh*
■ bread	**Brot** *broht*
■ rolls	**Brötchen** *BRERT-khen*
■ honey	**Honig** *HOHN-ikh*
■ lemon	**Zitrone** *tsi-TROHN-eh*

Medium-priced and expensive hotels may offer a veritable cornucopia for breakfast. A **Büfettfrühstück** (buffet breakfast) will include many varieties of cheeses, sausages, jams, preserves, and juices. If you enjoy gluttony, this is your opportunity. If you're informed that breakfast is served until 9:30 or 10:00, try to arrive at least a half hour before closing time, for the hotel staff is often anxious to dismantle the well-stocked breakfast tables.

If you arrive late, the following proverbs, may, alas, be appropriate:

Wer nicht kommt zu rechter Zeit, der muss essen was übrig bleibt.	Whoever shows up late gets the leftovers.
Morgenstund hat Gold im Mund. Wer verschläft sich geht zu Grund.	Golden are the morning hours. Over-sleepers come to grief.

If you want breakfast (or any meal) served in your room, ask:

Can I (we) be served in the room?	**Kann man es mir (uns) aufs Zimmer servieren?** *kahn mahn ehs meer (uns) owfs TSIM-uh zehr-VEER-en*
Do you have room service?	**Gibt es Zimmerbedienung?** *gipt ehs TSIM-uh-be-dien-ung*

HOTEL FEATURES

Many hotel rooms have a well-stocked **Mini-Bar.** In this small refrigerator you will find soft drinks, beer, and **Pikkolos** (diminutive bottles) of champagne (such as *Henkell Trocken*). You can check off what you consume on the list provided. At checkout time, payment is usually made on the honor system.

You can save money with a long stay by taking a room with full or half-board. There is usually a **Mindestaufenthalt** (minimum stay) requirement of three days, sometimes a week, if you want a reduced rate. The fare on these "contract feeding" programs is not always copious or succulent. It is of course always possible to order other items, but they will cost extra.

How much does it cost with full room and board?	**Wieviel kostet es mit voller Verpflegung?** *VEE-feel KOST-et ehs mit FOL-uh fehr-PFLAYG-ung*
How much is half-board?	**Was ist der Preis für Halbpension?** *vahs ist dehr preyes fewr HAHLP-pehn-zee-ohn*
How long must I stay before I can get a reduction in price?	**Wie lange muss ich bleiben, bevor ich eine Preisermäßigung bekommen kann?** *vee LAHNG-eh muss ikh BLEYEB-en beh-FOR ikh EYEN-eh PREYESS-ehr-mayss-ig-ung beh-KOM-en kahn*

Come in.	**Herein!** *heh-REYEN*
Put it ____.	**Stellen Sie es ____.** *SHTEL-en zee ehs*
■ over there	**da drüben** *daa DREWB-en*
■ on the table	**auf den Tisch** *owf dayn tish*
Just a minute.	**Augenblick nur.** *OWG-en-blik noor*

OTHER ACCOMMODATIONS

Is there a youth hostel (a castle hotel, an inn) here?	**Gibt es eine Jugendherberge (ein Schlosshotel, ein Gasthaus) hier?** *gipt ehs EYEN-eh YOOG-ent-hehr-behr-geh (eyen SHLOSS-ho-tel, eyen GAHST-hows) heer*
I'm looking for a room in a boarding-house.	**Ich suche ein Zimmer in einer Pension.** *ikh ZOOKH-eh eyen TSIM-uh in EYEN-uh penz-YOHN*
Where is the local tourist office?*	**Wo ist das Fremdenverkehrs-büro?*** *voh ist dahs FREMD-en-fehr-kayrs-bew-roh*
I'd like to rent a house (a furnished apartment).	**Ich möchte ein Haus (eine Ferien-wohnung) mieten.** *ikh MERKHT-eh eyen hows (EYEN-eh FEHR-yen-vohn-ung) MEET-en*
Are there reduced off-season rates?	**Gibt es eine Preisermäßigung außerhalb der Hauptsaison?** *gipt ehs EYEN-eh PREYESS-er-mayss-ig-ung OWSS-ehr-hahlp dehr HOWPT-zay-zon*

---

* The tourist office can also be called a **Verkehrsverein, Verkehrsamt** or **Amt für Touristik.** Many of them have a room reservations service. In spas, the **Kuramt** or **Kurkommission** will also make room referrals.

I'm looking for a hotel with ____.	**Ich suche ein Hotel mit ____ .** *ikh ZOOKH-eh eyen ho-TEL mit*
■ garage	**Garage** *gah-RAA-zheh*
■ parking	**eigenem Parkplatz** *EYE-ge-nem PAHRK-plahts*
■ indoor pool	**Hallenbad** *HAHL-en-baat*
I need a living room, bedroom, and kitchen.	**Ich brauche ein Wohnzimmer, Schlafzimmer, und Küche.** *ikh BROWK-eh eyen VOHN-tsim-uh, SHLAAF-tsim-uh unt KEW-kheh*
How much is the rent?	**Was ist die Miete?** *vah ist dee MEET-eh*
I'll be staying for ____.	**Ich bleibe ____.** *ikh BLEYEB-eh*
■ two weeks	**zwei Wochen** *tsveye VOKH-en*
■ one month	**einen Monat** *EYEN-en MOH-naat*
■ the whole season	**die ganze Saison** *dee GAHNTS-eh ZAY-zon*
I want something ____.	**Ich möchte etwas** *ikh MERKHT-eh ET-vahs*
■ downtown	**im Zentrum** *im TSENT-room*
■ in the old part of town	**in der Altstadt** *in dehr AHLT-shtaht*
■ with modern conveniences	**mit modernem Komfort** *mit mod-EHRN-em kom-FOHR*

If you're driving, you'll see many **Zimmer frei** (rooms to let) signs. **Gasthof** and **Gasthaus** both mean "inn." **Fremdenheim** is another word for **Pension**, or "boardinghouse."

Rooms in private homes normally include bed and breakfast (**Übernachtung mit Frühstück**).

DEPARTURE

We're checking out tomorrow.	**Wir reisen morgen ab.** *veer REYEZ-en MORG-en ahp*
Are there any letters (messages) for me?	**Gibt es Briefe (Nachrichten) für mich?** *gipt ehs BREEF-eh (NAHKH-rikht-en) fewr mikh*
Please prepare my bill.	**Bitte bereiten Sie meine Rechnung vor.** *BIT-eh beh-REYET-en zee MEYEN-eh REKH-nung for*
Can you give me information about train departures?	**Können Sie mir Auskunft über die Abfahrt der Züge geben?** *KERN-en zee meer OWSS-kunft EWB-uh dee AHP-faart dehr TSEWG-eh GAYB-en*
Where is the bus stop?	**Wo ist die Bushaltestelle?** *voh ist dee BUSS-hahl-teh-shteh-leh*
Please call a taxi for me.	**Besorgen Sie mir bitte ein Taxi.** *beh-ZORG-en zee meer BIT-eh eyen TAHK-see*
Here is my home (forwarding) address.	**Hier ist meine Heimat (Nach-sende) adresse.** *heer ist MEYEN-eh HEYEM-att (NAHKH-zehnd-eh) ah-DRESS-eh*
I'll recommend your hotel to my friends.	**Ich werde Ihr Hotel meinen Freunden empfehlen.** *ikh VAYRD-eh eer ho-TEL MEYEN-en FROYND-en emp-FAYL-en*
It was very nice.	**Es war sehr schön.** *ehs vaar zayr schern*
May I leave my luggage here until later?	**Darf ich mein Gepäck his später hier lassen?** *dahrf ikh meyen geh-PEHK bis SHPAYT-uh heer LASS-en*

GETTING AROUND TOWN

Most places, however small, are served by rail or by buses operated by the railway systems of Germany, Austria, and Switzerland. For intraurban traffic in cities, find out when the last bus, subway, or streetcar runs on specific lines. Or you may want to stroll around town.

PUBLIC TRANSPORTATION

Depending on the size of the city, the following modes of transport will appear:

Straßenbahn	Streetcar
Bus	Bus
U-Bahn	Subway (white *U* sign on blue background)
S-Bahn	Suburban commuter trains of German Rail (white *S* sign on green background)

SUBWAYS, BUSES, AND STREETCARS

Subways *(U-Bahn)* are usually closed between 1 and 5 A.M. Many cities offer booklets of tickets, which will provide some savings. It is often necessary to buy tickets in advance, either from an automatic dispenser or a newsstand. For **Schwarzfahrer** (those who ride without paying), there are stiff penalties if they are caught. So be sure to have your ticket.

Where can I buy a ticket?	**Wo kann ich eine Fahrkarte kaufen?** *voh kahn ikh EYEN-eh FAAR-kahr-teh KOWF-en*
What streetcar goes to Grinzing?	**Welche Straßenbahn fährt nach Grinzing?** *VELKH-eh SHTRAASS-en-baan fayrt nahkh GRINTS-ing*
How much does it cost to Grinzing?	**Was kostet es nach Grinzing?** *vahs KOST-et ehs nahkh GRINTS-ing*
When does the next bus leave?	**Wann fährt der nächste Bus?** *vahn fayrt dehr NAYKST-eh bus*
Where is the bus stop?	**Wo ist die Bushaltestelle?** *voh ist dee BUS-hahl-teh-shteh-leh*
When does the last streetcar leave?	**Wann geht die letzte Straßenbahn?** *vahn gayt dee LETST-eh SHTRAASS-en-baan*
Where is the nearest subway station?	**Wo ist die nächste U-Bahn Station (Untergrundbahn)?** *voh ist dee NAYKH-steh oo-baan shtah-TSYOHN (UNT-uh-grunt-baan)*
How much is the fare?	**Wieviel kostet die Fahrt?** *VEE-feel KOST-et dee faart*
Which is the line that goes to ____?	**Welche Linie fährt nach ____?** *VEHLKH-eh LEEN-yeh fehrt nahkh*
Does this train go to ____?	**Fährt dieser Zug nach ____?** *fehrt DEEZ-uh tsook nahkh*
What's the next stop?	**Was ist die nächste Haltestelle?** *vahs ist dee NEHKHST-eh HAHLT-eh-shtel-eh*
Where should I get off?	**Wo muß ich aussteigen?** *voh muss ikh OWS-shteyeg-en*

Do I have to change trains?	**Muß ich umsteigen?** *muss ikh UM-shteyeg-en*
Please tell me when we get there.	**Bitte sagen Sie mir, wann wir dort ankommen.** *BIT-eh ZAAG-en zee meer vahn veer dort AHN-kom-en*

TAXIS

Cabs are usually found at a taxi stand (**Taxistandplatz**), but they can also be hailed in the street.

Please call a taxi for me.	**Rufen Sie bitte eine Taxe fü mich.** *ROOF-en zee BIT-eh EYEN-eh TAHKS-eh fewr mikh*
How much is the ride to Wandsbek?	**Wieviel kostet die Fahrt nach Wandsbek?** *VEE-feel KOST-et dee faart nakh WAHNTS-behk?*
Drive me to the hotel (railroad station, airport).	**Fahren Sie mich zum Hotel (Bahnhof, Flughafen).** *FAAR-en zee mikh tsoom ho-TEL (BAAN-hohf, FLOOK-haa-fen)*
Please wait for me.	**Warten Sie auf mich bitte.** *VAART-en zee owf mikh BIT-eh*
I'm in a hurry.	**Ich hab's eilig.** *ikh hahps EYEL-ikh*
Is it still very far?	**Ist es noch sehr weit?** *ist ehs nokh zayr veyet*
Let me off at the next corner.	**Lassen Sie mich an der nächsten Ecke aussteigen!** *LASS-en zee mikh ahn dehr NAYKST-en EK-eh OWS-shteye-gen*

All taxis have meters. But if you are afraid that you may be "taken for a ride," check first at your hotel.

Approximately how long does a taxi ride to ____ take?	**Ungefähr wie lange davert eine Taxifahrt nach ____?** *UN-ge-fayr vee LAHNG-eh DOW-ehrt EYEN-eh TAHKS-ee-faart nakh*
And in heavy traffic?	**Und bei starkem Verkehr?** *unt beye SHTAHRK-em fehr-KAYR*
How much does a taxi ride to ____ cost?	**Wieviel kostet eine Taxifahrt nach ____?** *VEE-feel KOST-et EYEN-eh TAHKS-ee-faart nakh*

Most **Taxifahrer** (taxi drivers) are honest, and it is unlikely that you will meet any who will try to take you the long way around. As mentioned, you can ascertain price and duration of the trip before you go. But just in case:

I'm a foreigner. But	**Ich bin Ausländer(-in). Aber ich**

I'm not stupid.	**bin nicht dumm.** *ikh bin OWSS-lehnd-uh(-in, for women) AAB-uh* *ikh bin nikht dum*
Let me off at once!	**Lassen Sie mich sofort aussteigen!** *LAHSS-en zee mikh zoh-FORT OWS-shteye-gen*

SIGHTSEEING

I'm looking for the Tourist Office.	**Ich suche das Fremden-verkehrsbüro.** *ikh ZOOKH-eh dahs FREHM-den-fehr-kayrs-bew-roh*
Is there a guided tour of the city? (bus tour)	**Gibt es eine Stadtrundfahrt?** *gipt ehs EYEN-eh SHTAHT-runt-faart*
Is there an English-speaking tour?	**Gibt es eine englischsprachige Führung?** *gipt ehs EYEN-eh ENG-lish-shpraa-khi-geh FEWR-ung*
I need a guidebook.	**Ich brauche einen Reiseführer.** *ikh BROWKH-eh EYEN-en REYEZ-eh-few-ruh*
What are the chief sights?	**Was sind die Hauptsehenswürdig-keiten?** *vahs zint dee HOWPT-zay-ens-vewr-dikh-keye-ten DINGT geh-ZAY-en HAAB-en*
At what time is the city tour?	**Um wieviel Uhr ist die Rundfahrt?** *um VEE-feel oor ist dee RUND-faart*
Will they pick us up at the hotel?	**Holt man uns im Hotel ab?** *hohlt mahn uns im ho-TEL ahp*

Or do we have to go to the Tourist Office?	**Oder müssen wir zum Fremden-verkehrsbüro?** *OHD-uh MEWSS-en veer tsoom FREHM-den-fehr-kayrs-bew-roh*
Is (are) the ____ very far from here?	**Ist (sind) ____ sehr weit von hier?** *ist (zint) ____ zayr veyet fon heer*

- abbey — **die Abtei** *dee ahp-TEYE*
- amusement park — **der Vergnügungspark** *dehr fehr-GNEWG-ungks-paark*
- artists' quarter — **das Künstlerviertel** *dahs KEWNST-lehr-feer-tel*
- botanical garden — **der Botanische Garten** *dehr bo-TAAN-ish-eh GAART-en*
- castle — **das Schloss/die Burg, Festung** *dahs shloss/dee boork FEST-ung*
- cathedral — **der Dom/die Kathedrale** *dehr dohm/dee kaa-tayd-RAAL-eh*
- cemetery — **der Friedhof** *dehr FREET-hohf*
- city center — **die Stadtmitte/das Zentrum** *dee SHTAHT-mit-eh/dahs TSENT-rum*
- city hall — **das Rathaus** *dahs RAAT-hows*
- church — **die Kirche** *dee KEERKH-eh*
- commercial district — **das Geschäftsviertel** *dahs geh-SHEHFTS-feer-tel*
- concert hall — **die Konzerthalle** *dee kon-TSAYRT-hah-leh*
- docks — **die Hafenanlagen** *dee HAA-fen-ahn-laa-gen*
- fountain — **der Springbrunnen** *dehr SHPRING-bru-nen*
- gardens — **die Gärten/Günanlagen** *dee GEHRT-en/GREWN-ahn-laa-gen*
- library — **die Bibliothek** *dee bib-lee-oh-TAYK*
- market — **der Markt** *dehr maarkt*

■ monastery	**das Kloster**	*dahs KLOHST-uh*
■ monument	**das Denkmal**	*dahs DEHNK-maal*
■ museum	**das Museum**	*dahs moo-ZAY-um*
■ a nightclub	**ein Nachtlokal**	*eyen NAHKHT-lo-kaal*
■ old part of town	**die Altstadt**	*dee AHLT-shtaht*
■ open-air museum	**das Freilichtmuseum**	*dahs FREYE-likht-moo-zay-um*
■ opera	**das Opernhaus**	*dahs OH-pehrn-howss*
■ palace	**das Schloss/Palais/der Palast**	*dahs shloss/pah-LAY/dehr pah-LAHST*
■ ramparts	**die Stadtmauer**	*dee STAHT-mow-uh*
■ river	**der Fluss**	*dehr fluss*
■ ruins	**die Ruinen**	*dee roo-EEN-en*
■ stadium	**das Stadion**	*dahs SHTAAD-ee-ohn*
■ theater	**das Theater**	*dahs tay-AAT-uh*
■ the tower	**der Turm**	*dehr toorm*
■ the university	**die Universität**	*dee u-nee-vayr-zi-TAYT*

Museums offer guided tours, some in English. In some churches or parts of churches you must pay an admission and have a guide. But generally you can go through most museums and churches on your own. You must visit almost all palaces and castles with a group and a guide. If the wait for the guided tour group in German is shorter than the wait for the English tour and you want to test your German, go on the German tour. Or, if you have time, try both. During off-season, usually only the German tour is offered. But if most of the tourists are English-speaking, the guides usually relent and do the tour in English. Many churches have signs informing visitors, **Dies ist das Haus Gottes** (This is the house of God), and in a few cases tourist activities are interrupted by recorded voices delivering the same message. The sign **Kein Umhergehen während des Gottesdienstes** (No walking about during the service) is also frequently seen.

Can the castle (museum, monument) be visited without a guide?	**Kann man das Schloss (Museum, Denkmal) ohne Führung besichtig-en?** *kahn mahn dahs shloss (moo-ZAY-um, DENK-maal) OHN-eh FEWR-ung beh-ZIKHT-i-gen*
How long must one wait?	**Wie lange muss man warten?** *vee LAHNG-eh muss mahn VAART-en*
Is it all right to go in now?	**Darf man jetzt rein?** *dahrf mahn yetst reyen*
What time does it open (close)?	**Um wieviel Uhr wird geöffnet (geschlossen)?** *um VEE-feel oor veert geh-ERF-net (geh-SHLOSS-en)*
Must children (students) pay full price?	**Müssen Kinder (Studenten) den vollen Preis bezahlen?** *MEWSS-en KIND-uh (shtu-DENT-en) dayn FOL-en preyess beh-TSAAL-en*
I want three tickets.	**Ich möchte drei Eintrittskarten.** *ikh MERKH-teh dreye EYEN-trits-kaar-ten*
Two adults and one child at half price.	**Zwei Erwachsene und ein Kind zum halben Preis.** *tsveye ehr-VAHKS-en-eh unt eyen kint tsoom HAHLB-en preyess*
Is taking photographs allowed?	**Darf man fotografieren?** *dahr mahn foh-toh-grah-FEER-en*

RELIGIOUS SERVICES

With a little effort you will find Protestant services even in Catholic areas and vice versa. With a little more effort you will be able to find other religious services. Frederick the Great of Prussia welcomed persecuted Huguenots and declared that Turks could come and build mosques if they had something to contribute to the state. Many mosques now exist in German-speaking countries, and there are plans for more. Most large cities have Jewish communities. Buddhist zendos, Hindu ashrams, and meditation centers of a variety of creeds exist in most large cities. Many also have rural retreat houses. Ask at the Tourist Office.

Where is the Catholic/Protestant church?	**Wo ist die katholische/evangelische Kirche?** *voh ist dee kah-TOH-lish-eh/ay-vahn-GAY-lish-eh KEERKH-eh*
At what time does the service (mass) begin?	**Um wieviel Uhr beginnt der Gottesdienst (die Messe)?** *um VEE-feel oor beh-GINT dehr GOT-ehs-deenst (dee MESS-eh)*
Is there a synagogue (mosque) here?	**Gibt es eine Synagoge (Moschee) hier?** *gipt ehs EYEN-eh zew-nah-GOHG-eh (mo-SHAY) heer*
I'm looking for a minister (priest, rabbi, mullah) who speaks English.	**Ich suche einen Pfarrer (Priester, Rabbiner, Mullah) der Englisch spricht.** *ikh ZOOKH-eh EYEN-en PFAHR-uh (PREEST-uh, rah-BEEN-uh, MUL-ah) dehr EHNG-lish shprikht*
Is there a Buddhist Temple here?	**Gibt es einen buddhistischen Tempel hier?** *gipt ehs EYEN-en bud-IST-ish-en TEMP-el heer*
Is there a Vedanta Society in this town?	**Gibt es eine Wedanta Gesellschaft in dieser Stadt?** *gipt es EYEN-eh veh-DAHNT-ah geh-ZEL-shahft in DEEZ-uh shtaht*

Germany, Austria, and Switzerland have no pilgrimage sites in the same league with Rome, Jerusalem, Mecca, or Kapilavastu (Buddha's birthplace). But there are many

Wallfahrtskirchen (pilgrimage churches), such as the *Wieskirche*, *Vierzehnheiligen*, and *Einsiedeln*. Some people make pilgrimages to them more for esthetic than religious reasons.

The Alpine landscape is dotted with statuary and paintings on religious themes, and many of these Bavarian-Austrian-Swiss creations are of artistic interest.

Travel Tips Luggage is sometimes lost or arrives long after you do. To avoid problems, some people travel light and carry on everything. At the very least, take one complete change of clothing, basic grooming items, and any regular medication aboard with you. Because airlines will not replace valuable jewelry when paying for lost luggage, it should be carried on your person. Safer yet, select one set of basic, simple jewelry that can be worn everywhere and wear it during your whole trip. Remember, carry-on bags must be small enough to fit in overhead bins or to slide under your seat.

PLANNING TRIPS

During your stay you may want to plan some longer excursions. Tourists can get around Germany, Austria, and Switzerland by plane, train, car, or boat.

AT THE AIRPORT AND ON THE PLANE

Can I fly to Stuttgart directly from here?	**Kann ich von hier direkt nach Stuttgart fliegen?** *kahn ikh fon heer dee-REHKT naakh SHTUT-gahrt FLEEG-en*
Or do I have to change planes?	**Oder muss ich umsteigen?** *OHD-uh muss ikh UM-shteye-gen*
Please book a connecting flight to Karlsruhe for me.	**Buchen Sie bitte einen Anschlussflug nach Karlsruhe für mich.** *BOOKH-en zee BIT-eh EYEN-en AHN-shlus-flook nahkh KAALS-rooh-eh fewr mikh*
May I take this with me as carry-on luggage?	**Darf ich dies als Handgepäck mitnehmen?** *daarf ikh dees ahls HAHNT-ge-pehk MIT-nay-men*
How much is a one-way trip (a round-trip)?	**Was kostet ein einfacher Flug (ein Rückflug)?** *vahs KOST-et eyen EYEN-fahkh-uh flook (eyen REWK-flook)*
I want to fly to Hamburg and later to Berlin.	**Ich will nach Hamburg und anschließend nach Berlin.** *ikh vil nahkh HAHM-boork unt AHN-shleess-ent nahkh behr-LEEN*
When do I have to check in?	**Wann muss ich mich melden?** *vahn muss ikh mikh MEHLD-en*

Is there a direct flight to Brunswick?	**Gibt es einen Direktflug nach Braunschweig?** *gipt ehs EYEN-en dee-REHKT-flook nahkh BROWN-shveyek*
Please tell me the arrival and departure times again.	**Bitte sagen Sie mir noch einmal Ankunft- und Abflugzeiten.** *BIT-eh ZAAG-en zee meer noch EYEN-maal AHN-kunft unt AHP-flook-tseye-ten*
At what time does it leave?	**Um wieviel Uhr ist der Abflug?** *um VEE-feel oor ist dehr AHP-flook*
I want a seat next to the window in the (non)smoking section.	**Ich möchte einen Fensterplatz (Nicht)Raucher haben.** *ikh MERKH-teh EYEN-en FEHNST-uh-plahts (nikht)ROWKH-uh HAAB-en*

If you are not sure about what time zone the city of your destination is in, ask:

What time is it now in London (Paris)?	**Wieviel Uhr ist es jetzt in London (Paris)?** *VEE-feel oor ist ehs yehtst in london (pahr-EES)*
When do we land?	**Wann landen wir?** *vahn LAHND-en veer*
My ears hurt. Please give me something to drink.	**Meine Ohren tun mir weh. Bitte geben Sie mir etwas zu trinken.** *MEYEN-eh OHR-en toon meer vay. BIT-eh GAYB-en zee meer ET-vahs tsoo TRINK-en*
Is there a meal served on flight number ____?	**Gibt es eine Mahlzeit auf Flug Nummer ____?** *gipt ehs EYEN-eh MAAL-tseyet owf flook NUM-uh*
I have only carry-on baggage.	**Ich habe nur Handgepäck.** *ikh HAAB-eh noor HAHNT-geh-pehk*

Please pass my film (camera) through by hand.	**Bitte reichen Sie mir meinen Film (meine Kamera).** *BIT-eh REYEKH-en zee meer MEYEN-en film (MEYEN-eh KAA-meh-raa)*
Please don't let the film and camera go through the machine.*	**Bitte lassen Sie den Film und die Kamera nicht durch die Maschine laufen.** *BIT-eh LAS-en zee dayn film unt dee KAA-meh-raa nicht durkh dee mah-SHEEN-eh LOWF-en*

*NOTE: Some high-speed film can be damaged by airport security X rays. It is best to pack film in your suitcase, protected in a lead insulated bag. If you have film in your camera or carry-on baggage, avoid problems and ask the guard to pass it through by hand instead. If the guard refuses, bow to his wishes.

SHIPBOARD TRAVEL

Can I go by steamer from Düsseldorf to Cologne?	**Kann ich mit dem Rheindampfer von Düsseldorf nach Köln fahren?** *kahn ikh mit dem REYEN-dahmp-fuh fon DEWSS-el-dorf nahkh kerln FAAR-en*

NOTE: You can, but it will take a lot longer than the train, because there are many curves in the river in that stretch.

Does it take much longer by ship?	**Dauert es viel langer mit dem Schiff?** *DOW-ehrt ehs feel LEHNG-uh mit daym shif*
I prefer to go by ship.	**Ich fahre lieber mit dem Schiff.** *ikh FAAR-eh LEEB-uh mit daym shif*

When does the last ferry (the next boat) leave?	**Wann geht die letzte Fähre (das nächste Boot)?** *vahn gayt dee LEHTST-eh FAIR-eh (dahs NAYKST-eh boht)*
Is there also a hydrofoil (hovercraft)?	**Gibt es auch ein Luftkissenboot?** *gipt ehs owkh eyen LUFT-kissen-boht*
How long does the crossing to Helgoland take?	**Wie lange dauert die Überfahrt nach Helgoland?** *vee LAHNG-eh DOW-ehrt dee EWB-uh-faart nahkh HEHL-goh-lahnt*
I'd like a cabin ____.	**Ich möchte eine Kabine ____.** *ikh MERKHT-eh EYEN-eh kah-BEEN-eh*
■ in the luxury class	**in der Luxusklasse** *in dehr LUKS-us-klahss-eh*
■ in the first (second) class	**in der ersten (zweiten) Klasse** *in dehr EHRST-en (TSVEYET-en) KLAHSS-eh*

I want a luxury cabin in the Europe class (on Rhine steamers).	**Ich möchte eine Luxuskabine in der Europaklasse.** *ikh MERKHT-eh EYEN-eh LUKS-us-kah-been-eh in dehr oy-ROH-paa-klahss-eh*
I want a cabin in tourist class.	**Ich will eine Kabine in der Touristenklasse.** *ikh vil EYEN-eh kah-BEEN-eh in dehr too-RIST-en-klahss-eh*
When do we arrive in Cuxhaven?	**Wann kommen wir in Cuxhaven an?** *vahn KOM-en veer in CUKS-haaf-en ahn*
How long do we still have to stay on board?	**Wie lange müssen wir noch an Bord bleiben?** *vee LAHNG-eh MEWSS-en veer nokh ahn bort BLEYEB-en*
When do we have to board the ship again?	**Wann müssen wir wieder das Schiff besteigen?** *vahn MEWSS-en veer VEED-uh dahs shif be-STEYEG-en*
Do you have something for seasickness?	**Haben Sie etwas gegen Seekrank-heit?** *HAAB-en zee ET-vahs GAYG-en ZAY-krahnk-heyet*
I don't feel well.	**Ich fühle mich nicht wohl.** *ikh FEWL-eh mikh nikht vohl*
The sea air does wonders for me.	**Die Meeresluft tut Wunder für mich.** *dee MAYR-ehs-luft toot VUND-uh fewr mikh*

TRAINS

The fastest trains are the ICs and ICEs. You will have to pay a supplement for travel on them. German stations post timetables for departure **(Abfahrt,** yellow) and arrival

(Ankunft, white). *Before* you leave for Europe you may want to purchase a Eurail pass, or a more limited Euro or German Rail pass. Check with your travel agent.

Where are we now?	**Wo sind wir jetzt?** *voh zint veer yetst*
What's the name of this place?	**Wie heißt dieser Ort?** *vee heyest DEEZ-uh ort*
Can I go by train to Bruchhausen-Vilsen?	**Kann ich mit der Bahn nach Bruchhausen-Vilsen fahren?** *kahn ikh mit dehr baan nakh BRUKH-howz-en-FILZ-en FAAR-en*
Or must I take a bus?	**Oder muss ich einen Bus nehmen?** *OHD-uh muss ikh EYEN-en bus NAYM-en*

AT THE RAILROAD STATION AND ON THE TRAIN

The European railway system is extensive, and trains are fast and efficient. But if you are an old-time train buff and want to ride behind a steam locomotive, there are a number of them around too, for instance, in Austria's famed **Zillerthal.**

I'd like a rail trip with a steam locomotive.	**Ich möchte eine Eisenbahnreise mit einer Dampflokomotive.** *ikh MERKHT-eh EYEN-eh EYE-zehn-baan-reye-zeh mit EYEN-uh DAHMPF-lo-ko-mo-ti-veh*

You will probably be more interested in the fast TEE (Trans-Europe-Express) and Inter-City express trains. Both cost an extra fee **(Zuschlag).**

Must I pay a supplement?	**Muss ich einen Zuschlag bezahlen?** *muss ikh EYEN-en TSOO-shlahk be-TSAAL-en*

Please call me a taxi.	**Bitte besorgen Sie mir ein Taxi.** *BIT-eh beh-ZORG-en zee meer eyen TAHK-see*
Please help me with my luggage.	**Bitte helfen Sie mir mit meinem Gepäck.** *BIT-eh HELF-en zee meer mit MEYEN-em ge-PEHK*
Is there a baggage check office?	**Gibt es eine Gepäckaufbewahrung?** *gipt ehs EYEN-eh geh-PEHK-owf-be-vaar-ung*
Where are the luggage lockers?	**Wo sind die Schließfächer?** *voh zint dee SHLEESS-fekh-uh*
Can you give me change for them?	**Können Sie mir dafür Kleingeld geben?** *KERN-en zee meer daa-FEWR KLEYEN-gelt GAYB-en*
Where is the ticket office?	**Wo ist der Fahrkartenschalter?** *voh ist dehr FAAR-kahr-ten-shahl-tuh*
A one-way (a round-trip) ticket to Heidelberg.	**Eine einfache Fahrkarte (eine Rückfahrkarte) nach Heidelberg.** *EYEN-eh EYEN-fahkh-eh FAAR-kahr-teh (EYEN-eh REWK-faar-kahr-teh) nahkh HEYED-el-behrk*
Is there a price reduction for my daughter (my son)?	**Gibt es eine Preisermäßigung für meine Tochter (meinen Sohn)?** *gipt ehs EYEN-eh PREYESS-er-mayss-ig-ung fewr MEYEN-eh TOKHT-uh (MEYEN-en zohn)*
She is 11.	**Sie ist elf.** *zee ist elf*
He is 12.	**Er ist zwölf.** *air ist tsverlf*
Can children travel at half-price?	**Können Kinder zum halben Preis fahren?** *KERN-en KIND-uh tsoom HAHLB-en preyess FAAR-en*

What is the fare to Vienna?	**Was kostet die Fahrt nach Wien?** *vahs KOST-et dee faart nahkh veen*
Does the train stop in Linz?	**Hält der Zug in Linz?** *hehlt dehr tsook in lints*
On what platform does the train from Hamburg arrive?	**Auf welchem Bahnsteig kommt der Zug aus Hamburg an?** *owf WELKH-em BAAN-shteyek komt dehr tsook ows HAHM-boork ahn*
When does the next train for Zürich leave?	**Wann fährt der nächste Zug nach Zürich?** *vahn fehrt dehr NAYKST-eh tsook nahkh TSEW-rikh*
Has the last train for Marienbad already left?	**Ist der letzte Zug nach Marienbad schon abgefahren?** *ist dehr LETST-eh tsook nahkh maa-REE-en-baat shon AHP-ge-faar-en*
Is this car a smoker or nonsmoker?	**Ist dieser Wagen Raucher oder Nichtraucher?** *ist DEEZ-uh VAAG-en ROWKH-uh OHD-uh nikht ROWKH-uh*
Is this seat taken?	**Ist hier noch frei?** *ist heer nokh freye*
Do you have a time-table?	**Haben Sie einen Fahrplan?** *HAAB-en zee EYEN-en FAAR-plaan*
Is there a dining car?	**Gibt es einen Speisewagen?** *gipt ehs EIN-en SHPEYE-zeh-vaa-gen*
Is it up front or to the rear?	**Ist er vorne oder hinten?** *ist ehr FORN-eh OHD-uh HINT-en*
Is the train carrying a sleeping car?	**Führt der Zug einen Schlafwagen?** *fewrt dehr tsook EYEN-en SHLAAF-vaa-gen*

How much behind schedule will we arrive in Ulm?	**Mit wieviel Verspätung treffen wir in Ulm ein?** *mit VEE-feel fehr-SPAYT-ung TREHF-en veer in ulm eyen*
All aboard!	**Einsteigen!** *EYEN-shteye-gen*
Where should I get off?	**Wo soll ich aussteigen?** *voh zol ikh OWS-shteye-gen*
Must I change trains?	**Muss ich umsteigen?** *muss ikh UM-steye-gen*
Can I take the express from Osnabrück to Bassum?	**Kann ich mit dem Fernschnellzug von Osnabrück nach Bassum fahren?** *kahn ikh mit daym FEHRN-shnel-tsook fon oss-nah-BREWK nakh BAHSS-um FAAR-en*
Or must I change to a local train?	**Oder muss ich in einen Personenzug umsteigen?** *OHD-uh muss ikh in EYEN-en pehr-ZOHN-en-tsook UM-steye-gen*

A TOURING ITINERARY

The Rhine—fabled in song and story and heavy with wine and history—and the Alpine regions of Bavaria, Austria, and Switzerland are the most visited tourist areas. The flat north does not offer panoramic mountain views or exuberant baroque and rococo churches. Nevertheless, parts of Holstein and Saxony are so picturesque that they're known as **die Holsteinsche Schweiz** and **die Sächsische Schweiz** ("Holstein and Saxon Switzerland"). In addition, there are the North Sea and Baltic beaches and haunting landscapes of moor and marshland. Even in densely populated regions like the Ruhr basin, there is an abundance of museums, historic buildings, castles, parks, and other pleasant places worth visiting.

On the islands and in the coastal areas of the north, on Lake Constance (also known as "The Great Swabian Sea"), and on well over 1000 Alpine lakes in the south you can take many other boat trips besides the famous one on the Rhine. Most visitors to Hamburg take a **Hafenrundfahrt** (boat tour of the harbor), and many of the Alpine lakes have charming steamers. Since Germany, Austria, and Switzerland all border on the **Bodensee** (Lake Constance), you could visit all three countries in the same day. But there is such a wealth of sights—medieval, renaissance, and rococo monasteries, churches, castles, town halls, and palaces—that you will no doubt prefer to linger and savor as much as your time permits, rather than rush about. For good measure, there are vineyards (some dating back to medieval times), some citrus plantations on the island of Mainau, and prehistoric **Pfahlbauten** (palisade dwellings) on the water.

The source of the Danube in the Black Forest is not far from Lake Constance. And the Rhine, on its way to the North Sea from Switzerland, passes through it. You might well want to see the picturesque town of Stein am Rhein and the Rhine Falls near Schaffhausen, both in Switzerland. At Basel, and many other places, you can board a Rhine steamer either for a long tourist trip or for many shorter voyages. From Passau, on the Austrian border, you can take a Danube boat to Vienna and from there continue all the way to the Black Sea. When the Rhine steamers pass the fabled Lorelei Rock, bands often play the famous song about the siren who lured sailors to their doom. They also like to strike up Johann Strauss senior's **Lorelei Rheinklänge** waltz, and sometimes Johann Jr.'s renowned **An der Schönen Blauen Donau** ("On the Beautiful Blue Danube"). Johann Strauss also wrote a waltz, **An der Elbe**, and there are cruises on that river too. Many depart from Dresden.

Many hundreds of small towns all over Central Europe continue to cherish their cultural heritage. Some escaped wartime destruction; others have been lovingly restored. Large cities like Nuremberg, Munich, Vienna, and Dresden are filled with art treasures and look back on a past rich in achievement in technology, the crafts, and all the arts. The small area of Thuringia is associated with a wealth of great names, such as Bach, Luther, and Goethe. Many consider Austria's Großglockner mountain pass the most spectacular mountain drive in the world. Switzerland certainly does not lack for Alpine panoramas either and offers a variety of tours in trains like the "Glacier Express." In Switzerland you can also take a "Heidiland Tour" as well as a "chocolate" or a "cheese" tour. Everywhere in Central Europe you can tour spas or health resorts. In Hesse you can follow the **Hessische Bäder straße** (route of the spas). On it are famous old spas like Bad Homburg (Edward VII of England favored this one), Bad Ems (various emperors liked to hang out there), Bad Nauheim, Wiesbaden, and the isolated Schlangenbad (famous since Roman times for its huge but harmless snakes). But Hesse by no means has a monopoly on spas **(Kurorte).** You will find these elegant and restful watering places all over Germany, Austria, and Switzerland. Many, like Baden-Baden, are expensive, fashionable, and world-famous, but you will be able to select from hotels in various price categories there, too.

Germany offers many other vacation routes. One is even called the **Ferienstraße** (Vacation Road). The **Bergstraße** (Mountain Road) in the **Odenwald** (Odin's Wood) is renowned for its profusion of blossoms in the springtime. After visiting the famous Bavarian royal castles **(die Bayerischen Königsschösser),** you might want to take the **Deutsche Alpenstraße** (German Alpine Road), if you're driving, and either continue on to Lake Constance or journey north from Füssen to Würzburg on what is known as the **Romantische Straße** (Romantic Road). A great many tour buses take this route. Highlights on it are the medieval towns of Rothenburg, Dinkelsbühl, and Nördlingen. At the end of the **Romantische Straße** is Würzburg, a baroque-rococo jewel of a city. If you can, try to get to Veitzhöchheim, summer seat of the prince-bishops of Würzburg. You may have all you can handle visiting Würzburg's **Residenz** (the huge rococo palace) and the even larger medieval fortress-palace across the Main River, but the trip to Veitzhöchheim is worth the effort.

Another **Straße** (road) you might want to travel, perhaps after visiting Heidelberg, is the **Deutsche Weinstraße** (German Wine Road) in the Rhineland-Palatinate or the **Eichenlaubstraße** (Oak Leaf Road) in the nearby Saarland. It is a less traveled but charmingly rural tourist circuit.

There are many other off-the-beaten-track areas in Germany that you can set out to discover for yourself. Among these are the Lüneburg Heath and the Weser Bergland, where you can visit Hamelin (of "Pied Piper" fame) and many other storybook towns.

TRAVELING WITH PETS

Inquire at the consulate of every European country you plan to visit to find out what requirements you will have to meet to bring your pet. Proof of rabies vaccination is required everywhere.

Once at your destination, you will find that your pet is not welcome in all hotels and restaurants. But in those where it is, the following phrases may prove useful.

Bring a plate for my dog (my cat), please.	**Bringen Sie bitte einen Teller für meinen Hund (meine Katze).** *BRING-en zee BIT-eh EYEN-en TELL-uh fewr MEYEN-en hunt (MEYEN-eh KAHTS-eh)*
Would you be so kind as to give my dog (cat) some water (milk)?	**Würden Sie so lieb sein und meinem Hund (meiner Katze) etwas Wasser (Milch) geben?** *VEWRD-en zee zoh leep zeyen unt MEYEN-em hunt (MEYEN-uh KAHTS-eh) ET-vahs VAHSS-uh (milkh) GAYB-en*

In a grocery store you might ask:

What kind of dog food (cat food) do you have?	**Was für Hundefutter (Katzenfutter) haben Sie?** *vahs fewr HUND-eh-fut-uh (KAHTS-en-fut-uh) HAAB-en zee*

If your animal becomes ill:

Where can I find a veterinarian?	**Wo kann ich einen Tierarzt find-en?** *voh kahn ikh EYEN-en TEER ahrtst FIND-en*

In a hotel, you may want to ask:

How much extra for the night's lodging with the dog (the cat)?	**Wieviel extra kostet die Übernach-tung mit dem Hund (der Katze)?** *VEE-feel EHKS-tra KOST-et dee ew-ber-NAKH-tung mit daym hunt (dehr KAHTS-eh)*

Officially, dogs can travel on trains, but they must pay half a second-class-fare ticket. If someone complains, the dog must go to the baggage car.

DRIVING A CAR

At times you will find driving on the **Autobahnen** a less than restful experience. The recommended speed on them is 130 kilometers (80 mi.) per hour. But many vehicles (including military convoys) zoom by much faster. German **Landstraßen** (second-class main roads) and **Kreisstraßen** (district roads), as well as local roads, are all well maintained, and we recommend them for more scenic, stress-free driving.

ROAD SIGNS

You will recognize international road signs everywhere in German-speaking Europe. But you will also see signs written in German.

AUF 8 KM	For 8 Kilometers
AUSFAHRT FREI HALTEN	Keep Driveway Clear
BLAUE ZONE	Blue Parking Zone (requires special parking disk)
DURCHGANGS-VERKEHR	Through Traffic
EINBAHN-STRASSE	One-way Street
EINFAHRT FREI HALTEN	Do Not Block Entrance
EINORDNEN	Get in Lane
ENDE DES PARK-VERBOTS	End of No Parking Zone
____ (NICHT) ERLAUBT	____ (not) Allowed

Guarded railroad crossing

Yield

Stop

Right of way

Dangerous intersection ahead

Gasoline (petrol) ahead

Parking

No vehicles allowed

Dangerous curve

Pedestrian crossing

Oncoming traffic has right of way

No bicycles allowed

No parking allowed

No entry

No left turn

No U-turn

No passing

Border crossing

Traffic signal ahead

Speed limit

Traffic circle (roundabout) ahead

Minimum speed limit

All traffic turns left

End of no passing zone

One-way street

Detour

Danger ahead

Entrance to expressway

Expressway ends

FROSTSCHÄDEN	Frost Damage
FUSSGÄNGER-ZONE	Pedestrian Zone
GEFÄHRLICHES GEFÄLLE	Dangerous Descent
GEFÄHRLICHE STEIGUNG	Dangerous (steep) Hill
HALT, POLIZEI	Stop, Police
HUPEN VERBO-TEN	No Honking
KEIN DURCHGANG FÜR FUSSGÄNGER	Closed to Pedestrians
KURZPARKZONE	Limited Parking Zone
LANGSAM FAHREN	Drive Slowly
LAWINENGEFAHR	Danger of Avalanche
LINKS FAHREN	Keep Left
LKW	Alternate Truck Route
NUR FÜR ANLIEGER	Residents Only
PARKEN VERBOTEN	No Parking
RECHTS FAHREN	Keep Right
SCHLECHTE FAHRBAHN	Bad Road Surface
SCHULE	School
SPURRILLEN	Grooves in Road

STEINSCHLAG	Falling Rocks
STRASSENAR-BEITEN AUF 5 KILOMETER	Road Work for 5 Kilometers
UMLEITUNG	Detour
VERKEHRSSTAU AUF 15 KILOMETER	Traffic Backups (jams) for the Next 15 Kilometers
____ VERBOTEN	____ Not Allowed
VORSICHT	Caution

PARKING

In metropolitan areas there are parking sections known as "Blue Zones." To park there you must use a parking disk, which can be obtained free of charge at auto clubs, garages, gas stations, hotels, police stations, and tourist offices. You must set the time of your arrival, and the departure time will show automatically on the disk. The disk should be displayed on your windshield. Be careful to observe these regulations. Ignoring them may result in a fine.

CAR RENTALS

It may be a good idea to reserve your rental car at home before your trip, as the rates are often lower that way.

In major cities and terminals in German-speaking Europe, you can rent almost any model and make of American or European car. The legal driving age is 18, but some car rental companies have set higher limits. In Germany you may use your national driver's license to rent a vehicle. Many car rental agencies allow you to pick up and drop off cars at offices throughout Germany, but check with the individual agency about this.

Special arrangements can be made for chauffeur-driven cars with English-speaking drivers.

I need ___.	**Ich brauche ___.** *ikh BROWKH-eh*
■ a car	**einen Wagen** *EYEN-en VAAG-en*
■ a motorcycle	**ein Motorrad** *eyen moh-TOHR-raat*
■ a bicycle	**ein Fahrrad** *eyen FAAR-raat*
Is there a car rental office nearby?	**Gibt es eine Autovertmietung in der Nähe?** *gipt ehs EYEN-eh OW-toh-fehr-meet-ung in dehr NAY-eh*
Can they send somebody to pick me up at my hotel?	**Kann mich jemand im Hotel abholen?** *kahn mikh YAY-mahnt im ho-TEL AHP-hohl-en*
I need a big (small) car.	**Ich brauche einen grossen (kleinen) Wagen.** *ikh BROWKH-eh EYEN-en GROHSS-en (KLEYEN-en) VAAG-en*
What sort of cars do you have available?	**Was für Wagen haben Sie zu vermieten?** *vahs fewr VAAG-en HAAB-en zee tsoo fehr-MEET-en*

How much does it cost per ____?	**Wieviel kostet es pro ____?** *VEE-feel KOST-et ehs proh*
■ day	**Tag** *taak*
■ week	**Woche** *VOKH-eh*
■ month	**Monat** *MOH-naat*
■ kilometer	**Kilometer** *kee-loh-MAYT-uh*
How much is the insurance?	**Was kostet die Versicherung?** *vahs KOST-et dee fehr-ZIKH-ehr-ung*
Do I have to pay for gas?	**Muss ich das Benzin bezahlen?** *muss ikh dahs behn-TSEEN beh-TSAAL-en*
Do I have to leave a deposit?	**Muss ich etwas hinterlegen?** *muss ikh EHT-vahs hin-tehr-LAYG-en*
Even with this credit card?	**Selbst mit dieser Kreditkarte?** *zehlpst mit DEEZ-uh kray-DIT-kaart-eh*
I want to rent the car here and leave it in Munich.	**Ich will das Auto hier mieten und es in München wieder abgeben.** *ikh vil dahs OW-toh heer MEET-en unt ehs in MEWN-khen VEED-uh AHP-gayb-en*
Is there an additional charge for that?	**Entstehen mir dadurch zuätzliche Kosten?** *ehnt-SHTAY-en meer daa-DURKH TSOO-zehts-likh-eh KOST-en*
What kind of gasoline does it use?	**Mit welchem Benzin fährt der Wagen?** *mit VEHLKH-em behn-TSEEN fayrt dehr VAAG-en*
Here is my driver's license.	**Hier haben Sie meinen Führerschein.** *heer HAAB-en zee MEYEN-en FEWR-ehr-sheyen*

Do I have your telephone number?	**Habe ich Ihre Telefonnummer?** *HAAB-eh ikh EER-eh tay-leh-FOHN-num-uh*
Can I reach you day and night?	**Kann ich Sie Tag und Nacht erreichen?** *kahn ikh zee taak unt nahkht ehr-REYEKH-en*

ON THE ROAD

In mountainous Austria you can get information on road and traffic conditions by dialing 72 9 97 in Vienna (preceded by 0222 elsewhere in Austria). In Switzerland dial 163 for a recorded message in German. The Vienna number, you will be pleased to hear, provides information in English.

Pardon me.	**Entschuldigen Sie, bitte.** *ehnt-SHULD-ig-en zee BIT-eh*
Is this the road to ____?	**Ist dies die Straße nach ____?** *ist dees dee SHTRAASS-eh nahkh*
Where does this road lead?	**Wohin führt diese Straße?** *VOH-hin fewrt DEEZ-eh SHTRAASS-eh*
How do we get to ____?	**Wie kommen wir nach ____?** *Vee KOM-en veer nahkh*
Is this road shorter (longer)?	**Ist diese Straße kürzer (länger)?** *ist DEEZ-eh SHTRAASS-eh KEWRTS-ehr (LEHNG-ehr)*
Is it still very far to ____?	**Ist es noch sehr weit nach ____?** *ist ehs nokh zayr veyet nahkh*
What's the next town called?	**Wie heißt der nächste Ort?** *vee heyesst dehr NAYKST-eh ort*
Do you have a road map?	**Haben Sie eine Autokarte?** *HAAB-en zee EYEN-eh OW-toh-kaart-eh*

Can you show it to me on the map?	**Können Sie ihn mir auf der Karte zeigen?** *KERN-en zee een meer owf dehr KAART-eh TSEYEG-en*
Shall I drive straight ahead?	**Soll ich geradeaus fahren?** *zol ikh geh-RAAD-eh-owss FAAR-en*
Where must I turn?	**Wo muss ich abbiegen?** *voh muss ikh AHP-beeg-en*
Left?	**Links?** *links*
Right?	**Rechts?** *rehkhts*
At the next (second, third) traffic light?	**Bei der nächsten (zweiten, dritten) Ampel?** *beye dehr NAYKST-en (TSVEYE-ten, DRIT-en) AHMP-el*
Are there road signs, or should I ask again there?	**Ist es gut beschildert oder soll ich dort wieder fragen?** *ist ehs goot beh-SHILD-ehrt OHD-uh zol ikh dort VEED-uh FRAAG-en*
I got lost because of the detour.	**Wegen der Umleitung habe ich mich verfahren.** *VAYG-en dehr UM-leyet-ung haab ikh mikh fehr-FAAR-en*
Am I on the right road now?	**Bin ich jetzt auf der richtigen Straße?** *bin ikh yetst owf dehr RIKHT-ig-en SHTRAASS-eh*
■ highway exit	**Ausfahrt** *OWS-faart*

AT THE SERVICE STATION

Gasoline is sold by the liter in Europe, and if you are accustomed to gallons, it may seem confusing, especially if you want to calculate your mileage per gallon (kilometer per liter). See next page for some tips on making these conversions.

I'm looking for a gas station.	**Ich suche eine Tankstelle.** *ikh ZOOKH-eh EYEN-eh TAHNK-shtehl-eh*
Where is the nearest gas station (with service)?	**Wo ist die nächste Tankstelle (mit Bedienung)?** *voh ist dee NAYKST-eh TAHNK-shtehl-eh (mit beh-DEEN-ung)*

LIQUID MEASURES (Approximate)		
LITERS	US GALLONS	IMPERIAL GALLONS
10	2-3/4	2-1/4
20	5-1/4	4-1/2
30	8	6-1/2
40	10-1/2	8-3/4
50	13-1/4	11
60	15-3/4	13
70	19-1/8	15-1/2
80	21	17-1/2

DISTANCE MEASURES (Approximate)	
KILOMETERS	MILES
1	0.62
5	3
10	6-1/4
20	12-1/2
30	18-1/2
40	24-3/4
50	31
60	37-1/4
70	43-1/2
80	49-1/2
90	55-3/4
100	62

I don't want self-service.	**Ich will keine Selbstbedienung (SB).** *ikh vil KEYEN-eh ZEHLPST-beh-deen-ung (ess bay)*

(Although it is becoming increasingly difficult, many of you will want to make the effort to find full-service stations.)

Fill'er up, please.	**Voll, bitte.** *fol BIT-eh*
Give me twenty-five liters.	**Geben Sie mir fünfundzwanzig Liter.** *GAYB-en zee meer FEWNF-unt-tsvahn-tsikh LEET-uh*
■ regular	**Normal** *nor-MAAL*
■ super	**Super** *ZOOP-uh*
Please check the oil and water.	**Bitte kontrollieren Sie Ölstand und Wasser.** *BIT-eh kon-tro-LEER-en zee ERL-shtahnt unt VAHSS-uh*
Please check ____.	**Prüfen Sie bitte ____.** *PREWF-en zee BIT-eh*
■ the battery	**die Batterie** *dee bah-teh-REE*
■ the brakes	**die Bremsen** *dee BREHM-zen*
■ the carburetor	**den Vergaser** *dayn fehr-GAAZ-uh*
■ the spark plugs	**die Zündkerzen** *dee TSEWNT-kehrts-en*
■ the ignition system	**die Zündung** *dee TSEWND-ung*
■ the lights	**die Beleuchtung** *dee beh-LOYKHT-ung*
■ the tires	**die Reifen** *dee REYEF-en*
■ the spare tire	**den Ersatzreifen** *dayn ehr-ZATS-reyef-en*
■ the tire pressure	**den Reifendruck** *dayn REYEF-en-druk*
Can you change the tire (the oil) now?	**Können Sie den Reifen (das Öl) jetzt wechseln?** *KERN-en zee dayn REYEF-en (dahs erl) yetst VEHK-sehln*

Charge the battery, please.	**Bitte laden Sie die Batterie auf.** *BIT-eh LAAD-en zee dee bah-tay-REE owf*
Wash the car.	**Waschen Sie das Auto.** *VAHSH-en zee dahs OW-toh*
How long will it take?	**Wie lange wird es dauern?** *Vee LAHNG-eh veert ehs DOW-ehrn*
Please clean the windshield.	**Reinigen Sie bitte die Windschutz- scheibe.** *REYEN-ig-en zee BIT-eh dee VINT-shuts-sheyeb-eh*
Where are the rest rooms?	**Wo sind die Toiletten?** *voh zint dee toy-LET-en*
Do you have road maps? A telephone?	**Haben Sie Straßenkarten? Ein Telefon?** *HAAB-en zee SHTRASS- en-kaart-en eyen tay-leh-FOHN*

TIRE PRESSURE	
LB/SQ. IN.	KG/SQ. CM.
18	1.3
20	1.4
21	1.5
23	1.6
24	1.7
26	1.8
27	1.9
28	2.0
30	2.1
31	2.2
33	2.3
34	2.4
36	2.5
37	2.6
38	2.7
40	2.8

ACCIDENTS AND REPAIRS

My car has broken down.	**Mein Wagen hat eine Panne.** *meyen VAAG-en haht EYEN-eh PAHN-eh*
It overheats.	**Er ist überhitzt.** *ehr ist EWB-uh-hitst*
I have a flat tire.	**Der Reifen ist kaputt.** *dehr REYEF-en ist kah-PUT*
The car is stuck.	**Der Wagen ist verklemmt.** *dehr VAAG-en ist fehr-KLEHMT*
The radiator is leaking.	**Der Kühler ist undicht.** *dehr KEWL-uh ist UN-dikht*
The battery is dead.	**Die Batterie funktioniert nicht.** *dee bah-teh-REE funk-tsee-o-NEERT nikht*
The keys are locked inside the car.	**Die Schlüssel sind im Wagen und der Wagen ist abgeschlossen.** *dee SHLEWSS-el zint im VAAG-en unt dehr VAAG-en ist AHP-geh-shloss-en*
Is there a garage (for repairs) near here?	**Gibt es eine Reparaturwerkstatt in der Nähe?** *gipt ehs EYEN-eh reh-paa-rah-TOOR-vehrk-shtaht in dehr NAY-eh*
Can you help me?	**Können Sie mir helfen?** *KERN-en zee meer HELF-en*
I have no tools.	**Ich habe keine Werkzeuge.** *ikh HAAB-eh KEYEN-eh VEHRK-tsoyg-eh*
I can't change the tire.	**Ich kann den Reifen nicht wechsein.** *ikh kahn dayn REYEF-en nikht VEHKS-ein*

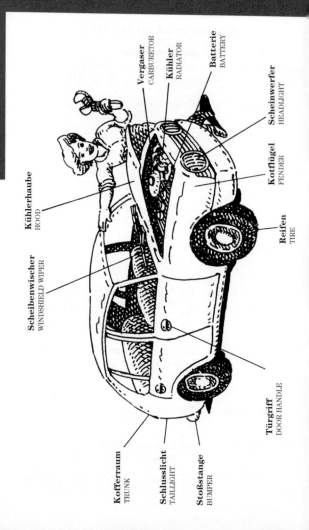

Verfaser CARBURETOR

Kühler RADIATOR

Batterie BATTERY

Scheinwerfer HEADLIGHT

Kühlerhaube HOOD

Kotflügel FENDER

Scheibenwischer WINDSHIELD WIPER

Reifen TIRE

Türgriff DOOR HANDLE

Kofferraum TRUNK

Schlusslicht TAILLIGHT

Stoßstange BUMPER

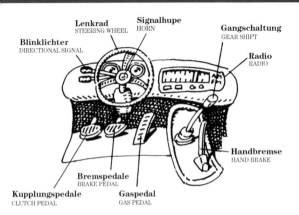

Lenkrad / STEERING WHEEL
Signalhupe / HORN
Gangschaltung / GEAR SHIFT
Blinklichter / DIRECTIONAL SIGNAL
Radio / RADIO
Handbremse / HAND BRAKE
Bremspedale / BRAKE PEDAL
Kupplungspedale / CLUTCH PEDAL
Gaspedal / GAS PEDAL

I need a mechanic (a tow truck).	**Ich brauche einen Mechaniker (Abschleppwagen).** *ikh BROWKH-eh EYEN-en meh-KHAA-nik-uh (AHP-shlehp-vaag-en)*
Can you lend me ___?	**Können Sie mir ___ leihen?** *KERN-en zee meer ___ LEYE-en*

- a flashlight **eine Taschenlampe** *EYEN-eh TAHSH-en-lahmp-eh*
- a hammer **einen Hammer** *EYEN-en HAHM-uh*
- a jack **einen Wagenheber** *EYEN-en VAAG-en-hayb-uh*
- a monkey wrench **einen Schraubenschlüssel** *EYEN-en SHROWB-en-shlewssel*
- pliers **eine Zange** *EYEN-eh TSAHNG-eh*
- a screwdriver **einen Schraubenzieher** *EYEN-en SHROWB-en-tsee-uh*

Can you fix the car?	**Können Sie den Wagen reparieren?** *KERN-en zee dayn VAAG-en ray-paa-REER-en*

Do you have the part?	**Haben Sie das Ersatzteil?** *HAAB-en zee dahs ehr-ZAHTS-teyel*
I need ____.	**Ich brauche ____.** *ikh BROWKH-eh*
■ a bulb	**eine Birne** *EYEN-eh BIRN-eh*
■ a filter	**einen Filter** *EYEN-en FILT-uh*
■ a fuse	**eine Sicherung** *EYEN-eh ZIKH-ehr-ung*
I think there's something wrong with ____.	**Ich glaube, es ist irgend etwas mit ____ verkehrt.** *ikh GLOWB-eh, ehs ist EER-gehnt EHT-vahs mit ____ fehr-KAYRT*
■ the directional signals	**den Blinklichtern** *dayn BLINK-likht-ehrn*
■ the door handle	**dem Türgriff** *daym TEWR-grif*
■ the electrical system	**der elektrischen Anlage** *dehr eh-LEHK-trish-en AHN-lahg-eh*
■ the fan	**dem Ventilator** *daym ven-ti-LAAT-ohr*
■ the fan belt	**dem Keilriemen** *daym KEYEL-reem-en*
■ the fuel pump	**der Benzinpumpe** *dehr behn-TSEEN-pump-eh*
■ the gear shift	**der Gangschaltung** *dehr GAHNG-shahlt-ung*
■ the headlights	**den Scheinwerfern** *dayn SHEYEN-vehr-fehrn*
■ the horn	**der Hupe** *der HOOP-eh*
■ the ignition	**der Zündung** *dehr TSEWND-ung*
■ the radio	**dem Radio** *daym RAA-dee-oh*
■ the starter	**dem Anlasser** *daym AHN-lahss-uh*
■ the steering wheel	**dem Steuerrad** *daym SHTOY-uh-raat*
■ the taillight	**dem Schlusslicht** *daym SHLUSS-likht*

■ the transmission	**dem Getriebe** *daym geh-TREEB-eh*
■ the water pump	**der Wasserpumpe** *dehr VAHSS-uh-pump-eh*
■ the windshield wiper	**dem Scheibenwischer** *daym SHEYEB-en-vish-uh*
Can you look at ____?	**Können Sie sich ____ ansehen?** *KERN-en zee zikh ____ AHN-zay-en*
■ the brakes	**die Bremsen** *dee BREHM-zen*
■ the bumper	**die Stoßstange** *dee SHTOHSS-shtahng-eh*
■ the exhaust	**dem Auspuff** *daym OWS-puf*
■ the fender	**den Kotflügel** *dayn KOT-flewg-el*
■ the gas tank	**den Benzintank** *dayn behn-TSEEN-tahnk*
■ the hood	**die Kühlerhaube** *dee KEWL-ehr-howb-eh*
■ the trunk	**den Kofferraum** *dayn KOHF-uh-rowm*
Can you repair it temporarily?	**Können Sie es provisorisch reparieren?** *KERN-en zee ehs pro-vi-ZOHR-ish ray-paa-REER-en*
How long will it take?	**Wie lange dauert's?** *vee LAHNG-eh DOW-ehrts*
Couldn't it possibly be done today?	**Geht's vielleicht doch heute noch?** *gayts fee-LEYEKHT dokh HOYT-eh nokh*
Is everything OK now?	**Ist jetzt alles in Ordnung?** *ist yetst AH-lehs in ORT-nung*
How much do I owe you?	**Was schulde ich Ihnen?** *vahs SHULD-eh ikh EEN-en*

ENTERTAINMENT AND DIVERSIONS

MOVIES, THEATER, CONCERTS, OPERA, BALLET

At the movies you will be surprised to see and hear the stars of American films all speaking German (although occasionally you will find foreign movies in the original language with German subtitles). Shows are on a fixed schedule, and you may buy your tickets in advance.

Large cities offer a wealth of theatrical and musical events, and even have a separate theater for operettas, such as Vienna's **Theater am Gärtnerplatz.** In medium-sized cities the **Stadttheater** (Municipal Theater) offers a mix of theater, opera, operetta, and ballet. In Berlin, Vienna, Hamburg, and Munich, opera is performed in the **Staatsoper** (State Opera). Many of the great opera houses were destroyed in World War II. Some have been restored, and some have been rebuilt in the modern style.

The **Festspielhaus** in Bayreuth is a place of summer pilgrimage for Wagnerites. Salzburg, Ansbach, Berlin, Schwetzingen, Donaueschingen, and Ludwigsburg also host famous music festivals. Castles and gardens everywhere resound with vocal and instrumental music. Choral and other concerts often take place in cathedrals and churches, too. Leipzig's **Thomaskirche** (St. Thomas Church) is closely associated with Bach, and that same city's concert hall, the **Gewandhous,** is historically linked to Mendelssohn, Schumann, and other famous musical figures.

Theater curtain time is 8 P.M. You'll do well to reserve in advance.

Let's go ____.	**Gehen wir ____.**	*GAY-en veer*
■ to the movies	**ins Kino**	*ins KEEN-oh*
■ to the museum	**ins Museum**	*ins moo-ZAY-um*
■ to the theater	**ins Theater**	*ins tay-AAT-uh*

■ to the opera · **in die Oper** · *in dee OHP-uh*

What sort of a movie is it? · **Was für eim Film ist es?** · *vahs fewr eyen film ist ehs*

It's ____. · **Est ist ____.** · *ehs ist*

■ a mystery · **ein Krimi** · *eyen KREEM-ee*

■ a comedy · **eine Komödie** · *EYEN-eh ko-MERD-yeh*

■ a drama · **ein Drama** · *eyen DRAAM-ah*

■ a musical · **ein Musical** · *eyen MYOOZ-ikal*

■ a romance · **eine Liebesgeschichte** · *EYEN-eh LEEB-es-ge-SCHIKHT-eh*

■ a war film · **ein Kriegsfilm** · *eyen KREEKS-film*

■ a science fiction film · **ein Science-fictionfilm** · *eyen SEYE ens-FICKSH-en-film*

■ a romantic movie · **ein romantischer Film** · *eyen roh-MAHNT-isch-uh film*

■ a horror film · **ein Horror film** · *eyen HOR-or-film*

Is it in English? · **Ist es in Englisch?** · *ist ehs in EHNG-lish*

Are there English subtitles? · **Hat er englischer Untertitel?** · *haht ehr EHNG-lish-eh UNT-uh-TEET-el*

Where is the time schedule? · **Wo ist der Zietplan?** · *voh ist dehr TSEIT-plaan*

What time does the (first) show begin? · **Wann beginnt die (erste) Vorstellung?** · *vahn beh-GINT dee (EHRST-eh) FOR-shtel-ung*

What time does the (last) show end? · **Wann endet die (letzte) Vorstellung?** · *vahn EHND-eht dee (LETST-eh) FOR-shtel-ung*

BUYING A TICKET

Can you get tickets for me?	**Können Sie Karten für mich besorgen?** *KERN-en zee KAART-en fewr mikh beh-ZORG-en*
I need two seats in the ___.	**Ich brauche zwie Sitze/Plätze im ___.** *ikh BROWKH-eh tsveye SITZ-eh/PLETS-eh im*

- orchestra   **Orchester** *or-KHES-tuh*
- balcony   **orbesten Rang** *OH-behrst-en rahng*
- first balcony   **ersten Rang** *EHRST-en rahng*
- mezzanine   **Mezzanin** *mehts-ah-NEEN*

I prefer ___.	**Ich höre am liebsten ___.** *ikh HEWR-eh am LEEP-sten*

- classical music   **klassische musik** *KLAHS-ish-eh mooz-EEK*
- popular music   **Popmusik** *POP-mooz-EEK*
- soft rock   **Softrock** *SOFT-rock*
- heavy metal   **Heavymetal** *heavy metal*
- opera   **Oper** *OHP-uh*
- ballet   **Ballett** *bah-LETT*
- folk dancing   **Volkstänze** *FOLKS-tehnts-eh*

What are they playing?	**Was spielt man?** *vahs shpeelt mahn*
Should I get tickets in advance?	**Sol ich Karten im voraus bestellen?** *zol ikh KAART-en im FOR-owss beh-SHTEL-en*
Do I have to dress formally?	**Wird Abendgarderobe verlangt?** *veert AAB-ent-gahr-deh-ROHB-eh ferh-LAHNKT*
How much are the front-row seats?	**Wieviel kosten die Plätze in der ersten Reihe?** *VEE-feel KOST-en dee PLETS-eh in derh EHRST-en REYE-eh*

What are the least expensive seats?	**Welche sind die billigsten Plätze?** *VELKH-eh zint dee BIL-ikhst-en PLETS-eh*
May I buy a program?	**Darf ich ein Program kaufen?** *dahrf ikh eyen proh-GRAHM KOWF-en*
When does the season begin (end)?	**Wann beginnt (endet) die Saison?** *vahn beh-GINT (END-eht) dee ZAY-zohn*
Who is the conductor?	**Wer dirigiert?** *vehr di-ree-GEERT*
Who's singing (tenor, soprano, baritone contralto)?	**Wer singt (Tenor, Sopran, Bariton, Alt)?** *vehr zinkt (ten-OHR, zo-PRAAN, bahry-TOHN, ahlt)*

NIGHTCLUBS

You will find **gemütlich** (homey, informal) sing-along places everywhere. The big cities cater to more bizarre tastes and offer an enormous variety of nightlife. Munich's Schwabing and Hamburg's notorious Sankt Pauli districts receive many visitors. Sankt Pauli's main street, the Reeperbahn, and the streets around it offer scores of clubs and dance halls. A word of caution to unattached gentlemen: In some places in Sankt Pauli and similar areas you may be staggered by the bill, especially if you have bought what you thought was a casual drink for a female habitué of the establishment.

I'd like to go to an interesting nightclub tonight.	**Ich möchte gerne in ein interessantes Nachtlokal heute abend gehen.** *ikh MERKHT-eh GEHRN-eh in eyen in-teh-ress-AHNT-es NAKHT-loh-kaal HOYT-eh AAB-ent GAY-en*
■ a beer or wine tavern with happy music.	**Eine Bier- oder Weinstube mit fröhlicher Musik.** *EYEN-eh beer OHD-uh VEYEN-shtoob-eh mit FRER-likh-ehr moo-ZEEK*
■ a discotheque with young people.	**Eine Diskothek mit jungen Leuten.** *EYEN-eh dis-koh-TAYK mit YUNG-en LOYT-en*
■ a lavish nightclub with a floor show.	**ein Nachtlokal von Format mit Attraktionen.** *eyen NAHKHT-lo-kaal fon for-MAAT mit aht-rahk-tsee-OHN-en*
Is a reservation necessary?	**Muss man reservieren lassen?** *muss mahn reh-zehr-VEER-en LASS-en*
Is evening dress required?	**Wird Abendgarderobe verlangt?** *veert AAB-ent-gaar-deh-roh-beh fehr-LAHNKT*
Where can I see folk dances?	**Wo kann ich Volkstänze sehen?** *voh kahn ikh FOLKS-tehn-tseh ZAY-en*

I'd like a good table.	**Ich möchte einen guten Tisch.** *ikh MERKHT-eh EYEN-en GOOT-en tish*
I want an adventure, but not an expensive evening.	**Ich will ein Abenteuer aber keinen teuren Abend.** *ikh vill eyen AAB-ehn-toy-uh AAB-uh KEYEN-en TOY-ren AAB-ent*
Is there a minimum?	**Gibt es eine Mindestgebühr?** *gipt ehs EYEN-eh MIND-ehst-geh-BEWR*

QUIET RELAXATION

Shall we play cards?	**Wollen wir Karten spielen?** *VOL-en veer KAART-en SHPEEL-en*
Do you have a deck of cards?	**Haben Sie Spielkarten?** *HAAB-en zee SHPEEL-kaart-en*
I'll shuffle.	**Ich mische.** *ikh MISH-eh*
You cut.	**Heben Sie ab.** *HAYB-en zee ahp*
Who dealt the cards?	**Wer hat die Karten gegeben?** *vehr haht dee KAART-en geh-GAYB-en*
What's trump?	**Was ist Trumpf?** *vahs ist trumpf*
■ hearts, diamonds, clubs, or spades?	**Herz, Karo, Kreuz, oder Pik?** *hehrts, KAA-roh, kroyts, OHD-uh peek*
You've got to show your cards now.	**Sie müssen jetzt Ihre Karten hinlegen.** *zee MEWSS-en yetst EER-eh KAART-en hin-LAYG-en*
I see the ____ is missing.	**Ich sehe ____ fehlt.** *ikh ZAY-eh ____ faylt*
■ the ace	**das As** *dahs ahss*
■ the king	**der König** *dehr KERN-ikh*

■ the queen	**die Dame**	*dee DAAM-eh*
■ the jack	**der Bube**	*dehr BOOB-eh*

Maybe you'd rather play gin rummy or 17 and 4 (21).	**Vielleicht spielten Sie lieber Rommé oder Siebzehn und Vier?** *FEEL-eyekht SHPEELT-en zee LEEB-uh ROM-may OHD-uh ZEEP-tsayn unt feer*
I'd like to play chess or checkers.	**Ich möchte Schach oder Dame spielen.** *ikh MERKHT-eh shakh OHD-uh DAAM-eh SHPEEL-en*
What are the names of the chess pieces in German?	**Wie heißen die Schachfiguren auf Deutsch?** *vee HEYESS-en dee SHAHKH-fi-goor-en owf doytsh*
They are called ____.	**Sie heißen ____.** *zee HEYESS-en*

■ the king	**der König**	*dehr KERN-ikh*
■ the queen	**die Dame**	*dee DAAM-eh*
■ the rook	**der Turm**	*dehr toorm*
■ the bishop	**der Läufer**	*dehr LOYF-uh*
■ the knight	**der Springer**	*dehr SHPRING-uh*
■ the pawn	**der Bauer**	*dehr BOW-uh*

Checkmate!	**Schachmatt!** *shahkh-MAHT*
You've won (lost) again.	**Sie haben wieder gewonnen (verloren).** *zee HAAB-en VEED-uh geh-VON-en (fehr-LOHR-en)*

SPORTS

As in the rest of Europe, Fußball (soccer) is by far the most popular sport. If you want to see some of the best teams in the world, you have come to the right place.

I would like to see a soccer match.	**Ich möchte ein Fußballmatch sehen.** *ikh MERKH-teh eyen FOOSS-bahl-mehch ZAY-en*
Where is the stadium?	**Wo ist das Stadion?** *voh ist dahs SHTAAD-ee-ohn*
What teams are going to play?	**Welche Mannschaften spielen?** *VELKH-eh MAHN-shahft-en SHPEEL-en*
What is the score?	**Wie ist der Spielstand?** *vee ist dehr SHPEEL-shtahnt*
How much is a ticket?	**Was kostet eine Eintrittskarte?** *vahs KOST-et EYEN-eh EYEN-trits-kaart-eh*

SPORTS VOCABULARY

I'd like to ___.	**Ich möchte ___.** *ikh MERKHT-eh*
■ do aerobics	**Aerobic betreiben** *ah-eh-ROHB-ik beh-TREYEB-en*
■ play baseball	**Baseball spielen** *BAYSS-bahl SHPEEL-en*
■ play basketball	**Baksetball spielen** *BAHS-keht-bahl SHPEEL-en*
■ go bicycling	**Rad fahren** *raat FAAR-en*
■ go boating	**Boot fahren** *boht FAAR-en*
■ do bodybuilding	**Bodybuilding betreiben** *BO-dee-bil-ding beh-TREYEB-en*
■ go canoeing	**Paddelboot fahren** *PAHD-el-boht faar-en*
■ go diving	**Wasser sprigen** *VAHSS-uh shpring-en*
■ fish	**angeln** *AHNG-eln*
■ play golf	**Golf spielen** *golf SHPEEL-en*

- play hockey **Hockey spielen** *HOK-eh SHPEEL-en*
- go horseback riding **reiten** *REYET-en*
- go hunting **auf die Jagd gehen** *owf dee jahkt GAY-en*
- ice-skate **Schlittschuh laufen** *SHLIT-shoo LOWF-en*
- go mountain climbing **bergsteigen** *BEHRK-shteyeg-en*
- parasail **parasegeln** *pah-rah ZAYG-eln*
- go roller skating **Rollschuh laufen** *ROL-shoo LOWF-en*
- go sailing **Segelsport fahren** *ZAYG-el-shport FAAR-en*
- scuba dive **Sporttauchen betreiben** *SHPORT-towkh-en beh-TREYEB-en*
- ski **Ski laufen** *skee LOWF-en*
- surf **surfen** *SERF-en*
- swim **schwimmen** *SHVIM-en*
- play tennis **Tennis spielen** *TEN-iss SHPEEL-en*
- play volleyball **Volleyball spielen** *VOL-ee-bahl SHPEEL-en*

PLAYING FIELDS

Shall we go ____. **Gehen wir ____.** *GAY-en veer*

- to the beach **an den Strand** *ahn dayn shtrahnt*
- to the court **auf den Platz** *owf dayn plahts*
- to the field **aufs Feld** *owfs felt*
- to the golf course **auf den Golfplatz** *owf dayn GOLF-plahts*
- to the gymnasium **in die Turnhalle** *in dee TOORN-hahl-eh*
- to the mountains **in die Berge** *in dee BEHRG-eh*

- to the ocean **an den Ozean** *ahn dayn ots-ay-AHN*
- to the park **in den Park** *in dayn pahrk*
- to the path **an den Pfad** *ahn dayn pfaat*
- to the pool **zum Schwimmbad** *tsoom SHVIM-baht*
- to the (roller-skating) rink **zur Rollschuhbahn** *tsoor ROL-shoo-baan*
- to the (ice-skating) rink **zur Schlittschuhbahn** *tsoor SHLIT-shoo-baan*
- to the sea **an die See** *ahn dee zay*
- to the stadium **zum Stadion** *tsoom SHTAAD-ee-ohn*
- to the track **zur Rennbahn** *tsoor REN-baan*

SPORTS EQUIPMENT

I need ___. **Ich brauche ___.** *ikh BROWKH-eh*

- a ball **einen ball** *EYEN-en bahl*
- a bat **ein Schlagholz** *eyen SHLAHK-holts*
- a bicycle **ein Fahrrad** *eyen FAAR-raht*
- a boat **ein Boot** *eyen boht*
- a canoe **ein Paddelboot** *eyen PAHD-el-boht*
- a diving suit **einen Taucheranzug** *EYEN-en TOWKH-uh-ahn-tsook*
- a fishing rod **eine Angelrute** *EYEN-eh AHNG-el-root-eh*
- golf clubs **Golfschläger** *golf-shlayg-uh*
- a hockey stick **einen Hockystock** *EYEN-en HOK-eh-shtok*
- ice skates **Schlittschuhe** *SHLIT-shoo-eh*
- jogging shoes **Joggingschuhe** *JOG-ing-shoo-eh*
- a jogging suit **einen Jogginganzug** *EYEN-en JOG-ing-ahn-tsook*
- mitts **Baseballhandschuhe** *BAYSS-bahl-hahnt-shoo-eh*

■ a net	**ein Netz** *eyen nets*
■ a puck	**einen Puck** *EYEN-en pook*
■ a racket	**einen Schläger** *EYEN-en SHLAYG-uh*
■ roller blades	**Inliner** *IN-leyen-uh*
■ a sailboard	**ein Windsurfbrett** *eyen VINT-serf-bret*
■ scuba gear	**Schwimmtauchausrüstung** *SHVIM-towkh-ows-rewst-ung*
■ a skateboard	**ein Skateboard** *eyen SKAYT-bohrd*
■ skis	**Skier** *SKEE-uh*
■ a surfboard	**ein Surfbrett** *eyen SERF-bret*
■ weights	**Gewichte** *geh-VIKHT-eh*
■ a wet suit	**einen Tauchanzug** *EYEN-en TOWKH-ahn-tsook*

SWIMMING

There has been a boom in the construction of swimming pools in recent years. Even small German, Austrian, and Swiss towns have large municipal pools. Increasingly popular are the **Thermalbäder** (thermal swimming pools), found especially in resort areas and spas.

The nudist movement, long an important one in Germany, especially in the north, is called **Freikörperkultur** (free physical culture). A number of lakes and North Sea and Baltic resorts have nudist (FKK) beaches.

It's terribly hot today!	**Welche Hitze heute!** *VELKH-eh HITS-eh HOYT-eh*
Where can I find a swimming pool?	**Wo kann ich ein Schwimmbad finden?** *voh kahn ikh eyen SHVIM-baat FIND-en*
Is it heated?	**Ist es geheizt?** *ist ehs geh-HEYETST*

What's the water temperature?	**Welche Temperatur hat das Wasser?** *VELKH-eh lem-pay-raa-TOOR haht dahs VAHSS-uh*
How do I get there?	**Wie komme ich dort hin?** *vee KOM-eh ikh dort hin*
When is low tide (high tide)?	**Wann ist Ebbe (Flut)?** *vahn ist EHB-eh (floot)*
Is there a lake in the area?	**Gibt es einen See in der Gegend?** *gipt ehs EYEN-en zay in dehr GAY-gent*
Is there a nudist beach in this area?	**Gibt es ein FKK Strandbad in dieser Gegend?** *gipt ehs eyen ef-koh-kah SHTRAHNT-baat in DEEZ-uh GAY-gent*
What's the admission charge?	**Was kostet der Eintritt?** *vahs KOST-et dehr EYEN-trit*
Is it safe to swim there?	**Kann man dort ohne Gefahr schwimmen?** *kahn mahn dort OHN-eh geh-FAAR SHVIM-en*
Is there a lifeguard?	**Gibt es einen Rettungsdienst?** *gipt ehs EYEN-en REHT-unks-deenst*
Can you swim in the river (pond)?	**Kann man im Fluss (Teich) schwimmen?** *kahn mahn im fluss (teyekh) SHVIM-en*
Is the water clean?	**Ist das Wasser rein?** *ist dahs VAHSS-uh reyen*
Where can I get ____?	**Wo kann ich ____ bekommen?** *voh kahn ikh ____ beh-KOM-en*
■ an air mattress	**eine Luftmatratze** *EYEN-eh luft-maht-rahts-eh*

- a bathing suit — **einen Badeanzug** *EYEN-en BAAD-eh-ahn-tsook*

- a chaise lounge — **einen Liegestuhl** *EYEN-en LEEG-eh-shtool*

- diving equipment — **eine Tauchausrüstung** *EYEN-eh TOWKH-owss-rewst-ung*

- sunglasses — **eine Sonnenbrille** *EYEN-eh ZON-en-bril-eh*

- suntan lotion — **Sonnencreme** *ZON-en-kraym*

WINTER SPORTS

Everyone has heard of skiing in the Bavarian, Austrian, and Swiss Alps. But a dozen other scenic areas, such as the Black Forest and the Harz Mountains in Germany, also have ski lifts.

Are the very high passes still open to traffic?	**Sind die ganz hohen Pässe noch dem Verkehr offen?** *zint dee gahnts HOH-en PEHSS-eh nokh daym fehr-KAYR OFF-en*
Can you take the train there?	**Kann man mit dem Zug dort hinfahren?** *kahn mahn mit daym tsook dort HIN-faar-en*
Is there a cable car or cogwheel railway?	**Gibt es eine Seilschwebe oder Bergbahn?** *gipt ehs EYEN-eh ZEYEL-shvayb-eh OHD-uh BAIRK-baan*
Are there ski lifts?	**Gibt es dort Schilifts?** *gipt ehs dort SHEE-lifts*
■ chair lifts or T-bars	**Sessel- oder Schlepplifts** *ZEHSS-el OHD-uh SHLEP-lifts*
I need skiing lessons.	**Ich brauche Schiunterricht.** *ikh BROWKH-eh SHEE-un-tehr-rikht*

■ skating lessons	**Unterricht im Schlittschuhlaufen** *UNT-ehr-rikht im SHLIT-shoo-lowf-en*
Is there an ice-skating rink?	**Gibt es eine Eisbahn?** *gipt ehs EYEN-eh EYESS-baan*
Is it possible to rent ____?	**Ist es möglich ____ zu mieten?** *ist ehs MERG-likh ____ tsoo MEET-en*
■ skiing equipment	**eine Schiausrüstung** *EYEN-eh SHEE-owss-rewst-ung*
■ a sled	**einen Schlitten** *EYEN-en SHLIT-en*
■ poles	**Schistöcke** *SHEE-shterk-eh*
■ boots	**Stiefel** *SHTEEF-el*

FISHING, RIDING, GAMBLING

Many areas offer good fishing (**Angeln,** *AHNG-eln*). Ask at the tourist office if you need a license (**Angelschein,** *AHNG-el-sheyen*).

You will find a racetrack (**Pferderennbahn**, *PFAYRD-eh-ren-baan*) in a number of large cities. Horses (**Pferde**, *PFAYRD-eh*) can be hired for riding (**Reiten**, *REYET-en*) in a number of resorts as well as from stables.

You need your passport to enter the casinos, of which there are almost 50 in Central Europe. All you can bet in Switzerland is five Swiss francs (about $2.50), but you can go broke much faster in German and Austrian casinos.

CAMPING

You'll find almost 3,000 camping sites in German-speaking Europe. Look for the blue signs bearing the international camping symbol, a black tent on a white background.

We're looking for a camping site around here.	**Wir suchen einen Campingplatz in der Nähe.** *veer ZUKH-en EYEN-en KEHMP-ing-plahts in dehr NAY-eh*
How far is it?	**Wie weit ist er?** *vee veyet ist ehr*
I hope it isn't too crowded.	**Hoffentlich ist er nicht zu voll.** *HOF-ent-likh ist ehr nikht tsoo fol*
Might it be possible to camp on your property?	**Dürften wir vielleicht auf Ihrem Grundstück zelten?** *DEWRFT-en veer feel-LEYEKHT owf EER-em GRUND-shtwek TSELT-en*
It's nice and quiet here (at your place).	**Bei Ihnen ist es schön ruhig.** *beye EEN-en ist ehs shern ROOH-ikh*
We're prepared to pay for peace and quiet.	**Wir sind bereit diese herrliche Ruhe zu bezahlen.** *veer zint beh-REYET DEEZ-eh HEHR-likh-eh ROO-eh tsoo beh-TSAAL-en*
Where can we spend the night?	**Wo können wir übernachten?** *voh KERN-en veer EWB-uh-nakht-en*

Where can we park our trailer?	**Wo können wir unseren Wohnwagen abstellen?** *voh KERN-en veer UN-zehr-en VOHN-vaag-en AHP-shtel-en*
How do we get to this camping place?	**Wie kommen wir zu diesem Campingplatz?** *vee KOM-en veer tsoo DEEZ-em KEHMP-ing-plahts*
Is there ____ there?	**Gibt es ____ dort?** *gipt ehs ____ dort*
■ drinking water	**Trinkwasser** *TRINK-vaass-uh*
■ running water	**fließendes Wasser** *FLEESS-end-es VAASS-uh*
■ a children's playground	**einen Spielplatz für Kinder** *EYEN-en SHPEEL-plahts fewr KIND-uh*
Are there ____?	**Gibt es ____?** *gipt es*
■ showers	**Duschen** *DOO-shen*
■ baths	**Bäder** *BAY-duh*
■ toilets	**Toiletten** *toy-LET-en*
■ tents	**Zelte** *TSELT-eh*
What does it cost per ____?	**Was kostet es pro ____?** *vahs KOST-et es proh*
■ person	**Person** *pehr-ZOHN*
■ car	**Wagen** *VAAG-en*
■ trailer	**Wohnwagen** *VOHN-vaag-en*
We'd like to stay ____ days (weeks).	**Wir möchten ____ Tage (Wochen) bleiben.** *veer MERKHT-en ____ TAAG-eh (VOKH-en) BLEYEB-en*
Where can I rent a car for the day (a week)?	**Wo kann ich ein Auto für einen Tag (eine Woche) mieten?** *voh kahn ikh eyen OW-toh fewr EYEN-en tahk (EYEN-eh VOKH-eh) MEET-en*

Are there tours to the country?	**Gibt es Ausflüge aufs Land?** *gipt ehs OWSS-flewg-eh owfs lahnt*
When do they leave?	**Wann fahren Sie ab?** *vahn FAAR-en zee ahp*
From where do they leave?	**Wo ist der Ausgangspunkt?** *voh ist dehr OWSS-gahngs-poonkt*
Is there anyone who can drive me?	**Gipt es jemanden, der mich fahren kann?** *gipt ehs YAY-mahnd-en dayr mikh FAAR-en kahn*
Look at ____.	**Sehen Sie ____ an.** *ZAY-en zee ____ an*
■ the bridge	**die Brücke** *dee BREWK-eh*
■ the brook	**der Bach** *dehr bahkh*
■ the birds	**die Vögel** *dee FERG-el*
■ the farm	**der Bauernhof** *dehr BOW-ehrn-hohf*
■ the fields	**die Felder** *dee FELD-uh*
■ the flowers	**die Blumen** *dee BLOOM-en*
■ the forest	**der Wald** *dehr vahlt*
■ the heath	**die Heide** *dee HEYED-eh*
■ the hut	**die Hütte** *dee HEWT-eh*
■ the lake	**der See** *dehr zay*
■ the mountains	**das Gebirge** *dahs geh-BEERG-eh*
■ the plants	**die Pflanzen** *dee PFLAHNTS-en*
■ the pond	**der Teich** *dehr teyekh*
■ the river	**der Fluss** *dehr fluss*
■ the sea	**das Meer** *dahs mayr*
■ the spring	**die Quelle** *dee KVEHL-eh*
■ the trees	**die Bäume** *dee BOYM-eh*
■ the village	**das Dorf** *dahs dorf*
■ the valley	**das Tal** *dahs taal*

I'm lost (driving).	**Ich habe mich verfahren.** *ikh HAAB-eh mikh fehr-FAAR-en*
I'm lost (walking).	**Ich habe mich verlaufen.** *ikh HAAB-eh mikh fehr-LOWF-en*
Can you show me the way to ____?	**Können Sie mir den Weg nach ____zeigen?** *KERN-en zee meer dayn vayk nahkh ____ TSEYFG-en*
Where does ____ lead to?	**Wohin führt ____?** *VOH-hin fewrt*
■ this path	**dieser Weg** *DEEZ-uh vayk*
■ this road	**diese Straße** *DEEZ-eh SHTRAASS-eh*
■ this brook	**dieser Bach** *DEEZ-uh bahkh*
■ this stream	**dieser Strom** *DEEZ-uh shtrom*
Could you accompany me a bit if you're going that way?	**Könnten Sie mich ein Stück begleiten, wenn Sie denselben Weg haben?** *KERNT-en zee mikh eyen shtewk beh-GLEYET-en ven zee dayn-ZELB-en vayk HAAB-en*

WALKING

The Germans, Austrians, and Swiss have a long tradition of walking, hiking, and romantic wandering. After winter's snow and ice, Goethe's Faust took a walk at Easter **(Osterspaziergang)** and so do millions of other Germans. Germany is a modern, industrialized country, but many vestiges of romantic nature mysticism remain. If you are in a hurry to cover long distances with various rail and bus passes or if you have time only for the major tourist circuits (the Romantic Road, the Rhine, the Bavarian castles), you will not be able to explore the extensive network of nature trails, where attractively lettered wooden signs indicate the distances to many places not found on most maps. If you spend time in and around university towns like Heidelberg or Tübingen, you will see paths once trod by famous philosophers and named for them.

In many wooded and scenic areas, you will find not only miles of hiking trails but also trails that are minicourses in natural history. There are also **Trimm dich Pfade** (keep-fit trails) where you can do the exercises shown on the signs. Organized walking tours of many areas are available. One such is the **Harzreise auf Schusters Rappen** (On shank's mare through the Harz Mountains).

Is there a nice walk I can take in the area?	**Kann man hier einen schönen Spaziergang machen?** *kahn mahn heer EYEN-en SHERN-en SHPAHTS-eer-gahng MAHKH-en*
Are there beautiful hiking trails in the area?	**Gibt es schöne Wanderwege in der Gegend?** *gipt ehs SHERN-eh VAHND-uh-vayg-eh in dehr GAYG-ent*

DRINKING AND DINING • 107

FOOD AND DRINK

DRINKING AND DINING

If you hanker for the cuisine of China, Japan, France, Italy, the Slavic countries, the Balkans, or the Middle East, you will have little trouble finding it in most large German cities. Occasionally, it's even easier to find restaurants offering exotic foreign fare than it is to come upon a traditional German restaurant. Our lists contain many traditional and typical German dishes, including regional specialties sometimes named in dialects. **Was der Bauer nicht kennt, frisst er nicht** (The farmer won't eat what he's unfamiliar with), declares an old proverb. We're certain, however, that you will want to try many specialties that you haven't eaten before. Many of these hearty dishes, incidentally, feature the word **Bauer** (farmer, peasant). Among them are **Bauernbrot, Bauernomelett, Bauernschmaus, Bauernsuppe, Bauernwürst.** We have described them for you in our lists. But like all dishes, they are best appreciated in the eating. **Guten Appetit!** *(GOOT-en ah-peh-TEET)*.

German meals normally consist of the following:

Frühstück **(breakfast)**	Can range from bread and butter basics to sumptuous buffets (generally included in hotel price).
Mittagessen **(lunch)**	The main meal in Germany (12:00 to 2:00 P.M.), generally consisting of soup, meat, and vegetables.
Kaffee (afternoon coffee)	Especially on weekends (approximately 4:00 to 5:00 P.M.), consisting of coffee/tea and cake/pastry. Known variously as **Nachmittagsimbiss**, **Vesperbrot**, **Jause** (Austria), and **Zvieri** (Switzerland), it can also consist of more copious fare such as cold meats, cheeses, etc.

Abendessen **(dinner)**	A light meal (6:00 to 9:00 P.M.); usually a variety of cold cuts with a basket of dark bread.

AT THE RESTAURANT

A Word of Caution. If you ask: **Wo ist das beste Restaurant?** (*voh ist dahs BEST-eh res-tow-RAHNT*—Where is the best restaurant?), you risk being steered to some high-priced, pretentious place that specializes in French phrases on the menu and small portions on the plate. You're not likely to get too many thin, circular slices of veal if the dish is called **Kalbsmedaillons,** and you'll probably get even fewer if it's called **medallions de veau.** To its admirers German cuisine is "hearty"; to its detractors it is "heavy." Whatever your opinion of it, you will certainly want to try German cooking in its natural habitat—a German, Austrian, or Swiss restaurant that specializes in the cuisine of the region. Ask, therefore, for such a restaurant.

Is there a restaurant that serves local specialties?	**Gibt es ein Restaurant, das einheimische Spezialitäten serviert?** *gipt ehs eyen res-tow-RAHNT dahs EYEN-heye-mish eh shpets-yah-li-TAYT-en zehr-VEERT*
Is there a good, not too expensive, German restaurant around here?	**Gibt es ein gutes, nicht zu teures deutsches Restaurant in der Nähe?** *gipt ehs eyen GOOT-es nikht tsoo TOYR-es DOY-ches res-tow-RAHNT in dehr NAY-eh*
Can you recommend an inexpensive restaurant ____?	**Können Sie mir ein preiswertes Restaurant empfehlen ____?** *KERN-en zee meer eyen PREYES-vehrt-es res-tow-RAHNT emp-FAYL-en*
■ with German specialties	**mit deutschen Spezialitäten** *mit DOY-chen shpehts-yah-li-TAYT-en*

■ with local   **mit hiesigen Spezialitäten** *mit*
specialties   *HEEZ-ig-en shpehts-yah-li-TAYT-en*

Many claim that organically grown and raised food tastes
better. If you're one of them, ask:

Is there a restaurant   **Gibt es hier ein Restaurant, das**
here that serves   **Biofleisch/Biogemüse serviert?** *gipt*
organically raised   *es heer eyen res-tow-RAHNT dahs*
meat/organically   *BEEO-fleyesh/BEEO-geh-MEWZ-eh*
grown vegetables?   *zehr-VEERT*

Do you carry bio-   **Führen Sie Bioprodukte?** *FEW-ren*
organic products?   *zee BEE-oh-pro-DOOKT-eh*

SOME PRELIMINARIES

You may be attracted by the exteriors of some German
restaurants. Half-timbered inns often have names like **Zum
Roten Ochsen** (The Red Ox), **Zum Goldenen Bären** (The
Golden Bear), or **Zum Schwarzen Adler** (The Black Eagle)
and a colorful sign portraying the animal for which the place
is named (**zum** means "at the"). Other places will proclaim
that they have a **gepflegte Küche** (carefully prepared cuisine)
or a **Gut bürgerliche Küche** (hearty middle-class cooking,
which can be quite elegant).

The **Speisekarte** (menu) is usually posted outside, and most
will include the service charge **(Bedienung inbegriffen).**
If not, ask:

Is service included?   **Ist die Bedienung inbegriffen?** *ist*
                        dee be-DEEN-ung in-beh-GRIF-en

It is not customary to leave a tip if service is included, but
some people leave a little change if they've been especially
pleased with the service.

"Waiter" in German is **Kellner,** and "waitress" is
Kellnerin, although she is always addressed as **Fräulein.** A
headwaiter is an **Oberkellner.** Perhaps to get better service
by pretending that each waiter is a "headwaiter," all waiters

are called **Herr Ober,** as in **"Herr Ober, zahlen bitte!"**
(Waiter, the check please"). If you specifically want the
headwaiter, say **Oberkellner.**

SOME BASICS

Do you have a table for me (us)?	**Haben Sie einen Tisch für mich (uns)?** *HAAB-en zee EYEN-en tish fewr mikh (uns)?*
Where are the toilets?	**Wo sind die Toiletten?** *voh zint dee toy-LET-en*
Where can I wash my hands?	**Wo kann ich mir die Hände waschen?** *voh kahn ikh meer dee HEHND-eh VAHSH-en*
Would we have to wait long?	**Müssten wir lange warten?** *MEWSST-en veer LAHNG-eh VAART-en*
I need (we need) another ____.	**Ich brauche (wir brauchen) noch ____.** *ikh BROWKH-eh (veer BROWKH-en) nokh*

- spoon **einen Löffel** *EYEN-en LERF-el*
- fork **eine Gabel** *EYEN-eh GAAB-el*
- knife **ein Messer** *eyen MESS-uh*
- glass **ein Glas** *eyen glaas*
- plate **einen Teller** *EYEN-en TEL-uh*
- chair **einen Stuhl** *EYEN-en shtool*
- ashtray **einen Aschenbecher** *EYEN-en AHSH-en-bekh-uh*
- napkin **eine Serviette** *EYEN-eh zehr-VYEHT-eh*

Some menus will list **fertige Speisen** (meals not cooked to order), others will indicate **20 Minuten Wartezeit** (20 minutes' waiting time).

If you are fond of long banquets with many courses, you may disagree with the well-known proverb: **In der Kürze liegt die Würze** (literally, "In brevity lies the spice") or, "Brevity is the soul of wit."

CONDIMENTS AND SPICES

On menus you will often see the words **Würze, Gewürz, gewürzt** (spices, spiced), **gespickt** (larded), **gefüllt** (stuffed), and **süß** and **sauer** (sweet, sour) to describe a particular item.

Salz	*zahlts*	salt
Pfeffer	*PFEHF-uh*	pepper
Senf	*zehnf*	mustard
Öl	*erl*	oil
Essig	*ESS-ikh*	vinegar
Zucker	*TSUHK-uh*	sugar
Würzkräuter	*VEWRTS-kroyt-uh*	aromatic herbs*
Sacharin	*zakh-ar-EEN*	saccharin
Tomatenketchup	*tom-AAT-en-keh-chup*	ketchup/catsup
Zitronenscheiben	*tsi-TROHN-en sheyeb-en*	slices of lemon
Meerrettich	*MAYR-reh-tikh*	horseradish
Kümmel	*KEWM-el*	caraway seeds (widely used in sauerkraut, etc.)

*NOTE: In some restaurants, especially in Switzerland, commercial preparations of aromatic herbs with salt, glutamate, etc., will be found on the table.

If you wish to avoid salt and all spices, say:

I'm on a diet. The meat without sauce, please.	**Ich lebe Diät. Das Fleisch ohne Soße, bitte.** *ikh LAY-beh dee-AYT dahs fleyesh OH-neh ZOHSS-eh BIT-eh*
Can they prepare a salt- and spice-free meal for me?	**Kann man mir ein Salz- und Gewürzfreies-Essen vorbereiten?** *kahn mahn meer eyen zahlts unt ge-VEWRTS-freye-ehs EHSS-en for-be-REYET-en*

APPETIZERS

Now that you are finally ensconced in the **Speisesaal** (dining room) at a table to your liking, you open the **Speisekarte** (menu) and peruse the **Vorspeisen** (appetizers). Sometimes these are divided into **kalte Vorspeisen** *(KAHLT-eh FOR-shpeyez-en)* and **warme Vorspeisen** *(VAARM-eh FOR-shpeyez-en)*.

I'd like an appetizer.	**Ich möchte gerne eine Vorspeise.** *ikh MERKHT-eh GEHRN-eh EYEN-eh FOR-shpeyez-eh*
What do you recommend to me?	**Was empfehlen Sie mir?** *vahs emp-FAYL-en zee meer*

SELECTIONS

Aal in Gelee *aal in zheh-LAY*	eel in aspic (ballotine of eel)
Appetithäppchen *ah-peh-TEET-hehp-khyen*	canapés
Artischockenherzen in Öl *ahr-ti-SHOK-en-herts-en in erl*	hearts of artichokes in oil
Bismarckhering *BIS-mahrk-hayr-ing*	marinated herring with onions

Bückling *BEWK-ling*	kipper, bloater
Fleischpastete *FLEYESH-pahs-tayt-eh*	meat pie, meat loaf
Froschschenkel *FROSH-shehnk-el*	frogs' legs
Gänseleberpastete *GEHN-zeh-lay-buh-pahs-tayt-eh*	goose liver pâté
Gänseleber im eigenen Fett *GEHN-zeh-lay-buh im EYEG-en-en fet*	goose liver (cold) in its own fat
Geräucherte Gänsebrust *geh-ROYKH-ert-eh GEHN-zeh-brust*	smoked breast of goose
Geftüllte Champignons *geh-FEWLT-eh shahm-pin-YONGS*	stuffed mushrooms
Hoppel-Poppel *HOP-pel-POP-pel*	bacon or sausages in scrambled eggs
Hummer *HUM-uh*	lobster
Käsehäppchen *KAY-zeh-hehp-khyen*	bits of cheese
Katenschinken *KAAT-en-shink-en*	lightly smoked Westphalian ham
Kaviar mit Zwiebeln und Zitrone *KAA-viah mit TSVEEB-eln unt tsit-ROHN-eh*	caviar with onions and lemon
Königinpastete *KERN-eeg-in-pahs-tayt-eh*	mushrooms and bits of chicken and tongue in a puff-pastry shell
Krabben *KRAHB-en*	tiny shrimps

Krebs *krayps*	crawfish, crayfish, crab
Lachs *lahks*	salmon
Languste *lahn-GUS-teh*	spiny lobster
Makrele *mah-KRAY-leh*	mackerel
Matjeshering *MAH-tyehs-hayr-ing*	"maiden herring" (a young, white, salted herring usually served with new potatoes)
Meefischli *MAY-fish-lee*	small baked fish from the Main River (a Würzburg specialty)
Ochsenmaulsalat *OKS-en-mowl-zah-laat*	ox-maw salad
Russische Eier *RUSS-ish-eh EYE-uh*	Russian eggs (hard-boiled eggs with mayonnaise)
Rehpastete *RAY-pahs-tayt-eh*	venison pâté
Sardellen *zahr-DEL-en*	anchovies
Schinken *SHINK-en*	ham
Schnecken *SHNEHK-en*	snails
Soleier *ZOHL-eye-uh*	eggs boiled in brine
Spargelspitzen *SHPAHRG-el-shpits-en*	asparagus tips

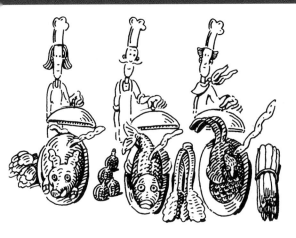

Strammer Max *STRAHM-uh mahks*

well-seasoned diced pork served with eggs and onions

Verschiedene kleine Vorspeisen *fer-SHEED-en-eh KLEYE-neh for-SHPEYEZ-en*

various little appetizers (hors d'oeuvres)

Wurstsalat *VOORST-zah-laat*

cold cuts chopped and served with onions and oil

BREADS, BAKED GOODS, PASTRIES

German bread is outstanding and varied. In a typical Stadt-bäckerei there will be 50 different types sold daily. An entire museum in Ulm is devoted to bread and its history.

Unless you order something like **Kalter Aufschnitt** (cold cuts), bread is not ordinarily served with a meal unless you ask for it. Many German breads are called **Schwarzbrot** *(SHVAHRTS-broht)*. They are black **(schwarz)** or brown in color. One variety you may have seen is called **Pumpernickel**.

Other breads are:

Vollkornbrot	*FOL-korn-broht*	whole-grain bread
Roggenbrot	*ROG-en-broht*	rye bread
Weizenkeimbrot	*VEYETS-en-keyem-broht*	wheat-germ bread
Weißbrot	*VEYESS-broht*	white bread

A **Schinkenbrot** is a ham sandwich. A **Wurstbrot** has sausage meat on it.

Waiter, please bring me some bread.	**Herr Ober, bringen Sie mir etwas Brot, bitte!** *hehrr OHB-uh BRING-en zee meer ET-vahs broht BIT-eh*
I'd like a piece of bread with it.	**Ich möchte ein Stück Brot dazu haben.** *ikh MERKH-teh eyen shtewk broht dah-TSOO HAAB-en*

You may not be able to get hot cross buns, but you can have crescent-shaped pastries called **Kipfel** or **Hörnchen.** The crescent is a symbol of Islam, and these pastries **(croissants),** like coffee, came to Europe with the Turks during and after their last siege of Vienna.

German breads are generally heavier than breads elsewhere. But German pastries are generally lighter. They are one of the chief glories of cuisine in German-speaking Europe, and to appreciate them in their full splendor, you will have to go to one of those pastry temples known as **Café-Konditoreien.** A number of elegant ones survive in spas **(Kurorte)** that escaped destruction by bombing. In the cities, too, shoppers seek out these oases of potted palms, crystal chandeliers, and marble pillars. A few **Konditoreien** have even retained string orchestras that play salon music as you sample your creamy pastries and drink your steaming coffee (or hot chocolate or tea). Some are modern, and a few have seen better days. But almost all of them make some attempt at elegance.

BEER

Beer may take a back seat to wine in the Rhineland and other wine-growing regions. Nevertheless, it is popular even there. Bavaria and Munich have long been associated with beer brewing, but Dortmund actually produces more beer than Munich. Local brews are found in all parts of German-speaking Europe. Some people affectionately refer to beer and other alcoholic beverages as **flüssiges Brot** (liquid bread).

Asking for a beer is simple:

Beer, please.	**Ein Bier, bitte.**	*eyen beer BIT-eh*

You can have either:

a bottle of beer	**eine Flasche Bier**	*EYEN-eh FLAH-sheh beer*
or		
draught beer	**Bier (frisch) vom Faß**	*beer (frish) fom fahss*

You may prefer dark (**dunkles,** *DUNK-les*) or light (**helles,** *HELL-es*) beer.

As to quantities, you can have:

a glass	**ein Glas**	*eyen glaas*
half a liter (about a pint)	**einen halben Liter**	*EYEN-en HAHLB-en LEET-uh*
a mug (liter)	**eine Maß**	*EYEN-eh maas*

You will also hear people ask for **ein Kleines** (a "short one") or **ein Seidel Bier,** which is usually about a pint, but that can vary. In many places you will see beer steins. They are often colorfully decorated and sport sayings in praise of drink and love. Unless they are valuable antiques, you may be able to drink from one of them.

May I please drink from the beautiful beer mug?	**Darf ich bitte aus dem schönen Steinkrug trinken?** *dahf ikh BIT-eh ows daym SHERN-en SHTEYEN-krook TRINK-en*

You may be familiar with some types of beer. Others may be new to you.

Altbier	*AHLT-beer*	A bitter beer high in hops (**Hopfen**), said by some to be a tranquilizer.
Alsterwasser	*AHL-stuh-vahss-uh*	A light beer with a dash of lemonade ("lime lager" in England, "panaché" *in* France); in southern Germany it's known as **Radlermaß** *(RAA-dluh-maass)*, but Hamburg's Alster river gives it its name in the north.
Bockbier	*BOK-beer*	Beers with a high alcohol and malt content.
Doppelbock	*DOPP-ehl-boh*	
Märzenbier	*MEHRTS-en-beer*	
Malzbier	*MAHLTS-beer*	A rather sweet, dark beer low in alcohol but not in calories.
Pilsener	*PILZ-en-uh*	A light beer originally brewed in Bohemia.
Schlenkerle	*SHLEHNK-ehr-leh*	A beer made of smoked hops, with a lightly smoked flavor, a specialty of Stuttgart.
Starkbier	*SHTAHRK-beer*	Strong, calorific beer, first brewed by Bavarian monks during Lent to keep up their strength and to keep from losing too much weight. Lent is still the Starkbier season.

| **Weißbier** | *VEYESS-beer* | A pale ale brewed from wheat. **Berliner Weiße mit Schuss** (with a shot) is **Weißbier** with a dash of **Himbeersaft** (raspberry juice). |

In places called **Biergarten, Bierhalle,** and **Bierhaus** you can get beer, of course, and food, usually sausages and hearty fare. A **Brauhaus** is similar to the above but connected with a brewery. A **Hofbräuhaus** is an establishment that was once a court brewery, furnishing beer to such worthies as the Electors of Bavaria in Munich and the prince-bishops of Würzburg. However, the atmosphere in such establishments is far from regal and quite down to earth.

Daniel Barenboim, director of the Berlin State Opera, declares that **die Kultur** is Germany's chief drawing card for foreigners. Germany is indeed famous for the "three B's" (Bach, Beethoven, Brahms). But for many, Bier, Bratwurst, and Blasmusik (oom-pah-pah) are equally, if not more, appealing, as numerous visitors to events such as Munich's Oktoberfest can attest.

ALCOHOLIC DRINKS

If you want bourbon, rum, scotch, sherry, whiskey and soda, or gin, just ask for them by name and most large bars will be able to accommodate you. You might prefer to try German gin, **Dornkaat** or **Steinhäger,** distilled from juniper berries.

Most drinkers in northern Germany are partial to **einen Korn** or **einen Klaren** (grain-distilled **Schnaps**), which they often gulp down (to keep warm, they say) and follow with a beer chaser. For less dedicated drinkers, a variety of liqueurs are available for sipping **(das Nippen).** Many monasteries are much visited by tourists (Kloster Ettal near King Ludwig's castle, Linderhof, is one) and various herbal liqueurs are offered for sale at them. These **Krauterliköre** are particularly popular in Alpine regions, although they are found elsewhere as well.

German for "brandy" is **Weinbrand** *(VEYEN-brahnt)*. Fruit brandies, however, often have names that end in **-geist, -schnaps,** or **-wasser.**

Apfelschnaps	*AHPF-el-shnahps*	apple jack
Birnenschnaps	*BEERN-en-shnahps*	pear brandy
Heidelbeergeist	*HEYED-el-bayr-geyest*	blueberry brandy
Himbeergeist	*HIM-bayr-geyest*	raspberry brandy
Kirschwasser	*KIRSH-vahs-uh*	cherry brandy
Pflümliwasser	*PFLEWM-lee-vahs-uh*	plum brandy
Zwetschgen-wasser	*TSVEHTSH-gen-vahs-uh*	plum brandy

Pflümli is a Swiss specialty. If there's a *k* instead of a *g* in **Zwetschgenwasser,** you know it's an Austrian specialty. Slavic **Sliwowitz,** another plum brandy, is also widely available. **Kirschwasser** is a Black Forest specialty, but is available everywhere. Ask the bartender or waiter about local specialties.

Are there alcoholic drinks from this area?	**Gibt es Spirituosen von hier?** *geept ehs spi-ri-tu-OH-zen fon heer*
What kind of local specialities do you have?	**Was für hiesige Spezialitäten haben Sie?** *vahs fewr HEEZ-ig-eh shpehts-yah-li-TAYT-en HAAB-en zee*
Is this cordial very sweet or just a bit sweet?	**Ist dieser Likör Sehr süß oder nur etwas süß?** *ist DEEZ-uh lee-KER zayr zews OHD-uh noor ET-vahs zews*

Two caraway-flavored brandies are **Bommerlunder** *(bomm-uh-LUND-uh)* and **Kümmel** *(KEW-mel)*. Other alcoholic drinks you may wish to try are:

Bärenfang	*BAHREN-fahng*	vodka, honey, and herbs
Danziger Goldwasser	*DAHNTS-ig-uh GOLT-vahs-uh*	a white liqueur with gold flakes floating in it
Eierlikör Goldschläger	*EYE-uh-lee-Ker GOLT-shlay-guh*	eggnog, eggflip, another liqueur with gold flakes, this one a cinnamon-flavored schnapps from Switzerland
Obstler	*OHPST-luh*	fruit brandy
Underbergs Magenbitter	*UND-uh-behrks MAAG-en-bitt-uh*	brandy with bitters

WINES

The best known, and the best, German wines are white, although some of the **Spätburgunder** reds from the Ahr Valley are notable. Imported red wines from other areas of Europe, Africa, and all over are abundantly available. Even though many German reds will seem like a rosé to you, you may nevertheless wish to try some from Baden-Württemberg, which are often put up in attractive monkey- or witch-shaped bottles **(Affenflasche, Hexenflasche).** Franconian wines, mostly white, can always be distinguished by their **Bocksbeutelflasche** (pouch-shaped bottle). Austria's Burgenland and parts of Switzerland also produce red wine. They can all be agreeable and pleasant, although you may find them wanting if you are having substantial fare such as game or heavier meats in strong sauces.

Rosé is sometimes called **Schillerwein,** not in honor of the famous writer but because its color is an iridescent blend of red, pink, and gray (**schillern** means "to be opalescent").

Punches made with fruit soaked first in brandy and then placed in wine are very popular in German homes. The **Erdbeerbowle** (wine with strawberries in it) is well known. **Kullerpfirsich** is a peach in a large champagne-filled goblet. "Cold duck," a mixture of sparkling white and red wines, is said to derive from the German **Kalte Ente** (cold duck), which was originally **Kaltes Ende** (cold end), referring to the custom of pouring together all the wines and other alcoholic drinks left over at the end of a party.

Most Europeans respect France's contention that only wines from the Rheims-Epernay region can be called champagne. A German sparkling wine will therefore be called either **Sekt** (zehkt) or **Schaumwein** *(SHOWM-veyen)*, although **Champagner** *(sham-PAAN-yuh)* is used colloquially. Some German sparkling wine is of superlative quality and can accompany any meal. Well-known ones are **Henkell, Fürst Metternich,** and **Kupferberg.**

Hundreds of songs exist praising the Rhine and its wines. (**Rhein** and **Wein** rhyme in German, too). One song holds that **Der Wein muss alt und jung das Mädchen sein** (the wine must be old and the girl young). But many disagree with that sentiment and seek out the new wines, variously called **Most, Reißer, Sauser** (depending on the region), and the famous Viennese **Heuriger.** You will see signs featuring the new wines during the fall. People often order **Zwiebelkuchen** *(TSVEEB-el-kookh-en)*, a rather heavy, fried-onion-and-cheese concoction, to enjoy with it. The new wine, still "working," doesn't seem very potent. But be careful!

There are many **Heurigen** taverns in famous suburbs of Vienna (such as Grinzing). One of the songs you're likely to hear there alleges that **Wenn man älter wird, ein wenig kälter wird, bleibt allein nur der Wein** (When one gets older, a bit colder, all that's left is wine).

The **Weinkarte** (wine list) in the better restaurants can often be very lengthy and complicated. Not only is the district of origin important, but also the vintage **(Jahrgang)** since Germany's northerly vineyards are much dependent on the weather.

Do you have a wine list?	**Haben Sie eine Weinkarte?** *HAAB-en zee EYEN-eh VEYEN-kaart-eh*
May I take a look at the wine list, please?	**Darf ich mir bitte die Weinkarte ansehen?** *daarf ikh meer BIT-eh dee VEYEN-kaart-eh AHN-zay-en*

If there is no wine list, ask:

What kinds of wine do you have?	**Was für Weine haben Sie?** *vahs fewr VEYEN-eh HAAB-en zee*

In places without a wine list, you may not be able to get:

a bottle of white wine (red wine).	**eine Flasche Weißwein (Rotwein).** *EYEN-eh FLAHSH-eh VEYESS-veyen (ROHT-veyen)*

But they will probably have **offene Weine** (open wines, i.e., wines sold by the glass). The glass is usually a green- or amber-colored goblet called a **Römer.** Open wines have the advantage of enabling you to try several different varieties. Many, however, find a particular pleasure and assurance in the presence of a wine bottle on the table. If an overanxious waiter is eager to spirit the bottle away, use one of the following phrases:

Leave the bottle, please.	**Lassen Sie die Flasche bitte!** *LAHSS-en zee dee FLAHSH-eh BIT-eh*
The bottle isn't empty yet.	**Die Flasche ist noch nicht leer.** *dee FLAHSH-eh ist nokh nikht layr*
Bring back the bottle.	**Bringen Sie die Flasche zurück!** *BRING-en zee dee FLAHSH-eh tsoo-REWK*

If you enjoyed your wine say:

Another ____.	**Noch ____.** *nokh*
■ glass	**ein Glas** *eyen glass*

- bottle   **eine Flasche**   *EYEN-eh FLAHSH-eh*
- half-pint glass   **ein Viertel**   *eyen FEERT-el*
- quarter-pint glass   **ein Achtel**   *eyen AHKHT-el*
- liter   **einen Liter**   *EYEN-en LEET-uh*
- carafe   **eine Karaffe**   *EYEN-eh kahr-AHF-eh*
- half bottle   **eine halbe Flasche**   *EYEN-eh HAHLB-eh FLAHSH-eh*

Or say simply:

The same, please.	**Dasselbe, bitte.** *dahs-ZEHLB-eh BIT-eh*

Most whites and rosés are served chilled. If you don't want your wine served chilled, say:

Not chilled.	**Nicht gekühlt** *nikht ge-KEWLT*
At room temperature, please.	**In Zimmertemperatur, bitte.** *in TSIM-uh-tem-pay-rah-toor BIT-eh*

Besides ordering small glasses of open wines, an even more attractive way of sampling a variety of wines from a particular region is to order a tray full of small glasses of different wines. Many hotels and restaurants along the **Deutsche Weinstraße** (German Wine Road) and other wine-growing regions feature these attractive trays, shaped like a violin, an artist's palette, or a swan. An accompanying menu will describe each wine with a battery of adjectives, such as **vollmundig** (full-bodied), **fruchtig** (fruity), and **lieblich** (endearing). The most important adjectives you will need are:

(very) dry	**(sehr) trocken** *(zayr) TRO-ken*
(rather) sweet	**(etwas) süß** *(ET-vahs) zews*
light	**leicht** *leyekht*

Wine labels can be visually and verbally picturesque. They can have words such as **Ritter** (knight), **Schloss** (castle), **Berg** (mountain), **Tal** (valley), and **Kloster** (monastery), and pictures of flowers, animals, and heavenly bodies.

If you are an aspiring **Weinkenner** (wine connoisseur), you may want to check to see if it's a **Naturwein** and not **verbessert** (improved) by adding sugar.

Many Moselle wines and some of the dry whites of the Rheingau can be outstanding. A superior wine is often labeled a **Qualitätswein** or a **Qualitätswein mit Prädikat.**

Other important wine terms denoting degree of sweetness are:

Spätlese *SHPAYT-layz-eh*	Used for dry wines made from grapes gathered later than those used for the normal vintage
Auslese *OWS-layz-eh*	Rather dry wines made from very ripe grapes
Beerenauslese *BAYR-en-ows-layz-eh*	Slightly sweet wines obtained from special overripe grapes
Trockenbeerenauslese *TROCK-en-bayr-en-ows-layz-eh*	As in the case of the best sauternes, these produce sweet, but not cloying, wines for which high prices are often paid

Many bus and Rhine steamer tours stop at Rüdesheim am Rhein, where festive crowds move from one tavern to the next on the **Drosselgasse.** You may want to join them, or you may prefer to seek out "temples of Bacchus" in more remote areas. Wherever you go and whatever you're drinking, we say:

To Your Health!	**Zum Wohl!**	*tsum vohl*

and

Cheers!	**Prost!**	*prohst*

NONALCOHOLIC BEVERAGES

hot chocolate	**heiße Schokolade** *HEYESS-eh SHO-ko-laad-eh*
(black, red) currant juice	**(schwarzer, roter) Johannisbeersaft** *(SHVAHRTS-uh ROHT-uh) yo-HAHN-is-bayr-zahft*
mineral water	**Mineralwasser** *min-eh-RAAL-vahs-uh*
orangeade	**Orangeade** *or-ahn-ZHAAD-eh*
soda water (artificially carbonated)	**Selterswasser** *ZEHLT-uhs-vahs-uh*
soda water	**Sprudelwasser** *SHPROOD-el-vahs-uh*
spring water	**Quellwasser** *KVEL-vahs-uh*
apple juice	**Apfelsaft** *AHPF-el-zahft*

SOUPS AND STEWS

German soups are often substantial, and the distinction between them and stews is not always clear. If you want a clear, uncluttered soup, ask for **Bouillon** *(BOO-yohn)*, chicken broth (**Hühnerbrühe,** *HEWN-uh-brew-eh*), or beef tea (consommé) with nothing in it (**Kraftbrühe ohne Einlage,** *KRAHFT-brew-eh OHN-eh EYEN-laag-eh*). But you will undoubtedly wish to sample many of the hearty soups listed here. Such old standbys as **Erbsensuppe** (pea soup) and **Linsensuppe** (lentil soup) often contain **Schinken** (ham), **Wurst** (sausage), or **Speck** (bacon). Sometimes there may be a special section called **Eintopfgerichte** (stews) on the menu. But usually soups and stews are grouped together. Remember that if you order an **Eintopf** ("one pot"), you will probably have little appetite left for subsequent courses.

If you want to know what the soup of the day is, ask:

What is the soup of the day?	**Was ist die Tagessuppe?** *vahs ist dee TAA-gehs-zup-eh*	
What soups do you have today?	**Was für Suppen gibt es heute?** *vas fewr ZUP-en geept ehs HOYT-eh*	

Aalsuppe *AAL-zup-eh* — eel soup

Backerbsensuppe *BAHK-ehrps-en-zup-eh* — broth with crisp, round noodles

Bauernsuppe *BOW-ern-zup-eh* — cabbage and sausage soup

Bohnensuppe *BOHN-en-zup-eh* — bean soup (usually with bacon)

Erbsensuppe *EHRP-sen-zup-eh* — pea soup

Fischsuppe *FISH-zup-eh* — fish soup

Fischbeuschelsuppe *FISH-boy-shel-zup-eh* — fish-roe soup with vegetables

Fridattensuppe *free-DAHT-en-zup-eh* — broth with pancake strips

Frühlingssuppe *FREW-lings-zup-eh* — spring vegetable soup

Grießnockerlsuppe *GREES-nok-ehrl-zup-eh* — semolina-dumpling soup

Gerstenbrühe *GEHRST-en-brew-eh* — barley broth

Gulaschsuppe *GOOL-ahsh-zup-eh* — stewed beef in a spicy soup

Hühnerreissuppe *HEWN-er-reyes-zup-eh* — chicken-rice soup

Hummersuppe *HUM-uh-zup-eh* — lobster soup

Kalte Obstsuppe, Kaltschale *KAHLT-eh OHPST-zup-eh, KAHLT-shahl-eh* — cold fruit soup, usually containing cream, beer, or wine

Kartoffelsuppe *kahr-TOF-el-zup-eh* — potato soup

Kartoffellauchsuppe *kahr-TOF-el-LOWKH-zup-eh* — potato-leek soup

Knödelsuppe *KNERD-el-zup-eh* — dumpling soup

Königinsuppe *KERN-ig-in-zup-eh* — contains beef, sour cream, and almonds

Kraftbrühe mit Ei *KRAFT-brew-eh mit eye* — beef consommé with raw egg

■ **mit Topfteigerbsen** *mit TOPF-teyek-ehrps-en* — with fried peas

■ **mit Markknochen Einlage** *mit MAHRK-knokh-en EYEN-laag-eh* — with bone marrow filling

Labskaus *LAAPS-kowss* — heavy stew of chopped, marinated meat with mashed potatoes and vegetables; the "fisherman's stew" version of this dish consists of herring and potatoes, red beets and onions, with a fried egg and pickles on the side

Leberknödelsuppe *LAY-behr-knerd-el-zup-eh* — liver dumpling soup

Linsensuppe *LINZ-en-zup-eh* — lentil soup

Mehlsuppe Basler Art *MAYL-zup-eh BAAZL-uh aart*	cheese soup with flour, Basle style
Nudelsuppe *NOO-del-zup-eh*	noodle soup
Ochsenschwanzsuppe *OK-sen-shvahnts-zup-eh*	oxtail soup
Pichelsteiner Eintopf *PIKH-el-shteyen-uh EYEN-topf*	meat and vegetable stew
Schildkrötensuppe *SHILT-krert-en-zup-eh*	turtle soup
Schweinsragoutsuppe *SHVEYENS-rah-goo-zup-eh*	pork-ragout soup
Semmelsuppe *ZEH-mel-zup-eh*	dumpling soup
Serbische Bohnensuppe *ZERB-ish-eh BOHN-en-zup-eh*	spicy bean soup
Spargelsuppe *SHPAHR-gel-zup-eh*	asparagus soup
Tomatensuppe *toh-MAAT-en-zup-eh*	tomato soup
Zwiebelsuppe *TSVEE-bel-zup-eh*	onion soup

You may wish to give yourself over entirely to the delights of the table and not think about language learning. But if you're studying German, even casually, you might like to ponder the following idioms and proverbs while you're having your soup:

Das macht die Suppe nicht fett. *dahs makht dee ZUP-eh nikht fet*	That won't make the soup fat. (That's of little use.)
Ein Haar in der Suppe. *eyen haar in dayr ZUP-eh*	A hair in the soup (a fly in the ointment).

Einem die Suppe versalzen.
EYEN-em dee ZUP-eh fehr-ZALTS-en

To ruin things for someone (by making the soup too salty).

MEATS

Very popular in restaurants in German-speaking areas are large selections of various meats. They can be fried, boiled, hot or cold, or all of these served together. Definitely not for vegetarians. What is called a **choucroute alsacienne** in France is to be found, with variations, in all German-speaking areas. Incidentally, French **quiche** and **quenelle** derive from German **Kuchen** (cake) and **Knödel** (dumpling). In Austria, sauerkraut with meat (pork, sausages) and potatoes is sometimes called a **Bauernchmaus;** in Switzerland it is called a **Berner Platte.** Sometimes other meats, such as tongue or ham, and a whole gamut of sausages can add to the garnishing of the sauerkraut. You can therefore get a monster meat platter, with or without sauerkraut or other garnishes (dumplings, red cabbage, etc.), in all German-speaking areas. Bremen's specialty is called **Kohl und Pinkel,** an ensemble of cabbage, potatoes, and smoked meat.

On some menus you will see the headings **vom Schwein, vom Kalb,** and **vom Rind** (from the pig, from the calf, and from beef), under which pork **(Schweinefleisch),** veal **(Kalbfleisch),** and beef **(Rindfleisch)** will be grouped.

Bauernomelett *BOW-ehrn-om-let*	bacon and onion omelette
Bauernschmaus *BOW-ehrn-shmowss*	sauerkraut with smoked pork, sausages, dumplings, and potatoes
Bauernwurst *BOW-ehrn-voorst*	pork sausage with mustard seeds and peppercorns

Berliner Buletten *behr-LEEN-uh bul-EHT-en* | fried meatballs, Berlin style

Beuschel (Aust.) *BOY-shel* | veal lungs and heart (often finely chopped, then stewed)

Bratwurst *BRAAT-voorst* | fried sausage

Bündnerfleisch (Swiss) *BEWND-nehr-fleyesh* | thinly sliced, air-dried beef

deutsches Beefsteak *DOY-ches BEEF-stayk* | Salisbury steak, hamburger

Eisbein *EYES-beyen* | pig's knuckle

Faschiertes (Aust.) *fah-SHEERT-es* | chopped meat

Fiakergulasch (Aust.) *fee-AHK-uh-goo-lahsh* | goulash topped with a fried egg

Frikadellen *fri-kah-DELL-en* | croquettes

gefülltes Kraut *geh-FEWLT-es krowt* | cabbage leaves stuffed with chopped meat, rice, eggs, and bread crumbs

Gehacktes *ge-HAHKT-es* | chopped meat

Geschnetzeltes (Swiss) *ge-SHNEH-tsel-tes* | braised meat tips

Geselchtes *ge-ZEHLKHT-es* | salty smoked meat

Gulasch *GOO-lahsh* | beef stew with spicy paprika gravy

Hackbraten *HAHK-braat-en*	meat loaf
Hackfleisch *HAHK-fleyesh*	chopped meat
Hammelbraten *HAHM-el-braat-en*	roast mutton
Hammelkeule, Hammelschlegel *HAHM-el-koyl-eh, HAHM-el-shlay-gel*	leg of mutton
Hammelrippchen *HAHM-el-rip-khen*	mutton chops
Herz *hehrts*	heart
Hoisteiner Schnitzel *HOL-shteyen-uh SHNITS-el*	breaded veal cutlet topped with a fried egg and often with bits of toast, anchovies, vegetables, etc.
Jungfernbraten *YUNG-fehrn-braat-en*	a crunchy roast suckling pig
Kalbsbraten *KAHLPS-braat-en*	roast veal
Kalbsbrust *KAHLPS-brust*	breast of veal
Kalbshachse *KAHLPS-hahks-eh*	veal shank
Kalbsmilch *KAHLPS-milkh*	sweetbreads
Karbonade *kahr-bo-NAAD-eh*	fried rib pork chops
Klöße *KLERSS-eh*	meatballs
Klößchen, Klößlein *KLERSS-khen, KLERSS-leyen*	small meatballs

Kohl und Pinkel	*kohl unt PINK-el*	smoked meat, cabbage, and potatoes
Kohlroulade	*KOHL-roo-laad-eh*	stuffed cabbage
Königsberger Klops	*KER-niks-behrg-uh klops*	meatballs in caper sauce
-kotelett	*-kot-LET*	chop, cutlet
Krenfleisch (Aust.)	*KRAYN-fleyesh*	pork (headcheese) with horseradish and shredded vegetables
Kutteln	*KUT-ehln*	tripe
Lammkotelett	*LAHM-kot-LET*	lamb chop
Leber	*LAY-buh*	liver
Leberkäs	*LAY-buh-kays*	meat loaf
Lendenbraten	*LEHND-en-braat-en*	roast sirloin, tenderloin
Medaillons	*mehd-EYE-yongs*	little discs of veal or pork
Naturschnitzel	*nah-TOOR-shni-tsel*	thick, unbreaded veal cutlet
Nieren	*NEER-en*	kidneys
Pöckelfleisch	*PER-kel-fleyesh*	pickled meat
Rinderbraten	*RIND-uh-braat-en*	roast beef
Rindsstück	*RINTS-shtewk*	steak, slice of beef

Rippensteak	*RIP-ehn-shtayk*	rib steak
Rouladen	*roo-LAAD-en*	vegetables rolled up in thick slices of beef or veal
Rumpfstück	*RUMPF-shtewk*	rump steak
Sauerbraten	*ZOW-ehr-braat-en*	marinated pot roast in a spicy brown gravy
Saure Nieren	*ZOW-reh NEER-en*	kidneys in a sauce containing vinegar
Schlachtplatte	*SHLAHKHT-plaht-eh*	mixed sausages and cold meats
Schmorfleisch	*SHMOHR-fleyesh*	stewed meat
Schnitzel	*SHNITS-el*	cutlet (usually veal)
Schweinskotelett	*SHVEYENS-kot-let*	pork chop
Spanferkel	*SHPAAN-fehr-kel*	suckling pig
Speck	*shpehk*	bacon
(Steierische) Brettjause	*SHTEYE-uh-rish-eh BREHT-yowz-eh*	(Styrian) cold cuts on a wooden platter
Sülze	*ZEWLTS-eh*	headcheese ("brawn" in Britain)
Tafelspitz	*TAAF-el-shpits*	Viennese boiled beef
Tartarensteak	*tahr-TAAR-en-shtayk*	ground raw beef, seasoned variously
Wiener Schnitzel	*VEEN-uh SHNITS-el*	breaded veal cutlet

Zigeuner Schnitzel *tsee-GOYN-uh SHNITS-el*	veal or pork cutlet in a sharp sauce
Zunge *TSUNG-eh*	tongue

SAUCES AND A NOTE ABOUT *ART*

The words **Tunke** (related to the English "dunk") and **Brühe** are occasionally used for "sauce," but most often **Soße** *(ZOH-sseh)*, the German transcription of "sauce," is used. Very often the word **Art,** sometimes preceded by **nach** (according to), will be used to express "in the style, manner of."

nach Pariser Art	Parisian style
nach Ungarischer Art	Hungarian style (i.e., with paprika, etc.)
nach Hausfrauenart	Sauce *bonne femme* (i.e., with apples and onions)
nach Jägerart	In the hunter's style (sauce *chasseur* or *cacciatore*–a blend of mushrooms, vegetables, and wine)
Hühnerbrust	Breast of chicken
Kiewer Art	Kiev

POULTRY, GAME

Goose and duck are more widely eaten in German-speaking Europe than in English-speaking countries. Chicken, of course, is universally popular. In Catholic Austria and in parts of Germany, goose is very widely eaten on St. Martin's Day in November. It is known as **Martinigansl.** Berliners, too, appreciate a well-roasted goose, and a **Weihnachtsgans** (Christmas goose) is traditional in many areas.

During the autumn hunting season, many restaurants feature **Wild** (game), Some even modify their decor with hunting motifs. Occasionally, while eating **Wildbret** (venison) or **Rebhuhn** (partridge), the diner will even find the bullet that brought the bird or animal down. So chew carefully!

Backhuhn *BAHK-hoon*	fried chicken
Brathuhn *BRAAT-hoon*	roast chicken
Entenbraten *EHNT-en-braat-en*	roast duck
Fasan *fah-ZAAN*	pheasant
Gänsebraten *GEHN-zeh-braat-en*	roast goose
Hähnchen *HAYN-khen*	small chicken
Hasenbraten *HAAZ-en-braat-en*	roast hare
Hasenpfeffer *HAAZ-en-pfeh-fuh*	spicy rabbit stew
Hirschbraten *HEERSH-braat-en*	venison
Hühnerbraten *HEWN-ehr-braat-en*	roast chicken
Hühnerkeule, Hühnerschlegel *HEWN-ehr-koyl-eh, hewn-ehr-SHLAY-gel*	drumstick, thigh
Kaninchen *kah-NEEN-khen*	rabbit
Rebhuhn *RAYP-hoon*	partridge
Rehrücken *RAY-rewk-en*	saddle of venison
Taube *TOW-beh*	pigeon, dove, squab
Truthahn *TROOT-haan*	turkey
Wachtel *VAHKHT-el*	quail

Wiener Backhendl	*VEEN-uh BAHK-hen-del*	"southern fried chicken," Viennese style
Wildbraten	*VILT-braat-en*	roast venison
Wildschweinrücken	*VILT-shveyen-rewk-en*	saddle of wild boar

If you have ordered your meat from listings under the heading **vom Grill** (from the grill) or **vom Spieß** (from the spit) you know how your meat will be prepared. In recent years various kabobs such as **Schaschlik am Spieß** have become popular in Germany. Anything listed as **am Spieß** means **en brochette**. When you order meat, you may add:

medium, please	**mittel, bitte**	*MIT-ehl BIT-eh*
rare (bloody)	**blutig**	*BLOOT-ikh*
underdone	**englisch**	*EHNG-lish*

You can have your meat prepared in the following ways:

baked	**gebacken**	*geh-BAH-ken*
boiled or cooked	**gekocht**	*geh-KOKHT*
stewed or braised	**geschmort**	*geh-SHMOHRT*
roasted	**geröstet**	*geh-RERST-et*
fried	**gebraten**	*geh-BRAAT-en*
steamed, stewed	**gedämpft**	*geh-DEHMPFT*
stuffed	**gefüllt**	*geh-FEWLT*
chopped	**gehackt**	*geh-HAHKT*

| breaded | **paniert** *pah-NEERT* |
| garnished | **garniert** *gahr-NEERT* |

A WORD ABOUT WURST

You are probably already familiar with liverwurst **(Leber-wurst)** and knockwurst **(Knackwurst**—from **knacken,** to burst). But there are many more **Würste** (sausages) made in German-speaking areas. They are a specialty. **Alles hat ein Ende und die Wurst hat zwei** (everything has an end and the sausage has two) declares the well-known proverb. But the variety of sausages, like links in an endless chain, sometimes seems to be without end.

Würste *(VEWRST-eh)* can be eaten as a **Vorspeise** (appetizer), in dishes such as **Wurstsalat** or **Wurstplatte,** or as part of the main course in elaborate platters (such as the **Schlachtplatte).** If Germans have had a large midday meal, it is common to serve cold cuts **(Kalter Aufschnitt)** with cheese **(Käse)** for the evening meal **(Abendessen).** Wurst varieties may be served hot (sometimes with other meats on a mixed grill) or cold. Hot wursts such as **Bauernwurst, Bockwurst,** and **Bratwurst** can be found on menus in cozy restaurants called **Weinstube, Gasthaus,** or **Gasthof.** Wursts are also sold in a **Würstchenstand** on busy streets in commercial areas. A **Schnellimbißstube** (snack bar) also offers wursts along with beer and (sometimes) wine. The more expensive and pretentious the restaurant, however, the fewer wursts you will see on the menu, although even there they will offer elaborate platters.

Some **Würste** you are not likely to find listed on a menu but that are offered for sale in butcher shops are:

Bierwurst	*BEER-voorst*	beer sausage
Blutwurst	*BLOOT-voorst*	blood sausage
Currywurst	*KUH-ree-voorst*	highly seasoned pork sausage

Mettwurst	*MEHT-voorst*	spicy, semisoft sausage for spreading on bread
Schlackwurst	*SHLAHK-voorst*	a fatty pork sausage
Weißwurst	*VEYESS-voorst*	delicate white sausage (a Munich specialty traditionally served in the morning)
Zervelatwurst	*TSEHR-vel-AAT-voorst*	salamilike sausage, saveloy
Zungenwurst	*TSUHNG-en-voorst*	tongue sausage
Zungenblutwurst	*TSUHNG-en-bloot-voorst*	tongue and blood pudding

There are a great many others. Frequently they are preceded by an adjective indicating the region they come from, as in **Braunschweiger Leberwurst** (from Brunswick), **Thüringer Blutwurst, Bremer Mettwurst,** and **Oldenburger Plockwurst.** The same wurst can be made according to many different recipes, and the **Wurstmacher,** if he makes a product appreciated by the local community, is held in high esteem. The great variety of German sausages is most apparent at the butcher's, where you may want to stock up on some for picnics. There you have the advantage of being able to point to what you want if you don't know its name. Point and say:

How about a few samples for tasting?	**Wie wär's mit einigen Kostproben?** *vee vayrs mit EYE-ni-gen KOST-prohb-en*
I would like a piece of that sausage there.	**Ich möchte ein Stück von der Wurst da.** *ikh MERKHT-eh eyen shtewk fon dehr voorst dah*

Cut off another piece for me.	**Schneiden Sie mir noch ein Stück ab!** *SHNEYE-den zee meer nokh eyen shtewk ahp*
■ a bigger piece	**ein größeres Stück** *eyen GRERSS-er-es shtewk*
■ a smaller piece	**ein kleineres Stück** *eyen KLEYEN-er-es shtewk*

Fleischer is the most common word for butcher, but you will also see the words **Metzger** and **Schlächter.** They all carry wursts, and a **Wurstmacher** (or **Selcher**) specializes in them. Remember that few wursts are low in calories, so after you've tried a few, make an effort to resist their spicy enticements. A diet of spicy wursts and sweet whipped cream desserts (another German staple) will wreak havoc with your waistline.

FISH, SEAFOOD

These are often grouped together under the heading **vom Meer** (from the Sea).

I like to eat fish.	**Ich esse gern Fisch.** *ikh EHSS-eh gehrn fish*
What is the catch of the day?	**Was ist der Tagesfang?** *vahs ist dehr TAAG-es-fahng*
Does the fish have many bones?	**Hat der Fisch viele Gräten?** *haht dehr fish FEEL-eh GRAYT-en*
Can you remove the fish bone for me?	**Können Sie mir die Gräte entfernen?** *KERN-en zee meer dee GRAY-teh ent-FEHRN-en*
Do you have only fish fillets?	**Haben Sie nur Fischfilets?** *HAAB-en zee nur FISH-fi-lays*
I want the whole fish. With head and tail.	**Ich will den ganzen Fisch. Mit Kopf und Schwanz.** *ikh vil dehn GAHN-tsen fish mit kopf unt shvants*

The following is a list of fish commonly found on menus. Restaurants near small, out-of-the-way lakes may sometimes use local-dialect variations. Often the name of the lake precedes the fish, as in **Bodensee Felchen** (Lake Constance whiting). Very often **Nordsee** (North Sea) or **Ostsee** (Baltic Sea) will precede the name of the fish. Menus almost always list **Kieler Sprotten** (Kiel sprats) rather than merely **Sprotten** (sprats).

Aal *aal*	eel
Austern *OW-stern*	oysters
Barsch *bahrsh*	(lake) perch
Brachse, Brasse *BRAHKS-ehl, BRAHSS-eh*	bream (similar to carp)
Brathering *BRAAT-hayr-ing*	fried sour herring
Dorsch *dorsh*	cod
Felchen *FEHL-khen*	whiting
Fischfrikadellen *FISH-fri-kah-dehl-en*	fish dumplings (croquettes)
Forelle *for-EHL-eh*	trout
Flunder *FLUND-uh*	flounder
Garnelen *gahr-NAYL-en*	shrimp, prawns
Haifischsteak *HEYE-fish-shtayk*	shark steak
Hecht *hekht*	pike
Heilbutt *HEYEL-but*	halibut
Hering *HAY-ring*	herring

Hummer	*HUM-uh*	lobster
Jakobsmuscheln	*YAA-kops-mush-eln*	scallops
Junger Hecht	*YUNG-uh hekht*	pickerel
Kabeljau	*KAA-bel-yow*	cod
Karpfen	*KAHR-pren*	carp
Kieler Sprotten	*KEEL-uh SHPROT-en*	(Kiel) sprats
Krabben	*KRAH-ben*	shrimp, prawn
Krebs	*krayps*	crab
Lachs	*lahks*	salmon
Languste	*lahn-GOOST-eh*	spiny lobster
Makrele	*mah-KRAY-leh*	mackerel
Muscheln	*MUSH-eln*	clams, cockles, mussels
Neunauge	*NOYN-owg-eh*	lamprey eel
Rauch-, Rächer-	*rowkh-, ROY-khuh-*	smoked
Rogen	*ROH-gen*	roe
Rotbarsch	*ROHT-bahrsh*	red sea bass
Schellfisch	*SHEHL-fish*	haddock
Scholle	*SHOL-eh*	flatfish, plaice
Schwertfisch	*SHVAYRT-fish*	swordfish

Seebarsch *ZAY-bahrsh*	sea bass
Seezunge *ZAY-tsung-eh*	sole
Sojawalfischsteak *ZOH-yah-vaal-fish-stayk*	soya whale steak

NOTE: Whales are mammals, not fish. But since our "whale steak" is made of soy beans, neither zoologists nor conservationists will object.

Steinbutt *SHTEYEN-but*	turbot
Stint *shtint*	smelt
Stör *shterr*	sturgeon
Tintenfisch *TINT-en-fish*	squid, cuttlefish
Weißfisch *VEYESS-fish*	whiting
Zander *TSAHND-uli*	pike-perch

Now, how would you like your fish?

With butter, lemon, and almonds	**Mit Butter, Zitrone, und Mandeln** *mit BUTT-uh tsi-TROHN-eh unt MAHN-deln*
With caper sauce	**Mit Kapernsoße** *mit KAAP-ehrn-zohss-eh*
Boiled (often in a *court bouillon* of herbs and onions)	**Blau** *blow*
Baked	**Gebacken** *geh-BAH-ken*
Fried	**Gebraten** *geh-BRAA-ten*

Deep fried	**In schwimmendem Fett gebacken** *in SHVIM-end-em feht ge-BAHK-en*
Sautéed	**In Butter geschwenkt** *in BUT-uh geh-SHVEHNGKT*
Grilled	**Gegrillt** *geh-GRILT*
Steamed	**Gedämpft** *geh-DEHMPFT*

Sometimes fish is served stuffed **(farciert** or **gefüllt).**

Flounder stuffed with shrimp and mushrooms	**Flunder mit Krabben und Champignons farciert** *FLUND-uh mit KRAH-ben unt sham-pin-YONGS fahr-SEERT*

VEGETABLES

I eat only vegetables.	**Ich esse nur Gemüse.** *ikh ESS-eh noor ge-MEWZ-eh*
I am a vegetarian.	**Ich bin Vegetarier(in).** *ikh bin veh-geh-TAAR yehr(in)*
What kind of vegetables are there?	**Was für Gemüse gibt es?** *vahs fewr ge-MEWZ-eh geept ehs*
What can you recommend?	**Was können Sie mir empfehlen?** *vahs KERN-en zee meer emp-FAYL-en*
There is:	**Es gibt:** *ehs geept*
We have:	**Wir haben:** *veer HAAB-en*

Auberginen *oh-behr-ZHEEN-en*		eggplant
Blumenkohl *BLOOM-en-kohl*		cauliflower
Bohnen *BOHN-en*		beans

Braunkohl *BROWN-kohl*	broccoli
Erbsen *EHRPS-en*	peas
Essiggurken *EHSS-ikh-goork-en*	sour pickles (gherkins)
Fisolen (Aust.) *fee-SOHL-en*	string beans, French beans
Gelbe Wurzeln *GEHLB-eh VOORTS-eln*	carrots
Gemischtes Gemüse *geh-MISHT-ehs ge-MEWZ-eh*	mixed vegetables
Grüne Bohnen *GREWN-eh BOHN-en*	green beans
Gurken *GOORK-en*	cucumbers
Häuptelsalat *HOYPT-el-zah-laat*	lettuce salad
Kabis, Kappes *KAHB-is, KAHP-es*	cabbage
Karfiol (Aust.) *kahr-fee-OHL*	cauliflower
Karotten *kahr-OT-en*	carrots
Knoblauch *KNOHP-lowkh*	garlic
Kohl, Kraut *kohl, krowt*	cabbage
Kren (Aust.) *krayn*	horseradish
Kürbis *KEWR-biss*	pumpkin
Kukuruz (Aust.) *KOOK-oor-oots*	corn, maize
Lauch *lowkh*	leeks

Leipziger Allerlei *LEYEPTS-eeg-uh AHL-uh-leye*		carrots, peas, and asparagus
Mais *meyess*		corn, maize
Meerrettich *MAYR-reh-tikh*		horseradish
Mohrrüben *MOHR-rewb-en*		carrots
Paradeiser (Aust.) *pah-rah-DEYEZ-uh*		tomatoes
Pfifferlinge *PFIF-ehr-ling-eh*		chanterelle mushrooms
Pilze *PILTS-eh*		mushrooms
Radieschen *rah-DEES-khen*		radishes
Rosenkohl *ROHZ-en-kohl*		brussels sprouts
Rote Beten (Rüben) *ROHT-eh BAYT-en (REWB-en)*		beets
Rotkohl (Rotkraut) *ROHT-kohl (ROHT-krowt)*		red cabbage
Rübenkraut *REWB-en-krowt*		turnip tops
Schnittbohnen *SHNIT-bohn-en*		French beans
Schwarzwurzeln *SHVAHRTS-voorts-eln*		salsify (vegetable oyster)
Spargelspitzen *SHPAARG-el-shpits-en*		asparagus tips

(You may also see **Schwetzinger Stangenspargel**, asparagus stalks from Schwetzingen, the asparagus capital of Germany, near Heidelberg. Tourists come not only to eat asparagus but also to visit the castle and attend concerts and music festivals.)

Spinat	*shpeen-AAT*	spinach
Tomaten	*to-MAAT-en*	tomatoes
Weiße Bohnen	*VEYESS-eh BOHN-en*	white beans
Weiße Rüben	*VEYESS-eh REWB-en*	turnips
Weißkohl	*VEYESS-kohl*	cabbage
Zwiebeln	*TSVEEB-eln*	onions

POTATOES, NOODLES

Bratkartoffeln	*BRAAT-kahr-tof-eln*	fried potatoes
Geröstel	*ge-RERST-el*	hash brown potatoes
Dampfnudeln	*DAHMPF-nood-eln*	steamed noodles
Fadennudeln	*FAAD-en-nood-eln*	vermicelli
Kartoffel(n)	*kahr-TOF-el(n)*	potato(es)
■ -**bälle**	*-behl-eh*	balls
■ -**brei**	*-breye*	mashed
■ -**flocken**	*-flok-en*	flakes (potato crisps)
■ -**klöße**	*-klewss-eh*	dumplings
■ -**kroketten**	*-kroh-keht-en*	croquettes
■ -**mus**	*-moos*	mashed
■ -**puffer**	*-puf-uh*	fritters, potato pancakes
Krautkrapfen	*KROWT-krahp-fen*	cabbage fritters

Pellkartoffeln *PEHL-kahr-tof-eln* unpeeled boiled potatoes

Petersilienkartoffeln *pay-tehr-ZEEL-yen-kahr-tof-eln* parsleyed potatoes

Pommes frites *pom frit* french fries

Röstkartoffeln *REWST-kahr-tof-eln* fried potatoes

Rösti (Swiss) *REWST-ee* hash brown potatoes

Salzkartoffeln *ZAHLTS-kahr-tof-eln* boiled potatoes

Schlutzkrapfen (a South Tyrol specialty) *SHLUTS-krahpf-en* ravioli filled with cottage cheese

Spätzle* *SHPEHTS-leh* thick noodles or Swabian dumplings

Teigwaren *TEYEKH-vaar-en* pasta products, noodles

*Spätzle, in numerous combinations and variations, can be a meal in themselves, as in the Vorarlberg (Austria) specialty, Käsespätzle (Spätzle with cheese).

SALADS

Salads with meat (**Wurstsalat, Ochsenmaulsalat**) or fish (**Hummersalat, Krabbensalat**) are eaten as appetizers or as a main course.

I would like a green (mixed) salad.	**Ich möchte bitte einen grünen (gemischten) Salat.** *ikh MERKHT-eh BIT-eh EYEN-en GREWN-en (geh-MISHT-en) zah-LAAT*
■ cucumber salad	**Gurkensalat** *GOORK-en-zah-laat*

■ lettuce salad	**Häuptelsalat, Kopfsalat, Staudensalat** *HOYPTL-zah-laat, KOPF-zah-laat, SHTOWD-en-zah-laat*
Bring me oil and vinegar.	**Bringen Sie mir Öl und Essig.** *BRING-en zee meer erl unt EHS-ikh*
I want to dress the salad myself.	**Ich will den Salat selber anmachen.** *ikh vill dayn zah-LAAT ZEHLB-uh AHN-mahkh-en*

CHEESES

You may see a German cheese called **Frühstückskäse** (breakfast cheese) on your breakfast table along with several others, such as **Schmierkäse** (Smear Cheese) or **Streichkäse**, processed cheeses for spreading on your bread. One popular cheese you'll have no trouble identifying is called "Bavaria Blue." Bavaria is to German cheeses what Normandy and Wisconsin are to French and American cheeses. Yet cheese is made in most areas of Germany.

Cheeses are sometimes classified according to their fat content. **Doppelfett** (65%), **Überfett** (55%), **Vollfett** (45%), **Dreiviertelfett** (35%), **Halbfett** (25%), **Viertelfett** (15%), and **Mager** (less than 15%).

Connoisseurs distinguish between **Aligüuer Bergkäse, Emmenthaler,** and **Greyerzer** (Gruyères), but most of us would call them "Swiss cheese." Other well-known German, Austrian, and Swiss cheeses are **Alpenkäse, Bierkäse,** and **Stangenkäse. Edelpilzkäse,** a fine sharp cheese, and **Mondseerkäse** (similar to Limburger) are Austrian specialties. To appreciate the full range of German, Austrian, and Swiss cheeses, drop into a **Käsegeschäft** (a store that specializes in cheese). You may want to try a few in a restaurant.

We'll have the cheese platter, please.	**Wir nehmen den Käseteller, bitte.** *veer NAY-men dehn KAY-zeh-tell-uh BIT-eh*

What kinds of cheeses are there on the cheese platter?	**Was für Käsesorten gibt es auf dem Käseteller?** *vahs fewr KAY-zeh-zort-en geept ehs owf dehm KAY-zeh-tell-uh*
Bring me a piece of cheese, please.	**Bringen Sie mir bitte ein Stück Käse!** *BRING-en zee meer BIT-eh eyen shtewk KAY-zeh*

"Cream cheese" is **Weichkäse** (literally, "soft cheese"), and another cheese is called **Hartkäse** (literally, "hard cheese"). You may wish to ask about other kinds:

Is the cheese soft or hard?	**Ist der Käse weich oder hart?** *ist dehr KAY-zeh veyekh OH-duh hahrt*
■ sharp or mild?	**scharf oder mild?** *shahrf OH-duh milt*

DESSERTS

Besides **Nachtische,** menu headings for desserts may be **Süßigkeiten** (sweets), **Mehlspeisen** (literally, "foods made with flour" but widely used in Austria for "dessert"), **Süßspeisen** (sweets), or **Nachspeisen** (remember **Vorspeisen,** "appetizers"?). Sometimes you will even see the word **Dessert** *(deh-SAYR)*. Occasionally, more fanciful captions, such as **Der letzte Schliff** (the finishing touch) are used.

The variety and quality of German, Swiss, and Austrian desserts are downright staggering. Many pastry connoisseurs, if stranded on a "dessert" island, would prefer it to be a German-speaking one. If your restaurant is connected to a **Café** or **Konditorei** (pastry shop), you are in luck.

What do you recommend?	**Was empfehlen Sie mir?** *vahs emp-FAYL-en zee meer*
Is there something particularly good?	**Ist etwas besonders zu empfehlen?** *ist EHT-vahs beh-ZOND-ehrs tsoo emp-FAYL-en*

Is dessert included in my menu?	**Ist der Nachtisch in meinem Gedeck mit einbegriffen?** *ist dehr NAHK-tish in MEYEN-em geh-DEHK mit EYEN-beh-grif-en*
I would like a:	**Ich möchte ein (eine)** *ikh MERKHT-eh eyen (EYEN-eh)*
■ strawberry ice cream	**Erdbeereis** *AYRT-bayr-eyess*
■ fruit-flavored berry pudding	**Rote Grütze** *ROHT-eh GREWTS-eh*

Fürst Pückler is vanilla, chocolate, and strawberry ice cream together (Neapolitan). Besides **Erdbeereis** (strawberry ice cream), you will also find **Mokka-** (coffee), **Schokoladen-** (chocolate), **Vanille-** (vanilla), and **Zitroneneis** (lemon ice cream), and occasionally more exotic flavors. The Empress Elizabeth of Austria was partial to a violet-colored ice cream crowned by a candied violet. Vienna's Demel's still serves it and it is enjoyed by all, not just those born to the purple. **Eis** *(eyess)* is used every-where for "ice cream," although occasionally **Glace** *(GLAHS-eh)* is heard in Switzerland.

Rote Grütze is a fresh berry pudding popular in the north. **Palatschinken** are particularly popular in the south. These crêpes can be filled with a variety of jams, cheeses, or even meats. **Apfelstrudel** is a popular delicate pastry filled with nuts, raisins, ham, and slices of apples. You may wish to try other varieties of strudel (poppy seed **[Mohn]**, cherry **[Kirsche]**, etc.) In wine-growing regions, **Apfeltorte** (apple tart) can be a marvelously light combination of a thin whisper of crust, wine-soaked apples, sugar, and cinnamon, all topped by the omnipresent **Schlag** (whipped cream). **Kaiserschmarren** (literally, "imperial scraps") are shredded pancakes with raisins.

Kuchen *(KOOKH-en)* means "cake," but you will see the word **Torte** *(TOHR-teh,* tart) more often. Many cakes have personalities and names of their own. For example:

Berliner *behr-LEEN-uh*	jelly doughnut
Bienenstich *BEEN-en-shtikh*	honey-almond cake (literally "bee sting")

Gugelhupf *GOOG-el-hupf*	a round pound cake with a hole in the middle, often containing raisins and almonds (a Bavarian-Austrian specialty)
Hefekranz *HAY-feh-krahnts*	circular coffee cake
Mannheimer Dreck *MAHN-heyem-uh drehk*	chocolate-covered almond paste
(Weihnachts) stollen *(VEYE-nahkhts)shtol-en*	fruity (Christmas) coffee cake

Schwarzwälder Kirschtorte (Black Forest cherry tart) is very popular all over Europe, not just in the Black Forest **(Schwarzwald).** It is more like a creamy chocolate cake with cherries than a "tart." Austria offers a great many **Torten** and is so proud of one creamy one that it calls it an **Austria Torte.** Another favorite is the **Linzer Torte** (crushed almonds in a crumbly cake covered with raspberry jam).

Perhaps the most famous chocolate cake in the world is the **Sachertorte** (subject of lengthy lawsuits disputing the name and the recipe). It contains a thin layer of apricot jam along with chocolate filling and icing.

Here are some other pastries that you may like:

Cremeschnitte *KRAYM-shnit-eh*	napoleon
Mohrenkopf *MOHR-en-kopf*	chocolate meringue
Windbeutel *VINT-boyt-el*	cream puff

They already have cream in them, but it is not uncommon to ask for them **mit Schagsahne,** that is, topped with whipped cream. You, too, may wish to have your cake, pastry, or **Obsttorte** (fruit tart) inundated with whipped cream.

It is a pity to have to pass up dessert, but if you don't want it, say:

Nothing more, thank you.	**Nein danke, nichts mehr.** *neyen DAHNK-eh nikhts mayr*
Unfortunately, I can't eat any more.	**Leider kann ich nichts merh essen.** *LEYED-uh kahn ikh nikhts mayr ESS-en*

COFFEE AND TEA

You can get other things to drink in a **Café** or **Kaffeehaus,** but coffee is their specialty.

I would like ____.	**Ich möchte bitte ____.** *ikh MERKHT-eh BIT-eh*
■ a cup of coffee	**eine Tasse Kaffee** *EYEN-eh TAHSS-eh KAH-fay*
■ with cream	**mit Sahne** *mit ZAAN-eh*
■ with milk	**einen Milchkaffee** *EYEN-en MILKH-kah-fay*
■ black coffee	**einen Schwarzen** *EYEN-en SHVAHRTS-en*
■ coffee with cream	**Braunen** *BROWN-en*
■ espresso	**Espresso** *es-PREHSS-oh*
■ iced coffee	**Eiskaffee** *EYES-kah-fay*

There are many refinements and variations on these basics, particularly in Vienna, which is famous for its coffeehouses.

black coffee with rum or brandy	**Mocca gespritzt** *MOK-ah ge-SHPRITST*
Turkish coffee	**Türkischer** *TEWRK-ish-uh*

Vienna also offers **Einspänner, Konsul, Mélange, Piccolo,** etc., terms denoting the kind and quantity of coffee. Many have cream blended with them and are often crowned with **Schlag,** or whipped cream (also called **Schlagobers**).

Coffeehouses were the scene of concerts in Bach's day and sometimes still are today. It is doubtful that Bach would have written his *Coffee Cantata* in praise of any of the numerous *ersatz* coffees available in Germany, but many people find them quite palatable. They are mixtures of beet roots, figs, chicory, and grains and are widely available. Many German homes have a **Kaffeemühle** (coffee mill) and make their own **Bohnenkaffee** (coffee from beans).

Herbal tea is very popular in Europe, and you can get many varieties at pharmacies and health-food stores (called **Reformhäuser,** or less dauntingly, **Bioläden** or **Ökoläden**), which carry many fine products, including wines low in tannin. Most restaurants and coffeehouses carry the more common varieties, such as:

peppermint tea	**Pfefferminztee**	*pfehf-uh-MINTS-tay*
linden-blossom tea	**Lindenblütentee**	*LIND-en-blewt-en-tay*
rosehip tea	**Hagebuttentee**	*HAAG-eh-but-en-tay*
chamomile tea	**Kamillentee**	*kah-MIL-en-tay*

For ordinary tea, just ask for:

A cup of tea ____.	**Eine Tasse Tee ____.**	*EYEN-eh TAHSS-eh tay*
■ with milk	**mit Milch**	*mit milkh*
■ with lemon	**mit Zitrone**	*mit tsi-TROHN-eh*

In recent years bookstores dealing with oriental culture and religions have proliferated, and many of them offer several varieties and blends of tea.

FRUITS AND NUTS

Ananas *AHN-ah-nahss*   pineapple

Apfel *AHPF-el*   apple

Apfelsine *ahpf-el-ZEEN-eh*	orange
Aprikosen *ahp-ree-KOHZ-en*	apricots
Banane *bah-NAAN-eh*	banana
Birne *BEERN-eh*	pear
Blaubeeren *BLOW-bayr-en*	blueberries (bilberries)
Brombeeren *BROM-bayr-en*	blackberries
Datteln *DAHT-ehln*	dates
Erdbeeren *AYRT-bayr-en*	strawberries
Feigen *FEYEG-en*	figs
Gemischte Nüsse *geh-MISHT-eh NEWSS-eh*	mixed nuts
Granatapfel *grah-NAAT-ahpf-el*	pomegranate
Haselnüsse *HAAZ-el-newss-eh*	hazelnuts
Heidelbeeren *HEYED-el-bayr-en*	blueberries
Himbeeren *HIM-bayr-en*	raspberries
Holunderbeeren *hol-UND-uh-bayr-en*	elderberries
Johannisbeeren *yoh-HAHN-is-bayr-en*	currants
Kastanien *kahst-AAN-yen*	chestnuts
Kirschen *KEERSH-en*	cherries

Kokosnuß *KOHK-os-nuus*		coconut
Mandarine *mahn-dah-REEN-eh*		tangerine
Mandeln *MAHND-eln*		almonds
Marillen (Aust.) *mah-RIL-en*		apricots
Melone *meh-LOHN-eh*		cantaloupe
Nüsse *NEWSS-eh*		nuts
Pampelmuse *PAHMP-el-mooz-eh*		grapefruit
Pfirsich *PFEER-zikh*		peach
Pflaumen *PFLOW-men*		plums
Preiselbeeren *PREYE-zel-bayr-en*		cranberries
Quitte *KVIT-eh*		quince
Rauschbeeren *ROWSH-bayr-en*		cranberries, crawberries
Rhabarber *rah-BAHRB-uh*		rhubarb
Rosinen *roh-ZEEN-en*		raisins
Stachelbeeren *SHTAH-khel-bayr-en*		gooseberries
Studentenfutter *shtu-DENT-en-fut-uh*		"student fodder" (assorted nuts, raisins, seeds)
Südfrüchte *ZEWT-frewkht-eh*		tropical fruits
Trauben *TROWB-en*		grapes
Walnüsse *VAHL-newss-eh*		walnuts

Wassermelone *VAHSS-uh-meh-lohn-eh*	watermelon
Weichselkirschen *VEYEKS-el-keersh-en*	(sour) morello cherries
Weintrauben *VEYEN-trowb-en*	grapes
Zuckermelone *TSUK-uh-meh-lohn-eh*	honeydew melon
Zwetschgen *TSVEHTSH-gen*	plums

APROPOS OF APPLES

In den sauren Apfel beißen *in dayn ZOWR-en AHPF-el BEYESS-en*	To bite into the sour apple (swallow a bitter pill; perhaps appropriate when it's time to pay the bill)
Der Apfel fällt nicht weit vom Stamm (Baum). *dehr AHPF-el fehlt nikht veyet fom shtahm (bowm)*	The apple doesn't fall far from the trunk (tree). (Like father like son.)

GEOGRAPHY

Sometimes menu listings have fanciful names. If you see **Himmel und Erde** (Heaven and Earth) on the menus of restaurants in North Rhine–Westphalia, the words refer to blood sausage served with potatoes and applesauce. In the same region, don't miss an opportunity to try the **Bergische Kaffeetafel**, a Westphalian version of English "high tea." It consists of raisin bread, rice pudding, honey, black bread, cottage cheese, butter, waffles, sugar and cinnamon, soft German pretzels, crabapples, and coffee. Geographical names are frequently included in describing the specialty— for example, **Neuenahrer Rauchfleisch** (smoked meat from the Neuenahr region), **Pfälzer Saumagen** (hog belly from the Palatinate), or **Hunsrücker Spieß- und Schaukelbraten** (meats roasted and turned in the Hunsrück style).

For many, collecting culinary souvenirs is as important a part of travel as sightseeing or shopping. If the restaurant is located in a historic site (a castle or an old inn) or if there are several restaurants from which to choose, elements of sightseeing and shopping can be combined in the restaurant experience. After a ride through Old Vienna in a horse-drawn open cab, you may enjoy **Fiakergulasch** ("Coachman's Beef"), a dish of beef chunks in a spicy paprika gravy, topped with a fried egg and usually served with **Knödel** (dumplings) and **Wiener Würstchen** ("wieners"). You can, of course, get **Wiener Schnitzel** (veal cutlet fried in egg and breadcumbs) anywhere. But if it's good and if you're eating it in Vienna, your meal may be enhanced by an on-the-spot sense of satisfaction.

COMPLAINTS

We hope that your memory albums will be filled with souvenirs of many delectable meals. We hope not only that the meals will be memorable but also that they will be beautifully and promptly served. But sometimes they aren't. If you're kept waiting and you don't want to wait any longer, select from the following phrases:

We're in a hurry.	**Wir haben's eilig.** *veer HAAB-ens EYEL-ikh*
I'm in a hurry.	**Ich hab's eilig.** *ikh hahps EYEL-ikh*
Why is it taking so long?	**Warum dauert es so lange?** *vaar-UM DOW-ehrt ehs zoh LAHNG-eh*
I can't (we can't) wait any longer.	**Ich kann (wir können) nicht länger warten.** *ikh kahn (veer KERN-en) nikht LEHNG-uh VAART-en*
I'm leaving.	**Ich gehe.** *ikh GAY-eh*
We're leaving.	**Wir gehen.** *veer GAY-en*

You don't like what you see? Here are some useful expressions:

The tablecloth isn't clean.	**Das Tischtuch ist nicht sauber.** *dahs TISH-tookh ist nikht ZOWB-uh*
This is dirty.	**Dies ist schmutzig.** *dees ist SHMUTS-ikh*

The food is ____.

Das Essen ist ____. *dahs ESS-en ist*

■ cold   **kalt** *kahlt*

■ not very hot   **nicht sehr heiß** *nikht zayer heyess*

■ not even warm   **nicht einmal warm** *nikht EYEN-mahl vahrm*

There's too much fat in it.	**Da ist zu viel Fett drin.** *dah ist tsoo feel feht drin*

This is too ____.

Dies ist zu ____. *dees ist tsoo*

■ salty   **salzig** *ZAHLTS-ikh*

■ dried out   **dürr** *dewr*

■ sweet   **süß** *zews*

■ sour   **sauer** *ZOW-uh*

■ bitter   **bitter** *BIT-uh*

The meat is ____.

Das Fleisch ist ____. *dahs fleyesh ist*

■ overdone   **zu stark gebraten** *tsoo shtahrk ge-BRAAT-en*

■ too tough   **zu zäh** *tsoo tsay*

■ too rare   **zu roh** *tsoo roh*

The milk is sour.	**Die Milch hat einen Stich.** *dee milkh haht EYEN-en shtikh*
The butter isn't fresh.	**Die Butter ist nicht frisch.** *dee BUT-uh ist nikht frish*

I want to talk to the head waiter.	**Ich möchte mit dem Oberkellner sprechen.** *ikh MERKHT-eh mit daym OH-buh-keln-uh SHPREHKH-en*

RESTRICTIONS

You may be a traveler with special dietary requirements, so here are a few phrases that might help you get what you need or avoid what does not agree with you.

I am on a diet.	**Ich mache eine Schlankheitskur.** *ikh MAHKH-eh EYEN-eh SHLAHNK-heyets-koor*
I am a vegetarian.	**Ich bin Vegetarier(in).** *ikh bin veh-geh-TAAR-yehr(in)*
I can't have ___.	**Ich vertrage ___.** *ikh fehr-TRAAG-eh*
■ any dairy products	**keine Milchprodukte** *KEYEN-eh MILKH-pro-dookt-eh*
■ any alcohol	**keinen Alkohol** *KEYEN-en ahl-ko-HOHL*
■ any saturated fats	**keine gesättigten Fette** *KEYEN-eh geh-ZEHT-ikht-en FET-eh*
■ any seafood	**keine Meeresfrüchte** *KEYEN-eh MAYR-ehs-frewkht-eh*
■ any nuts	**keine Nüsse** *KEYEN-eh NEWSS-eh*
■ any MSG	**kein Glutamat** *keyen Gloot-ah-MAAT*
I'm looking for a dish ___.	**Ich suche ein ___ Gericht.** *ikh ZOOKH-eh eyen ___ geh-RICHT*
■ high in fiber	**ballaststoffreiches** *bah-LAHST-shtof-reyekh-es*
■ low in cholesterol	**cholesterinarmes** *ko-lest-ehr-EEN-ahrm-es*

■ low in fat	**fettarmes**	*FETT-ahrm-es*
■ low in carbohydrates	**kohlenhydratarmes**	*KOHL-en-hew-draat-ahrmes*
■ low in sodium	**natriumarmes**	*NAA-tree-um-ahrm-es*
■ nondairy	**milchfreies**	*MILKH-freyes-es*
■ salt-free	**salzfreies**	*ZAHLTS-freye-es*
■ sugar-free	**zuckerfreies**	*ZOOK-ehr-freye-es*

I'm looking for a dish/food without ____.	**Ich suche ein Gericht/Essen ohne ____.** *ikh ZOOKH-eh eyen geh-RIKHT/ESS-en OHN-eh*
■ preservatives	**Konservierungsmittel** *kohn-zayr-VEER-ungs-mit-el*
■ artificial coloring	**Kunstfarbstoff** *KOONST-fahrp-shtoff*

EATING IN

Although hotels frown on it, you might occasionally want to eat in your room. Whether you're setting up housekeeping or just going on a picnic, you'll find not only staples but, in many stores, luxury items such as salads, wursts, and smoked fish in great variety. There is a number code indicating what coloring and preserving agents, if any, have been used. If you have a background in chemistry, you will recognize them. In many areas you will find colorful indoor or outdoor markets. Outdoor markets are often held only on a particular day; indoor markets can offer a profusion of shops and wares. Look for local specialties, such as Aachen's crisp **Printen** (cookies with designs) and Basel's even crisper **Leckerli** (honey-ginger biscuits).

I need ____.	**Ich brauche ____.** *ikh BROWKH-eh*
■ bread	**Brot** *broht*
■ butter	**Butter** *BUT-uh*

■ cheese	**Käse**	*KAYZ-eh*
■ cold cuts	**Kalter Aufschnitt**	*KHALT-uh OWF-shnit*
■ cookies	**Kekse**	*KAYKS-eh*
■ candy	**Konfekt**	*kon-FEHKT*
■ a chocolate bar	**eine Tafel Schokolade**	*EYEN-eh TAAF-el sho-ko-LAAD-eh*
■ a dozen eggs	**ein Dutzend Eier**	*eyen DUTS-ent EYE-uh*
■ fruit	**Obst**	*ohpst*
■ a bottle of milk	**eine Flasche Milch**	*EYEN-eh FLAHSH-eh milkh*

If you ask for a **Pfund** or a **halbes Pfund** of something, you'll be getting more than a pound or half a pound, since the German **Pfund** is 500 grams (half a **Kilo**) and the American/English pound is 454 grams.

Travel Tips Every traveler has a few small items that he or she never fails to carry along on a trip. Some of these are a small flashlight, a tiny tube of spot remover, a Swiss army knife, some twine, Scotch tape, a small screwdriver, a corkscrew, a sewing kit, rubber bands and paper clips, extra plastic bags, and a washcloth.

MEETING PEOPLE

GREETINGS AND INTRODUCTIONS

What's your name?	**Wie heißen Sie?**	*vee HEYESS-en zee*
My name is ____.	**Ich heiße ____.**	*ikh HEYESS-eh*
Pleased to meet you.	**Sehr erfreut.**	*zayr ehr-FROYT*
How do you do?	**Wie geht es Ihnen?**	*vee gayt es EEN-en*
How are things?	**Wie geht's?**	*vee gayts*
May I introduce ____?	**Darf ich ____ vorstelien?**	*dahrf ikh ____ FOHR-shtehl-en*
■ my husband	**meinen Mann**	*MEYEN-en mahn*
■ my wife	**meine Frau**	*MEYEN-eh frow*
■ my son	**meinen Sohn**	*MEYEN-en zohn*
■ my daughter	**meine Tochter**	*MEYEN-eh TOKHT-uh*
■ my friend	**meinen Freund**	*MEYEN-en froynd*
What's ____ name?	**Wie heißt ____?**	*vee heyesst*
■ your son's	**Ihr Sohn**	*eer zohn*
■ your daughter's	**Ihre Tochter**	*EER-eh TOKHT-uh*
■ your dog's	**Ihr Hund**	*eer hunt*

CONVERSATION

We have children the same age as yours.	**Wir haben Kinder im selben Alter.** *veer HAAB-en KIND-uh im ZEHLB-en AHLT-uh*

Where are you from?	**Wo sind Sie her?** *voh zint zee hayr*
I'm ___.	**Ich bin ___.** *ikh bin*
■ from America	**aus Amerika** *owss ah-MAY-ree-kah*
■ from the South	**aus den Südstaaten** *ows dayn ZEWT-shtaat-en*
■ from New England	**aus Neuengland** *ows noy-EHNG-lahnt*
■ from the Midwest	**aus dem Mittelwesten** *ows daym MIT-el-vehst-en*
■ from England	**aus England** *ows EHNG-lahnt*
■ from Canada	**aus Kanada** *ows KAH-nah-dah*
■ from Australia	**aus Australien** *ows ows-TRAAL-yen*
This is my first time in Germany.	**Dies ist das erste Mal, das ich in Deutschland bin.** *dees ist dahs EHRST-eh maal dahs ikh in DOYCH-lahnt bin*
I like many things.	**Mir gefällt vieles.** *meer geh-FELT FEEL-es*
I think it's ___.	**Ich finde es ___.** *ikh FIND-eh ehs*
■ a bit strange	**etwas komisch** *ET-vahss KOHM-ish*
■ beautiful	**schöh** *shern*
■ interesting	**interessant** *in-tehr-eh-SAHNT*
■ magnificent	**herrlich** *HEHR-likh*
■ unique	**einzigartig** *EYEN-tsikh-ahrt-ikh*
I will be staying ___.	**Ich bleibe ___.** *ikh BLEYEB-eh*
■ a few days	**einige Tage** *EYEN-ig-eh TAAG-eh*
■ a week	**eine Woche** *EYEN-eh VOKH-eh*
■ a month	**einen Monat** *EYEN-en MOHN-aat*

Is your hotel far?	**Ist Ihr Hotel weit entfernt?** *ist eer ho-TEL veyet ehnt-FEHRNT*
Would you like a picture?	**Möchten Sie ein Bild?** *MERKHT-en zee eyen bilt*
Stand here (there).	**Stellen sie sich dorthin.** *SHTEHL-en zee zikh dort hin*
Don't move.	**Keine Bewegung!** *KEYEN-eh beh-VAYG-ung*
Smile. That's it!	**Lächeln. Genau! (Richtig!)** *LEHKH-eln geh-NOW (RIKHT-ikh)*
Would you take a picture of me (us)?	**Wurden Sie mich (uns) photographieren?** *VEWRD-en zee mikh (uns) foh-toh-grah-FEER-en*
I'd like a picture of you, as a remembrance.	**Ich möchte ein Bild von Ihnen, als Andenken.** *ikh MERKHT-eh eyen bilt fon EEN-en, ahls AHN-denk-en*

DATING AND SOCIALIZING

Are you alone?	**Sind Sie allein?** *zint zee ah-LEYEN*
Or with your family?	**Oder mit der Familie?** *OHD-uh mit dehr fah-MEEL-yeh*
May I have this dance?	**Darf ich um diesen Tanz bitten?** *dahrf ikh um DEEZ-en tahnts BIT-en*
Would you like a drink (cigarette)?	**Möchten Sie ein Getränk (eine Zigarette)?** *MERKHT-en zee eyen geh-TREHNK (EYEN-eh tsi-gah-REHT-eh)*

Do you have a light?	**Haben Sie Feuer?** *HAAB-en zee FOY-uh*
Do you mind if I smoke?	**Macht es Ihnen etwas aus, wenn ich rauche?** *mahkht ehs EEN-en EHT-vahs ows vehn ikh ROWKH-eh*
Are you free this evening?	**Sind Sie heute Abend frei?** *zint zee HOYT-eh AAB-ent freye*
Would you like to go for a walk with me?	**Möchten Sie einen Spaziergang mit mir machen?** *MERKHT-en zee EYEN-en shpah-TSEER-gahng mit meer MAHKH-en*
What's your telephone number?	**Wie ist Ihre Telephonnummer?** *vee ist EER-eh TAY-leh-fohn-num-uh*
May I invite you for ___?	**Darf ich Sie zu ___ einladen?** *dahrf ikh zee tsoo ___ EYEN-laad-en*
■ a glass of wine	**einem Glas Wein** *EYEN-em glaass veyen*
■ a cup of coffee	**einer Tasse Kaffee** *EYEN-uh TASS-eh KAH-fay*
What is your profession?	**Was sind Sie von Beruf?** *vahs zint zee fon beh-ROOF*
I'm a ___.	**Ich bin ___.** *ikh bin*
■ doctor	**Arzt (Ärztin)** *ahrtst (EHRTST-in)*
■ accountant	**Buchhalter(in)** *BOOKH-hahlt-ehr(in)*
■ musician	**Musiker(in)** *MOOZ-ik-ehr(in)*
■ hairdresser	**Friseur (Friseuse)** *free-ZEWR (free-ZEWZ)*
■ police officer	**Polizeibeamte** *pol-its-EYE-beh-ahmt-uh*
■ engineer	**Ingenieur(in)** *in-jen-EWR(in)*

- scientist **Wissenschaftler(in)** *VISS-ent-shahft-lehr(in)*
- clerk **Verkäufer(in)** *fehr-KOYF-ehr(in)*
- secretary **Sekretär(in)** *zehk-reh-TAYR(in)*
- manager **Geschäftsführer(in)** *geh-SHEFTS-fewr-ehr(in)*
- mechanic **Mechaniker(in)** *meh-KHAA-ni-kehr(in)*
- teacher **Lehrer(in)** *LAY-rehr(in)*
- lawyer **Rechtsanwalt (Rechtsanwältin)** *REHKHTS-ahn-vahlt (REHKHTS-ahn-vehlt-in)*
- gardener **Gärtner(in)** *GEHRT-nehr(in)*
- dentist **Zahnarzt (Zahnärztin)** *TSAAN-aartst (TSAAN-ehrtst-in)*
- writer **Schriftsteller(in)** *SHRIFT-shteh-lehr(in)*

■ nurse	**Krankenpfleger(in)** *krahnk-en-PFLAY-gehr(in)*
■ secretary	**Sekretär(in)** *zeh-kreh-TAYR(in)*
■ salesperson	**Verkäufer(in)** *fehr-KOY-fehr(in)*
■ businessperson	**Geschäftsmann(frau)** *geh-SHEHFTS-mahn(frow)*
■ student	**Student(in)** *shtoo-DEHNT(in)*

Do you love music (the theater, films)?
Lieben Sie Musik (Theater, Filme)? *LEEB-en zee moo-ZEEK (TAY-aat-uh, FILM-eh)*

I'll pick you up at your house (hotel).
Ich hole Sie in Ihrem Haus (Hotel) ab. *ikh HOHL-eh zee in EER-em hows (ho-TEL) ahp*

I'll wait for you in front of the theater (café).
Ich warte auf Sie vor dem Theater (Café). *ikh VAART-eh owf zee for daym TAY-aat-uh (kah-FAY)*

I thank you for your wonderful hospitality.
Ich danke Ihnen für Ihre wunderbare Gastfreundlichkeit. *ikh DAHNK-eh EEN-en fewr EER-eh VUND-uh-baar-eh GAHST-froynt-likh-keyet*

It was very nice (pleasant, fantastic, unforgettable).
Es war sehr schön (angenehm, fabelhaft, unvergesslich). *ehs vaar zayr shern (AHN-geh-naym, FAAB-el-hahft, un-fehr-GEHSS-likh)*

Next year you'll come and visit me at my place.
Nächstes Jahr kommen Sie zu mir auf Besuch. *NAYKST-es yaar KOM-en zee tsoo meer owf beh-ZOOKH*

The pleasure was all mine.
Die Freude war ganz meinerseits. *dee FROYD-eh vaar gahnts MEYEN-ehr-zeyets*

In most German restaurants (all but the most expensive) and in a **Brauhaus** or a **Bierhalle**, it is common for people to be seated together at large tables. This can make for **Gemütlichkeit**, or chummy togetherness. **Gemütlichkeit** has traditionally been said to increase as one goes south, reaching its high point in Austria. Franconia is in northern Bavaria, and some southerners call its inhabitants the "Prussians of Bavaria," citing the saying **Zehn Franken, zehn Tische** (ten Franconians, ten tables). Some sociologists claim, however, that today northerners have lost much of their standoffishness and that southerners have lost some of their **Gemütlichkeit**. You will undoubtedly make friends everywhere, particularly if you try out your German.

SAYING GOOD-BYE

Nice to have met you.	**Nett, dass ich Sie kennen gelernt habe.** *neht dahss ikh zee KEHN-en-geh-lehrnt HAAB-eh*
Regards to ___.	**Grüße an ___.** *GREWSS-eh ahn*
I must go now.	**Ich muss jetzt gehen.** *ikh muss yehtst GAY-en*
We'd like to hear from you.	**Wir würden gerne von Ihnen hören.** *veer VEWRD-en GEHRN-eh fon EEN-en HER-en*
You must come to visit us.	**Sie müssen uns besuchen.** *zee MEWSS-en uns beh-ZOOKH-en*
Do you have a home page on the Internet?	**Haben Sie eine Home-Page im Internet?** *HAAB-en zee EYEN-eh hohm paych im IN-ter-net*
E-mail us often.	**E-mailen Sie uns oft!** *EE-mayl-en zee uns oft*

Travel Tips   Save receipts on foreign purchases for declaring at customs on re-entry to the U.S. Some countries return a sales or value-added tax to foreign visitors. Take receipts to a special office at the store or to a tax rebate window at the airport of departure. Americans who buy costly objects abroad may be surprised to get a bill from their state tax collector. Most states with a sales tax levy a "use" tariff on all items bought outside the home state, including those purchased abroad. Most tax agencies in these states will send a form for declaring and paying the assessment.

SHOPPING

SHOPS AND STORES

In German-speaking Europe, shops generally open between 8 and 9 A.M. and close around 6 P.M. On Saturdays most shops close around 1 P.M. Many close for a lunch break of approximately two hours, a custom difficult for some American shoppers to adjust to.

In many cities and towns, stores offering plentiful and attractive wares are located on streets under romantic stone archways, where you can do your shopping no matter what the weather. Berne's **Marktgasse** is such a street. Other noted shopping streets are Düsseldorf's **Königsallee**, and Cologne's **Hohe Straβe**. Many streets are dazzling to behold in December. There are department store chains, small, elegant boutiques, stores in modern complexes and in quaint corners. Whatever articles you're looking for, you will find them in abundance.

Even if you think you know your clothes sizes, you may have trouble finding the right size even in your own country. This is all the more true in a foreign country. So whenever possible, try on before you buy. See the Size Guide in the clothing section (pages 181–183).

There is a value-added tax on all purchases, which will be refunded to shoppers living outside Germany. If the store agrees, you fill out a form and the amount of the tax will be mailed to your home.

GOING SHOPPING

I must do some shopping today.	**Ich muss heute einige Einkäufe machen.** *ikh muss HOY-teh EYE-ni-geh EYEN-koy-feh MAH-khen*
I'm looking for ___.	**Ich suche ___.** *ikh ZOOKH-eh*
■ an antique shop	**ein Antiquitätengeschäft** *eyen ahn-ti-kvi-TAYT-en-geh-shehft*

- an art dealer **einen Kunsthändler** *EYEN-en KUNST-hehnt-luh*

- a bookstore **eine Buchhandlung** *EYEN-eh BOOKH-hahnt-lung*

- a china shop **einen Porzellanladen** *EYEN-en por-tseh-LAAN-laad-en*

- a camera shop **ein Photogeschäft** *eyen FOH-toh geh-shehft*

- a bakery **eine Bäckerei** *EYEN-eh beh-keh-REYE*

- a butcher shop **einen Fleischerladen** *EYEN-en FLEYESH-ehr-laa-den*

- a candy store **einen Süßwarenladen** *EYEN-en SEWSS-vaa-ren-laa-den*

- a clothing store **ein Bekleidungsgeschäft** *eyen beh-KLEYED-ungs-geh-shehft*

   for children **Kinderbekleidungsgeschäft** *KIND-ehr-beh-kleyed-ungs-geh-shehft*

   for women **Damenbekleidungsgeschäft** *DAH-men-beh-kleyed-ungs-geh-shehft*

   for men **Herrenbekleidungsgeschäft** *HEHR-en-beh-kleyed-ungs-geh-shehft*

- a delicatessen **ein Delikatessengeschäft** *eyen deh-li-kah-TEHSS-en-geh-shehft*

- a department store **ein Warenhaus** *eyen VAAR-en-hows*

- a drugstore **eine Drogerie/Apotheke** *EYEN-eh dro-geh-REE/ah-poh-TAYK-eh*

NOTE: A **Drogerie** carries over-the-counter drugs as well as toiletries and sundries. However, if you need *prescription* drugs you will have to go to **eine Apotheke**.

■ a dry cleaner's	**eine chemische Reinigung** *EYEN-eh KHAY-mi-sheh REYE-ni-gung*
■ a flower shop	**ein Blumengeschäft** *eyen BLOOM-en-geh-shehft*
■ a furrier	**einen Kürschner** *EYEN-en KEWRSH-nuh*
■ a gift (souvenir) shop	**einen Andenkenladen** *EYEN-en AHN-dehnk-en-laad-en*
■ a gourmet grocery store	**eine Feinkostwarenhandlung** *EYEN-eh FEYEN-kost-vaar-en-hahnt-lung*
■ a grocery store	**ein Lebensmittelgeschäft** *eyen LAYB-ens-mit-el-geh-shehft*
■ a hardware store	**eine Eisenwarenhandlung** *EYEN-eh EYEZ-en-vaar-en-hahnt-lung*
■ a health-food store	**ein Reformhaus** *eyen reh-FORM-hows*
■ a jewelry store	**einen Juwelier** *EYEN-en yu-veh-LEER*
■ a liquor store	**eine Spirituosenhandlung** *EYEN-eh shpee-ree-tu-OHZ-en-hahnt-lung*
■ a market	**einen Markt** *EYEN-en mahrkt*
■ a newsstand	**einen Zeitungsstand** *EYEN-en TSEYET-unks-shtahnt*
■ a pastry shop	**eine Konditorei** *EYEN-eh kon-dee-to-REYE*
■ a record store	**ein Schallplattengeschäft** *eyen SHAHL-plaht-en-geh-shehft*
■ a shoe store	**ein Schuhgeschäft** *eyen SHOO-geh-shehft*
■ a shopping center	**ein Einkaufszentrum** *eyen EYEN-kowfs-tsent-rum*
■ a supermarket	**einen Supermarkt** *EYEN-en ZOOP-uh-mahrkt*

- a tobacco shop **einen Tabakladen** *EYEN-en TAA-bahk-laad-en*

- a toy shop **ein Spielwarengeschäft** *eyen SHPEEL-vaar-en-geh-shehft*

- a wine merchant **eine Weinhandlung** *EYEN-eh VEYEN-hahnt-lung*

Can you help me? **Können Sie mir helfen?** *KERN-en zee meer HEHLF-en*

BOOKS

Germans buy a lot of books. It is therefore not surprising that there are a lot of bookstores. In Mainz you will want to visit the **Gutenberg Haus** and the Museum of Printing.

Where is the largest bookstore here? **Wo ist hier die größte Buchhandlung?** *voh ist heer dee GRERST-eh BOOKH-hahnt-lung*

I'm looking for a copy of ___. **Ich suche ein Exemplar von ___.** *ikh ZOOKH-eh eyen eks-ehm-PLAAR fon*

The title (author) of the book is ___. **Der Titel (Autor) des Buches ist ___.** *dehr TEET-el (OWT-or) dehs BOOKH-es ist*

I've forgotten the title and author. **Titel und Autor hab ich vergessen.** *TEET-el unt OWT-or hahb ikh fehr-GESS-en*

I'm just browsing. **Ich sehe mich nur um.** *ikh ZAY-eh mikh noor um*

Do you have books (novels) in English? **Haben Sie Bücher (Romane) in Englisch?** *HAAB-en zee BEWKH-uh (roh-MAAN-eh) in EHNG-lish*

I'd like an English and German edition of *Grimm's Fairy Tales*.	**Ich möchte eine englische und eine deutsche Ausgabe von *Grimms Märchen*.** *ikh MERKHT-eh EYEN-eh EHNG-lish-eh unt EYEN-eh DOYCH-eh OWSS-gaab-eh fon grimms-MAYRKH-en*
I need a guidebook.	**Ich brauche einen Reiseführer.** *ikh BROWKH-eh EYEN-en REYEZ-eh-fewr-uh*
Can you recommend a good grammar book to me?	**Können Sie mir eine gute Grammatik empfehlen?** *KERN-en zee meer EYEN-eh GOOT-eh grah-MAH-tik ehmp-FAYL-en*
I'm looking for ___.	**Ich suche ___.** *ikh ZOOKH-eh*
■ a pocket dictionary	**ein Taschenwörterbuch** *eyen TAHSH-en-vert-ehr-bookh*
■ a German-English dictionary	**ein deutsch-englisches Wörterbuch** *eyen doytsh-EHNG-lishes vert-ehr-bookh*
Would you have ___?	**Hätten Sie ___?** *HEHT-en zee*
■ a map of the city	**einen Stadtplan** *EYEN-en SHTAHT-plaan*
■ a good mystery story?	**einen guten Krimi** *EYEN-en GOOT-en KREE-mee*
■ old books	**alte Bücher** *AHLT-eh BEWKH-uh*
■ bilingual editions of poetry (by Goethe, Rilke, Heine)	**zweisprachige Ausgaben von Gedichten (von Goethe, Rilke, Heine)** *TSVEYE-shpraa-khi-geh OWS-gaab-en fon geh-DIKHT-en (fon GERTH-eh, RILK-eh, HEYEN-eh)*

CLOTHING

Please show me ___.	**Zeigen Sie mir bitte ___.**	*TSEYEG-en zee meer BIT-eh*
◼ a belt	**einen Gürtel**	*EYEN-en GEWRT-el*
◼ a blouse	**eine Bluse**	*EYEN-eh BLOOZ-eh*
◼ a cap	**eine Mütze**	*EYEN-eh MEWTS-eh*
◼ a brassiere	**einen Büstenhalter**	*EYEN-en BEWST-en-hahlt-uh*
◼ a coat	**einen Mantel**	*EYEN-en MAHNT-el*
◼ a dress	**ein Kleid**	*eyen kleyet*
◼ furs	**Pelze**	*PELTS-eh*
◼ an evening gown	**ein Abendkleid**	*eyen AAB-ent-kleyet*
◼ gloves	**Handschuhe**	*HAHNT-shoo-eh*
◼ a hat	**einen Hut**	*EYEN-en hoot*
◼ a jacket	**eine Jacke**	*EYEN-eh YAHK-eh*
◼ knitwear	**Stricksachen**	*SHTRIK-zahkh-en*

■ lingerie	**Damenunterwäsche**	*DAAM-en-un-tehr-vehsh-eh*
■ pants	**eine Hose**	*EYEN-eh HOHZ-eh*
■ a mink coat	**einen Nerzmantel**	*EYEN-en NEHRTS-mahn-tel*
■ panties	**einen Schlüpfer**	*EYEN-en SHLEWPF-uh*
■ panty hose	**eine Strumpfhose**	*EYEN-eh SHTRUMPF-hohz-eh*
■ a raincoat	**einen Regenmantel**	*EYEN-en RAYG-en-mahn-tel*
■ a scarf	**ein Halstuch**	*eyen HAHLS-tookh*
■ a shirt	**ein Hemd**	*eyen hemt*
■ a pair of shoes	**ein Paar Schuhe**	*eyen paar SHOO-eh*
■ shorts	**kurze Unterhosen**	*KURTS-eh UN-tehr-hohz-en*
■ a skirt	**einen Rock**	*EYEN-en rok*
■ a slip	**einen Unterrock**	*EYEN-en UN-tehr-rok*
■ slippers	**Hausschuhe**	*HOWS-shoo-eh*
■ socks	**Socken**	*ZOK-en*
■ stockings	**Strümpfe**	*SHTREWMPF-eh*
■ a man's suit	**einen Anzug**	*EYEN-en AHN-tsook*
■ a woman's suit	**ein Kostüm**	*eyen kos-TEWM*
■ a sweater	**einen Pullover**	*EYEN-en pul-OHV-uh*
■ a tie	**eine Krawatte**	*EYEN-eh krah-VAHT-eh*
■ an undershirt	**ein Unterhemd**	*eyen UN-tehr-hehmt*
■ underwear	**Unterwäsche**	*UN-tehr-vehsh-eh*
Is there a sale today?	**Gibt's heute einen Verkauf?**	*gipts HOYT-eh EYEN-en fehr-KOWF*

Is this really a close-out sale?	**Ist das wirklich ein Schlussverkauf?** *ist dahs VIRK-likh eyen SHLUSS-fehr-kowf*
Are there any special sale items?	**Was für Angebote gibt's?** *vahs fewr AHN-geh-boht-eh gipts*
Do you carry underwear made of natural fibers?	**Führen Sie Unterwäsche aus natürlichen Fasern?** *FEWR-en zee UN-tehr-vehsh-eh ows nah-TEWR-likh-en FAAZ-ehrn*
Do you know of a store that might have a large stock of ____.	**Kennen Sie ein Geschäft, das ein reichhaltiges Lager an ___ hätte?** *KEN-en zee eyen geh-SHEHFT dahs eyen REYEKH-hahl-ti-ges LAAG-uh ahn ___ HEHT-eh*
Do you have the same thing with short (long) sleeves?	**Haben Sie dasselbe mit kurzen (langen) Ärmeln?** *HAAB-en zee dahs-ZELB-eh mit KOORTS-en (LAHNG-en) EHRM-ehln*
I'd like something ____.	**Ich möchte etwas ___.** *ikh MERKHT-eh EHT-vahs*
■ less expensive	**Billigeres** *BIL-ig-ehr-es*
■ more elegant	**Eleganteres** *eh-lay-GAHNT-ehr-es*
■ of better quality	**von besserer Qualität** *fon BEHSS-ehr-uh kvah-li-TAYT*
■ more cheerful	**Heitereres** *HEYET-ehr-ehr-es*
■ more youthful	**Jugendlicheres** *YOOG-ent-li-kher-es*
■ else	**anderes** *AHND-ehr-es*
■ bigger	**Größeres** *GRERSS-ehr-es*
■ smaller	**Kleineres** *KLEYEN-ehr-es*
I (don't) like it.	**Es gefällt mir (nicht).** *ehs geh-FEHLT meer (nikht)*

This is too ___.	**Dies ist zu ___.** *deess ist tsoo*
■ thick	**dick** *dik*
■ thin	**dünn** *dewn*
■ expensive	**teuer** *TOY-uh*
■ dark	**dunkel** *DUNK-el*
■ light	**hell** *hel*

It's very elegant, but I don't want to spend a fortune on it.	**Es ist sehr elegant, aber ich will kein Vermögen dafür ausgeben.** *ehs ist zayr eh-lay-GAHNT AAB-uh ikh vil keyen fehr-MERG-en dah-FEWR OWS-gay-ben*

COLORS

I like the material, but I don't like the color.	**Der Stoff gefällt mir, aber nicht die Farbe.** *dehr shtof geh-FEHLT meer, AAB-uh nikht die FAARB-eh*

Would you have it in ___?	**Hätten Sie es vielleicht in ___?** *HEHT-en zee ehs fee-LEYEKHT in*
■ black	**schwarz** *shvaarts*
■ blue	**blau** *blow*
■ brown	**braun** *brown*
■ gray	**grau** *grow*
■ green	**grün** *grewn*
■ pink	**rosa** *ROH-zaa*
■ red	**rot** *roht*
■ white	**weiß** *veyess*
■ yellow	**gelb** *gehlp*

There are many additional shades and hues. **Bläulich** (*BLOY-likh*) and **grünlich** (*GREWN-likh*) are "blueish" and "greenish." If you want a darker or lighter shade, say:

■ A lighter (darker) blue (brown, green).	**Ein helleres (dunkleres) Blau (Braun, Grün).** *eyen HEL-ehr-es (DUNK-lehr-es) blow (brown, grewn)*

FIT, ALTERATIONS

Please take my measurements (for a dress).	**Bitte nehmen Sie mir Maß (zu einem Kleid).** *BIT-eh NAYM-en zee meer maass (tsoo EYEN-em kleyet)*
I think my size is 40.	**Ich glaube, ich habe Größe vierzig.** *ikh GLOWB-eh ikh HAAB-eh GRERSS-eh FEER-tsikh*
I'd like to try it on.	**Ich möchte es anprobieren.** *ikh MERKHT-eh ehs AHN-proh-beer-en*
It fits badly in the shoulders.	**Es sitzt schlecht in den Schultern.** *ehs zitst shlehkht in dayn SHUL-tehrn*
The sleeves are too narrow (wide).	**Die Ärmel sind zu eng (weit).** *dee EHRM-el zint tsoo ehng (veyet)*
It needs alterations.	**Es braucht Änderungen.** *ehs browkht EHND-eh-rung-en*
Can you alter it?	**Können Sie es ändern?** *KERN-en zee ehs EHND-ehrn*
Can I return this?	**Kann ich dies zurückgeben?** *kahn ikh dees tsoo-REWK-gayb-en*
It fits very well.	**Es passt sehr gut.** *ehs pahsst zayr goot*
It doesn't fit.	**Es passt nicht.** *ehs pahsst nikht*
I'll take it.	**Ich nehm's.** *ikh naymss*
Please wrap it well.	**Bitte packen Sie es gut ein.** *BIT-eh PAHK-en zee ehs goot eyen*
Please giftwrap it.	**Bitte packen Sie es als Geschenk ein.** *BIT-eh PAHK-en zee ehs ahls geh-SHEHNK eyen*

SALE SIGNS

AUSVERKAUF	(Sale)
SCHLUSSVERKAUF	(Close-out, clearance sale)
SONDERANGEBOT	(Special sale items)

SHOES

I need a pair of shoes (boots).	**Ich brauche ein Paar Schuhe (Stiefel).** *ikh BROWKH-eh eyen paar SHOO-eh (SHTEEF-el)*
Those over there in the window.	**Die da im Schaufenster**. *dee daa im SHOW-fenst-uh*
My size is ___.	**Ich habe Nummer ___.** *ikh HAAB-eh NUM-uh*

SIZE GUIDE FOR READY-MADE WEAR

WOMEN					
DRESSES, COATS, SUITS, AND SKIRTS					
American	10	12	14	16	18	20
German	38	40	42	44	46	48
DRESSES, COATS, SUITS, AND SKIRTS (MEDIUM AND LARGE)					
American	34	36	38	40	42	44
German	42	44	46	48	50	52

WOMEN (continued)

JUNIOR MISS DRESSES, COATS, SUITS, AND SKIRTS

American	7	9	11	13	15	17
German	34–36	36–38	38–40	40–42	42–44	44–46

BLOUSES, SWEATERS, AND CARDIGANS

American	30	32	34	36	38	40	42	44
German	38	40	42	44	46	48	50	52

SHOES

American	2	2-1/2	3-1/2	4	5	5-1/2	6-1/2	7-1/2	8
German	34	35	36	37	38	39	40	41	42

MEN

SHOES

American	9	9-1/2	10-1/2	11	12	13
German	43	44	45	46	47	48

SUITS, COATS, SWEATERS, CARDIGANS, AND PAJAMAS

American	34	36	38	40	42	44	46	48
German	44	46	48	50	52	54	56	58

SHIRTS

American	14	14-1/2	15	15-1/2	16	16-1/2	17	17-1/2
German	36	37	38	39	40	41	42	43

HATS

American	6-7/8	7	7-1/8	7-1/4	7-3/8	7-1/2	7-5/8	7-3/4
German	55	56	57	58	59	60	61	62

CHILDREN					
DRESSES AND SUITS					
American	2	4	6	8	10	12
German	40–45	50–55	60–65	70–75	80–85	90–95

They're too narrow (wide).	**Sie sind zu eng (weit).** *zee zint tsoo eng (veyet)*
They pinch in front (in back).	**Sie drücken vorne (hinten).** *zee DREWK-en FORN-eh (HINT-en)*
They fit fine.	**Sie passen gut.** *zee PAHSS-en goot*
I'll take them.	**Ich nehme sie.** *ikh NAYM-eh zee*
Please give me some shoelaces, too.	**Geben Sie mir bitte auch Schnürsenkel.** *GAYB-en zee meer BIT-eh owkh SHNEWR-zenk-el*
That's all I need today.	**Heute brauche ich sonst nichts mehr.** *HOYT-eh browkh ikh zonst nikhts mayr*

REGIONAL CLOTHES

Trachten (local peasant costumes) are still seen in various parts of German-speaking Europe. Best known are the **Lederhosen** and **Dirndlkleider** of the Alpine areas, standard apparel for performers and vocalists in Bavarian bands in nightspots all over the world. Adaptations of **Dirndl** dresses often appear in the collections of prominent designers.

Where can I buy regional costumes?	**Wo kann ich hier Trachten kaufen?** *voh kahn ikh heer TRAHKHT-en KOWF-en*
I'm looking for ___.	**Ich suche ___.** *ikh ZOOKH-eh*
■ a dirndl dress	**ein Dirndlkleid** *eyen DEERNDL-kleyet*

- leather short pants **Lederhosen** *LAYD-uh-hohz-en*
- a loden cloak **einen Lodenmantel** *EYEN-en*
  (flowing, and *LOHD-en-mahnt-el*
  usually hunter's
  green)
- a Tyrolean hat **einen Tirolerhut** *EYEN-en tee-*
  ROHL-uh-hoot
- a waterproof **einen Wetterfleck** *EYEN-en*
  woolen overcoat *VEHT-uh-flehk*
- embroidered **Stickereien** *SHTIK-eh-reye-en*
  articles
- linen goods **Leinenzeug** *LEYEN-en-tsoyk*

You may want a **Tiroler Pfeife** (pipe) to accompany your
Tyrolean hat, and perhaps a **Gamsbart** (chamois brush) to
pin on the hat. They are widely sold in souvenir shops.

ELECTRICAL APPLIANCES

Electric current in the U.S. is 110V AC, whereas in Germany
it is 220V AC. Unless your electric shaver or alarm clock is
able to handle both currents, you will need to purchase an
adapter. When making a purchase, please be aware that *some*
German products are engineered to work with either system
whereas others will require an adapter. When making a
purchase, be careful to check the warranty to ensure that the
product is covered internationally.

I'm looking for ___. **Ich suche ___.** *ikh ZOOKH-eh*
- an electric **einen Adapter** *EYEN-en ahd-*
  adapter *AHPT-uh*
- an alarm clock **einen Wecker** *EYEN-en VEK-uh*
- a battery **eine Batterie** *EYEN-eh bah-tay-*
  REE
- a blender **einen Mixer** *EYEN-en MIKS-uh*

■ a can opener	**einen Büchsenöffner**	*EYEN-en BEWKS-en-erf-nuh*
■ an electric shaver	**einen Rasierapparat**	*EYEN-en rah-ZEER-ah-pah-raut*
■ a hair dryer	**einen Haartrockner**	*EYEN-en HAAR-trok-nuh*
■ an electric heater	**ein Heizungsgerät**	*eyen HEYETS-unks-geh-rayt*
■ an immersible heater (for liquids)	**einen Tauchsieder**	*EYEN-en TOWKH-zee-duh*
■ a curling iron	**einen Lockenschere**	*EYEN-en LOK-en-shay-reh*
Can you repair this?	**Können Sie dies reparieren?**	*KERN-en zee dees reh-pah-REER-en*
How much would a new one cost?	**Was kostet das neu?**	*vahs KOST-et dahs noy*

JEWELRY

Many tour buses stop at Idar-Oberstein on the Nahe, south of the Moselle river. It is a diamond-cutting center but offers gemstones of all kinds in many shops. The **Schwarzwald** (Black Forest) is famous for cuckoo clocks, and Switzerland for watches.

What sort of jewelry do you have?	**Was für Schmucksachen haben Sie?** *vahs fewr SHMUK-zahkh-en HAAB-en zee*
Please show me ___.	**Zeigen Sie mir bitte ___.** *TSEYEG-en zee meer BIT-eh*
■ a bracelet	**ein Armband** *eyen AHRM-bahnt*
■ a brooch	**eine Brosche** *EYEN-eh BROSH-eh*
■ a chain	**ein Kettchen** *eyen KET-khen*

■ cuff links	**Manschettenknöpfe** *mahn-SHEHT-en-knerpf-eh*
■ a goblet	**einen Becher** *EYEN-en BEHKH-uh*
■ earrings	**Ohrringe** *OHR-ring-eh*
■ a necklace	**eine Halskette** *EYEN-eh HAHLS-ket-eh*
■ a pin	**eine Anstecknadel** *EYEN-eh AHN-shtehk-naad-el*
■ a ring	**einen Ring** *EYEN-en ring*
■ an engagement ring	**einen Verlobungsring** *EYEN-en fehr-LOHB-unks-ring*
■ a wedding ring	**einen Ehering** *EYEN-en AY-eh-ring*
■ a tie pin	**eine Krawattennadel** *EYEN-eh krah-VAHT-en-naad-el*
■ a tiara	**eine Tiara** *EYEN-eh tee-AAR-ah*
■ a wristwatch	**eine Armbanduhr** *EYEN-eh AHRM-bahnt-oor*

Is this ___?	**Ist dies in ___?** *ist dees in*
■ gold	**Gold** *golt*
■ platinum	**Platin** *plah-TEEN*
■ silver	**Silber** *ZILB-uh*
■ stainless steel	**rostfreiem Stahl** *ROST-freye-em shtahl*

Is it gold or just gold plate?	**Ist es in Gold oder nur vergoldet?** *ist ehs in golt OHD-uh noor fehr-GOLD-et*
■ silver plate	**versilbert** *fehr-ZILB-ehrt*
How many carats is it?	**Wieviel Karat hat es?** *VEE-feel kah-RAAT haht ehs*
I collect precious stones.	**Ich sammle Edelsteine.** *ikh ZAHM-leh AY-del-shteyen-eh*

- semiprecious stones, too

  Halbedelsteine auch *HAHLP-ay-del-shteyen-eh owkh*

I'm looking for ___.

Ich suche ___. *ikh ZOOKH-eh*

- amber jewelry

  Bernsteinschmuck *BEHRN-shteyen-shmuk*

- an amethyst

  einen Amethyst *EYEN-en ah-meh-THEWST*

- diamonds

  Diamanten *dee-ah-MAHNT-en*

- emeralds

  Smaragde *smah-RAHKT-eh*

- hematite

  Blutstein *BLOOT-shteyen*

- ivory

  Elfenbein *EHLF-en-beyen*

- jade

  Jade *YAAD-eh*

- onyx

  Onyx *OH-niks*

- pearls

  Perlen *PEHRL-en*

- rubies

  Rubine *ru-BEEN-eh*

- sapphires

  Saphire *zah-FEER-eh*

- topazes

  Topase *toh-PAAZ-eh*

- turquoises

  Türkise *tewr-KEEZ-eh*

How much are you asking for this ruby?

Wieviel verlangen Sie für diesen Rubin? *VEE-feel fehr-LAHNG-en zee fewr DEEZ-en ru-BEEN*

I don't want it at that price.

Ich mag ihn zu diesem Preise nicht nehmen. *ikh maak een tsoo DEEZ-em PREYEZ-eh nikht NAYM-en*

I'm looking for a suitable gift for a ten-year-old girl.

Ich suche ein passendes Geschenk für ein zehnjähriges Mädchen. *ikh ZOOKH-eh eyen PASS-end-es geh-SHEHNK fewr eyen TSAYN-yehr-ig-es MAYT-khen*

All that glitters is not gold.

Es ist nicht alles Gold, was glänzt. *ehs ist nikht AHL-es golt vahs glehntst*

MUSIC EQUIPMENT

Is there an audio/video store in the neighborhood?	**Gibt es einen Audiovisuell-Laden hier in der Gegend?** *gipt ehs EYEN-en OW-dee-o-viz-oo-el-laad-en heer in dehr GAYG-ent*
I'm looking for ___.	**Ich suche ___.** *ikh ZOOKH-eh*
■ an amplifier	**einen Verstärker** *EYEN-en fehr-SHTERK-uh*
■ analog cassettes	**Analogkassetten** *ahn-ah-LOK-kahss-ET-en*
■ a CD player	**einen CD-Speiler** *EYEN-en tsay day SHPEEL-uh*
■ a CD recorder	**einen CD-Rekorder** *EYEN-en tsay day re-KORD-uh*
■ CDs	**CDs** *tsay dayss*
■ DAT cassettes	**DAT-Kassetten** *day ah tay kahss-ET-en*
■ headphones	**Kopfhörer** *KOPF-hewr-uh*
■ a minidisk player	**einen Mini-Disketten-Spieler** *EYEN-en mini-dis-KET-en-shpeel-uh*
■ minidisks	**Mini-Disketten** *mini-dis-KET-en*
■ a receiver	**einen Empfänger** *EYEN-en emp-FENG-uh*
■ recordable CDs	**Aufnahme CDs** *OWF-naam-eh tsay dayss*
■ a small cassette player	**einen kleinen Kassettenspieler** *EYEN-en KLEYEN-en kahss-ET-en-shpeel-uh*
■ a small cassette recorder	**einen kleinen Kassettenrekorder** *EYEN-en KLEYEN-en kahss-ET-en-re-kord-uh*
■ speakers	**Lautsprecher** *LOWT-shprekh-uh*
■ a tuner	**einen Tuner** *EYEN-en TOON-uh*

■ wireless headphones	**drahtlose Kopfhörer** *DRAAT-lohz-eh KOPF-hewr-uh*
I'm looking for a CD by ___.	**Ich suche eine CD von ___.** *ikh ZOOKH-eh EYEN-eh tsey-day fon*
I'm interested in ___.	**Ich interessiere mich für ___.** *ikh in-teh-reh-SEER-eh mikh fewr*
■ brass-band music	**Blasmusik** *BLAAS-moo-zeek*
■ chamber music	**Kammermusik** *KAHM-uh-moo-zeek*
■ classical music	**klassische Musik** *KLAHS-ish-eh moo-ZEEK*
■ folk music	**Volksmusik** *FOLKS-moo-zeek*
■ folksongs (dances)	**Volkslieder (tänze)** *FOLKS-leed-uh (TEHNTS-eh)*
■ the latest hits	**die allerneusten Schlager** *die AHL-ehr-noyst-en SHLAAG-uh*
■ golden oldies	**"Evergreens"** *Evergreens*
■ easy listening	**Unterhaltungsmusik** *UNT-ehr-hahlt-unks-moo-zeek*
■ pop music	**Pop-Musik** *POP-moo-zeek*
Do you have historic recordings of DGG and Telefunken?	**Haben Sie historische Aufnahmen von DGG und Telefunken?** *HAAB-en zee his-TOHR-ish-eh OWF-naam-en fon DAY-gay-gay unt TAY-leh-funk-en*
Do you have albums of opera highlights?	**Haben Sie Opernquerschnitte?** *HAAB-en zee OHP-ehrn-kvehr-shnit-eh*

VIDEO EQUIPMENT

Please see the note under Electrical Appliances on page 184. In addition, Europe uses broadcasting and recording systems that are often incompatible with those of the U.S. German TVs, VCRs, VCR tapes, computers, and telephone answering systems will not operate properly in the U.S.

I need ___.	**Ich brauche ___.** *ikh BROWKH-eh*
■ a camcorder	**einen Camcorder** *EYEN-en KAHM-kord-uh*
■ a digital camcorder	**einen digitalen Camcorder** *EYEN-en dig-it-AAL-en KAHM-kord-uh*
■ digital videofilm	**digitalen Videofilm** *dig-it-AAL-en VEE-day-oh-film*
■ DVD movies	**DVD Spielfilme** *day vay day SHPEEL-film-eh*
■ a DVD player	**einen DVD-Spieler** *EYEN-en day vay day SHPEEL-uh*
■ videofilm	**Videofilm** *VEE-day-oh-film*
■ a VCR	**einen VCR** *EYEN-nen vay-tsay-ehr*
■ VCR tape	**VCR-Tonband** *vay-tsay-ehr TOHN-bahnt*

Do you have VCR or DVD movies with subtitles in English?	**Haben sie VCR oder DVD Spielfilme mit englischen Untertiteln?** *HAAB-en zee vay-tsay-ehr OHD-uh day-vay-day SHPEEL-film-eh mit EHNG-lish-en UNT-ehr-teet-eln*
Will the warranty be honored in the U.S.?	**Ist die Garantie auch in den USA gültig?** *ist dee gah-rehn-TEE owkh in dehn oo-ess-aa GEWLT-ikh*
Whom should I contact if this malfunctions?	**Wen soll ich anrufen, wenn dies defekt ist?** *vayn zol ikh AHN-roof-en ven deess de-FEHKT ist*

PHOTOGRAPHIC EQUIPMENT

| Where can I find a camera shop? | **Wo finde ich ein Fotogeschäft?** *voh FIND-eh ikh eyen FOH-toh-geh-sheft* |

I would like ___.	**Ich möchte ___.** *ikh MERKHT-eh*
■ black-and-white film	**Schwarzweißfilm** *SHVAHRTS-veyess-film*
■ a camera bag	**eine Kameratasche** *EYEN-eh KAHM-eh-raa-tah-she*
■ camera batteries	**Kamerabatterien** *KAHM-eh-raa-bah-tehr-ee-en*
■ camera film	**Kamerafilm** *KAHM-eh-raa-film*
■ digital camera film	**digitalen Kamerafilm** *di-gi-taal-en KAHM-eh-raa-film*
■ a disposable camera	**eine Einwegkamera** *EYEN-eh EYEN-vayk-kahm-eh-raa*
■ film	**Film** *film*
■ a flash	**ein Blitzlicht** *eyen BLITS-likht*
■ a lens	**ein Objektiv** *eyen ob-yek-TEEF*
■ a point-and-shoot camera	**eine Richt-und-Knips-Kamera** *EYEN-eh rikht-unt-knips-kahm-eh-raa*
■ slide film	**Diafilm** *DEE-ah-film*
■ an SLR camera	**eine Spiegelreflexkamera** *EYEN-eh SHPEEG-el-reh-flex-kahm-eh-raa*
■ a tripod	**ein Stativ** *eyen shtaht-EEF*
■ a slide projector	**einen Diaprojektor** *EYEN-en DEE-ah-proh-yek-tohr*
■ a zoom lens	**ein Zoomobjektiv** *eyen ZOOM-ob-yek-TEEF*
How quickly can you develop these films?	**Wie schnell können Sie diese Filme entwickeln?** *vee shnel KERN-en zee DEEZ-eh FILM-eh ehnt-VIK-ehln*
Here are a black-and-white and two color films.	**Hier haben Sie einen schwarz-weißen und zwei Farbfilme.** *heer HAAB-en zee EYEN-en SHVAHRTS-veyess-en unt tsveye-FAHRP-film-eh*

| I want a print of each negative. | **Ich möchte einen Abzug von jedem Negativ.** *ikh MERKHT-eh EYEN-en AHP-tsook fon YAYD-em NEH-gah-teef* |
| I want this picture enlarged. | **Ich möchte dieses Bild vergrößern lassen.** *ikh MERKHT-eh DEEZ-es bilt fehr-GRERSS-ehrn LASS-en* |

- with a glossy finish **Hochglanz** *HOHKH-glahnts*
- with a matte finish **matt** *maht*

| Is there an extra charge for developing? | **Kostet das Entwickeln extra?** *KOST-et dahs ehnt-VIK-eln EKS-traa* |
| I want prints only of the exposures that turned out well. | **Ich möchte nur von den gut gelungenen Aufnahmen Abzüge haben.** *ikh MERKHT-eh noor fon dayn goot geh-LUNG-en-en OWF-naam-en AHP-tsewg-eh HAAB-en* |

NEWSPAPERS, MAGAZINES, AND POSTCARDS

Do you have stamps?	**Haben Sie auch Briefmarken?** *HAAB-en zee owkh BREEF-maark-en*
Do you sell booklets of tickets for the streetcars?	**Verkaufen Sie Fahrscheinhefte für die Straßenbahnen?** *fehr-KOW-fen zee FAAR-sheyen-heft-eh fewr dee SHTRAASS-en-baan-en*
Do you have newspapers (magazines, periodicals) in English?	**Haben Sie Zeitungen (Illustrierten, Zeitschriften) in Englisch?** *HAAB-en zee TSEYET-ung-en (il-us-TREERT-en, TSEYET-shrift-en) in EHNG-lish*

Do you have other postcards besides these?	**Haben Sie noch andere Postkarten als diese?** *HAAB-en zee nokh AHND-eh-reh POST-kaart-en ahls DEEZ-eh*
How much is that?	**Was macht das?** *vahs mahkht dahs*

HANDICRAFTS, TOYS, SOUVENIRS

Tourist souvenir shops offering mass-produced trinkets are found everywhere. However, all items sold in Austria's **Heimatwerk** (handicraft) shops are handmade. Branches exist in most Austrian cities. Switzerland offers similar arts and crafts of high quality. You can even get Alpine cowbells, as well as the more traditional dolls, carvings, and fabrics. The inventiveness, variety, and craftsmanship of German toys have long been held in great esteem. At Christmastime (from late November on), outdoor markets are set up in German-speaking European cities. You will find many interesting wares on display there. The Christmas markets in Munich, Vienna, and Nuremberg are the best known, and Nuremberg produces some of the most ingenious and elaborate toys ever made. You will, of course, find toys in all price ranges.

(See also Regional Clothes on pages 183–184 and Porcelain, Fine Arts on pages 194–197.)

I'd like to buy a gift (souvenir).	**Ich möchte gerne ein Geschenk (Andenken) kaufen.** *ikh MERKHT-eh GEHRN-eh eyen geh-SHENK (AHN-dehnk-en) KOWF-en*
I don't want to spend more than ___ on it.	**Ich will nicht mehr als ___ dafür ausgeben.** *ikh vil nikht mayr ahls ___ dah-FEWR OWS-gayb-en*
What do you have in ___?	**Was haben Sie an ___?** *vahs HAAB-en zee ahn*
■ leather goods	**Lederwaren** *LAYD-uh-vaar-en*
■ glassware	**Glaswaren** *GLAAS-vaar-en*

Are these little spoons genuine silver?	**Sind diese Löffelchen echt Silber?** *zint DEEZ-eh LERF-el-khen ehkht ZILB-uh*
How old is this beer stein?	**Wie alt ist dieser Bierkrug?** *vee ahlt ist DEEZ-uh BEER-krook*
Is this ___ ?	**Ist dies ___?** *ist dees*
■ handcarved	**handgeschnitzt** *HAHNT-geh-shnitst*
■ handpainted	**handgemalt** *HAHNT-geh-maalt*
How much is this little cup?	**Was kostet dieses Tässchen?** *vahs KOST-et DEEZ-es TEHS-khen*
Do you have dolls in peasant costumes?	**Haben Sie Puppen in Trachten?** *HAAB-en zee PUP-en in TRAHKHT-en*
How much does this set of tableware (cutlery) cost?	**Wieviel kostet dieses Essbesteck?** *VEE-feel KOST-et DEEZ-es EHSS-beh-shtek*
Is this made of wood (paper, metal, copper, pewter)?	**Ist dies aus Holz (Papier, Metall, Kupfer, Zinn)?** *ist dees ows holts (pah-PEER, meh-TAHL, KUP-fuh, tsin)*
What kinds of toys do you have?	**Was für Spielzeuge haben Sie?** *vahs fewr SHPEEL-tsoyg-eh HAAB-en zee*
■ For a ten-year-old child.	**Für ein zehnjähriges Kind.** *fewr eyen TSAYN-yay-rig-es kint*
■ Nothing dangerous!	**Nichts Gefährliches!** *nikhts geh-FAYR-likh-es*

PORCELAIN, FINE ARTS

Ever since the alchemists **Böttger** and **Tschirnhaus** (working for the Electors of Saxony) succeeded in duplicating the Chinese formulas in the West, Dresden china (**Meißner Porzellan**) has been world famous.

Some early porcelain pieces are very costly and can be found in antique shops. The modern Hummel figures enjoy great popularity. Berlin's **Flohmarkt U-Bahnhof Nollendorf Platz** (flea market at the Nollendorf Platz subway station) offers masses of bric-a-brac. Vienna's Dorotheum, with branches throughout Austria, also offers a great variety of assorted antiques, sometimes at auction.

The English "bull in a china shop" becomes in German **der Elefant im Porzellanladen**. You can buy bulls, elephants, Lipizzaner stallions, unicorns, and entire menageries in glass or porcelain everywhere in German-speaking Europe. Happy Antiquing!

Is this shepherdess genuine Dresden china?	**Ist diese Schäferin echtes Meißner Porzellan?** *ist DEEZ-eh SHAYF-ehr-in EHKHT-es MEYESS-nuh por-tseh-LAAN*
How old is this statue?	**Wie alt ist diese Statue?** *vee ahlt ist DEEZ-eh SHTAA-tu-eh*
How much do these Hummel figures cost?	**Wieviel kosten diese Hummel-figuren?** *VEE-feel KOST-en DEEZ-eh HUM-el-fi-goor-en*
Have you something smaller (bigger, cheaper, older)?	**Haben Sie etwas Kleineres (Größeres, Billigeres, Älteres)?** *HAAB-en zee EHT-vahs KLEYEN-eh-res (GRERSS-eh-res, BIL-ig-eh-res, EHLT-eh-res)*
That's too much to carry.	**Das ist zu viel zu tragen.** *dahs ist tsoo feel tsoo TRAAG-en*
I just want a small souvenir.	**Ich möchte nur ein kleines Andenken.** *ikh MERKHT-eh noor eyen KLEYEN-es AHN-dehnk-en*
What sort of trinkets do you have?	**Was für Nippsachen haben Sie?** *vahs fewr NIP-zahkh-en HAAB-en zee*

What are the shipping charges to America (England, Canada, Australia)?	**Was sind die Versandkosten nach Amerika (England, Kanada, Australien)?** *vahs zint dee fehr-ZAHNT-kost-en nakh ah-MEH-ree-kah (EHNG-lahnt, KAH-nah-dah, ows-TRAA-lyen)*
I'm interested in classical (medieval, modern) art.	**Ich interessiere mich für antike (mittelalterliche, moderne) Kunst.** *ikh in-teh-reh-SEER-eh mikh fewr ahn-TEEK-eh (MIT-el-ahl-tehr-likh-eh, mo-DEHRN-eh) kunst*
Do you have ___?	**Haben Sie ___?** *HAAB-en zee*
■ woodcarvings by Riemenschneider and Stoss	**Holzschnitzereien von Riemenschneider und Stoß?** *HOLTS-shnits-eh-reye-en fon REEM-en-shneyed-uh unt shtohss*
■ engravings by Dürer and Schongauer	**Stiche von Dürer und Schongauer** *SHTIKH-eh fon DEWR-uh unt SHOHN-gow-uh*
■ paintings by Holbein and other old masters	**Gemälde von Holbein und anderen alten Meistern** *geh-MAYLD-eh fon HOL-beyen unt AHN-dehr-en AHLT-en MEYE-stern*
■ Russian icons	**russische Ikonen** *RU-ssi-sheh ee-KOHN-en*
■ handcarved crucifixes and angels	**handeschnitzte Kruzifixe und Engel (Putten)** *HAHNT-geh-shnitst-eh kru-tsee-FIKS-eh unt EHNG-el (PUT-en)*
■ bronzes of Shiva, Buddha, and others from the Orient	**Bronzen von Schiwa, Buddha, und anderen aus dem Orient** *BRONTS-en fon SHEE-vaa, BU-dah, unt AHN-deh-ren ows daym oh-ree-EHNT*
Please receipt this bill.	**Bitte, quittieren Sie diese Rechnung.** *BIT-eh kvi-TEER-en zee DEEZ-eh REHKH-nung*

| I don't want any trouble at customs. | **Ich will keine Schwierigkeiten beim Zoll haben.** *ikh vil KEYEN-eh SHVEE-rikh-keyet-en beyem tsol HAAB-en* |

STATIONERY ITEMS

I'm looking for ___.	**Ich suche ___.** *ikh ZOOKH-eh*
■ ball-point pens	**Kugelschreiber** *KOOG-el-shreyeb-uh*
■ a deck of playing cards	**Spielkarten** *SHPEEL-kaart-en*
■ envelopes	**Umschläge** *UM-shlayg-eh*
■ an eraser	**einen Radiergummi** *EYEN-en rah-DEER-gu-mee*
■ glue	**Leim** *leyem*
■ notebooks	**Notizhefte** *noh-TEETS-hehft-eh*
■ pencils	**Bleistifte** *BLEYE-shtift-eh*
■ a ruler	**ein Lineal** *eyen lee-nay-AAL*
■ tape	**Klebestreifen** *KLAYB-eh-shtreyef-en*
■ some string	**Schnur** *schnoor*
■ thumbtacks	**Reißzwecken** *REYESS-tsvehk-en*
■ typing paper	**Schreibmaschinenpapier** *SHREYEP-mah-sheen-en-pah-peer*
■ a writing pad	**einen Schreibblock** *EYEN-en SHREYEP-blok*
■ airmail writing paper	**Luftpost Briefpapier** *LUFT-post BREEF-pah-peer*
■ Scotch tape	**Tesafilm** *TAY-zaa-film*

TOBACCO

Cigarettes are widely sold in cigarette machines. So, nicotine craving can be calmed even when the tobacco shop is closed.

Can you give me change for the machine?	**Können Sie mir Kleingeld für den Automaten geben?** *KERN-en zee meer KLEYEN-gehlt fewr dayn ow-toh-MAAT-en GAYB-en*
I'd like a pack (carton) of cigarettes.	**Ich möchte eine Schachtel (Stange) Zigaretten.** *ikh MERKHT-eh EYEN-eh SHAHKHT-el (SHTAHNG-eh) tsee-gah-REHT-en*
■ filtered	**mit Filter** *mit FILT-uh*
■ unfiltered	**ohne Filter** *OHN-eh FILT-uh*
■ menthol	**Mentholzigaretten** *mehn-TOHL-tsee-gah-REHT-en*
■ king-size	**extra lang** *EKS-traa lahng*
■ reduced nicotine	**nikotinarm** *ni-koh-TEEN-ahrm*
What American cigarettes do you have?	**Was für amerikanische Zigaretten haben Sie?** *vahs fewr ah-meh-ree-KAAN-ish-eh tsee-gah-REHT-en HAAB-en zee*
Do you carry Cuban cigars?	**Führen Sie Havannas?** *FEWR-en zee hah-VAHN-ahs*
What sort of pipe tobacco do you have?	**Was für Pfeifentabak haben Sie?** *vahs fewr PFEYEF-en-tah-bahk HAAB-en zee*
Can you prepare a special blend for me?	**Können Sie mir eine besondere Mischung vorbereiten?** *KERN-en zee meer EYEN-eh beh-ZOND-eh-reh MISH-ung FOR-beh-reyet-en*

I need ___.	**Ich brauche ___.** *ikh BROWKH-eh*
■ chewing tobacco	**Kautabak** *KOW-tah-bahk*
■ cigars	**Zigarren** *tsee-GAHR-en*
■ snuff	**Schnupftabak** *SHNUPF-tah-bahk*
■ a cigarette holder	**eine Zigarettenspitze** *EYEN-eh tsee-gah-REHT-en-shpits-eh*
■ flints	**Feuersteine** *FOY-uh-shteyen-eh*
■ a cigarette lighter	**ein Feuerzeug** *eyen FOY-uh-tsoyk*
■ pipe cleaners	**Pfeifenreiniger** *PFEYEF-en-reye-nig-uh*
■ matches	**Streichhölzer** *SHTREYEKH-herlts-uh*
What do you recommend?	**Was empfehlen Sie mir?** *vahs ehm-PFAYL-en zee meer*

FOOD AND HOUSEHOLD ITEMS

It would be a good idea to take your own shopping bag or basket, as not all markets give out bags. See also the Food and Drink chapter (page 107) and the dictionary (pages 281–313) for more food words.

I'd like ___.	**Ich möchte ___.** *ikh MERKHT-eh*
■ a bar of soap	**ein Stück Seife** *eyen shtewk ZEYEF-eh*
■ a bottle of juice	**eine Flasche Saft** *EYEN-eh FLAHSH-eh zahft*
■ a box of cereal	**ein Karton Müsli** *eyen kahr-TONG MEWS-lee*
■ a can (tin) of tomato sauce	**eine Dose Tomatensoße** *EYEN-eh DOHZ-eh toh-MAAT-en-zohss-eh*
■ a dozen eggs	**ein Dutzend Eier** *eyen DUTS-ehnt EYE-uh*
■ a jar of coffee	**ein Glas Kaffee** *eyen glahs KAH-fay*

- a kilo of potatoes (just over 2 pounds) **ein Kilo Kartoffeln** *eyen KEE-loh kahr-TOF-eln*

- a half-kilo of cherries (just over 1 pound) **ein halbes Kilo Kirschen** *eyen HAHLB-es KEE-loh KEERSH-en*

- a liter of milk (about 1 quart) **ein Liter Milch** *eyen LEET-uh milkh*

- a package of candies **ein Paket Bonbons** *eyen pah-KAYT bohn-BOHNS*

METRIC WEIGHTS AND MEASURES

Solid Measures
(approximate measurements only)

OUNCES	GRAMS (GRAMM)	GRAMS	OUNCES
1/4	7	10	1/3
1/2	14	100	3-1/2
3/4	21	300	10-1/2
1	28	500	18

POUNDS	KILOGRAMS (KILOGRAMM)	KILOGRAMS	POUNDS
1	1/2	1	2-1/4
5	2-1/4	3	6-1/2
10	4-1/2	5	11
20	9	10	22
50	23	50	110
100	45	100	220

METRIC WEIGHTS AND MEASURES			

Liquid Measures
(approximate measurements only)

OUNCES	MILLILITERS (**MILLILITER**)	MILLILITERS	OUNCES
1	30	10	1/3
6	175	50	1-1/2
12	350	100	3-1/2
16	475	150	5

GALLONS	LITERS (**LITER**)	LITERS	GALLONS
1	3-3/4	1	1/4 (1 quart)
5	19	5	1-1/3
10	38	10	2-1/2

■ 100 grams of cheese (about 1/4 pound) **hundert Gramm Käse** *HUN-dehrt grahm KAYZ-eh*

■ a roll of toilet paper **eine Rolle Toilettenpapier** *EYEN-eh ROL-eh toy-LEHT-en-pah-peer*

■ a kilo of butter **ein Kilo Butter** *eyen KEE-loh BUT-uh*

■ 200 grams (about 1/2 pound) of cookies **zweihundert Gramm Kekse** *TSVEYE-hun-dehrt grahm KAYKS-eh*

■ 100 grams of bologna **hundert Gramm Fleischwurst** *HUN-dehrt grahm FLEYESH-voorst*

NOTE: Common measurements for purchasing foods are a kilo or fractions thereof, and 100 (**einhundert**), 200 (**zweihundert**), and 500 (**fünfhundert**) grams. See also the pages on Numbers (14–17).

TOILETRIES

For prescription drugs you need an **Apotheke** (see Pharmacy section, pages 216–219). For toilet and household articles, and patent medicines, go to a **Drogerie**.

I'm looking for ___.	**Ich suche ___.** *ikh ZOOKH-eh*
■ a brush	**eine Bürste** *EYEN-eh BEWRST-eh*
■ cleansing cream	**Reinigungscreme** *REYEN-ig ungs-kraym*
■ cologne	**Kölnisch Wasser** *KERLN-ish VAHS-uh*
■ condoms	**Kondome** *KON-dohm-eh* **Präservative** *pray-zayr-vah-TEEV-eh*
■ dental floss	**Zahnseide** *TSAAN-zeyed-eh*
■ (disposable) diapers	**(wegwerfbare) Windeln** *(VEHK-vehrf-baar-eh) VIND-eln*
■ a file	**eine Feile** *EYEN-eh FEYEL-eh*
■ eyeliner	**einen Lidstift** *EYEN-en LEED-shtift*
■ eye shadow	**einen Lidschatten** *EYEN-en LEED-shaht-en*
■ an eyebrow pencil	**einen Augenbrauenstift** *EYEN-en OWG-en-brow-en-shtift*
■ foot powder	**Fußpuder** *FOOSS-pood-uh*
■ hairpins	**Haarklemmen** *HAAR-klem-en*
■ hair spray	**Haarspray** *HAAR-shpray*
■ lipstick	**einen Lippenstift** *EYEN-en LIP-en-shtift*
■ mascara	**Wimperntusche** *VIMP-ehrn-tush-eh*
■ a mirror	**einen Spiegel** *EYEN-en SHPEEG-el*

■ mouthwash	**Mundwasser**	*MUNT-vahs-uh*
■ nail clippers	**eine Nagelzange**	*EYEN-eh NAAG-el-tsahng-eh*
■ nail polish	**Nagellack**	*NAAG-el-lahk*
■ nail polish remover	**Nagellackentferner**	*NAAG-el-lahk-ehnt-fehrn-uh*
■ nail scissors	**eine Nagelschere**	*EYEN-eh NAAG-el-shayr-eh*
■ a razor	**einen Rasierapparat**	*EYEN-en rah-ZEER-ah-pah-raat*
■ razor blades	**Rasierklingen**	*rah-ZEER-kling-en*
■ rouge	**Schminke, Rouge**	*SHMINK-eh, roozh*
■ sanitary napkins	**Damenbinden**	*DAAM-en-bind-en*
■ shampoo	**ein Haarwaschmittel**	*eyen HAAR-vahsh-mit-el*
■ shaving lotion	**Rasierwasser**	*rah-ZEER-vahs-uh*
■ shaving cream	**Rasiercreme**	*rah-ZEER-kraym*
■ soap	**Seife**	*ZEYEF-eh*
■ a sponge	**einen Schwamm**	*EYEN-en shvahm*
■ tissues	**Papiertücher**	*pah-PEER-tewkh-uh*
■ toilet paper	**Toilettenpapier**	*toy-LEHT-en-pah-peer*
■ a toothbrush	**eine Zahnbürste**	*EYEN-eh TSAAN-bewrst-eh*
■ toothpaste	**Zahnpaste**	*TSAAN-pahs-teh*
■ tweezers	**eine Pinzette**	*EYEN-eh pin-TSEHT-eh*

Travel Tips Touring on a budget? Then it pays to do your homework. Look for hotels or bed-and-breakfast establishments that include a morning meal in the price of a room. Often the breakfast is hearty enough to allow a light lunch. Carry nutrition bars from home in your tote bag for snacking when only expensive airport or restaurant food is available. Use public transportation whenever possible. Rail and air passes are sold for Europe and other regions but often can only be purchased in the U.S. before departure. If you must rent a car and have booked one from home, double-check local prices. Sometimes better deals can be arranged on the spot. When you first arrive in a country, check with a visitors' bureau. Agents there will explain discount cards or money-saving packets offered by local governments or merchants. The discount plans often cover transportation, food, lodging, museums, concerts, and other entertainment.

PERSONAL CARE AND SERVICES

If your hotel doesn't offer personal services, ask the desk clerk to recommend someone nearby.

THE BARBER SHOP

I must go to the barber.	**Ich muss zum Friseur.**	*ikh muss tsoom free-ZEHR*
Is there one in the hotel?	**Gibt's einen im Hotel?**	*gipts EYEN-en im ho-TEL*
I don't want to wait long.	**Ich will nicht lange warten.**	*ikh vil nikht LAHNG-eh VAART-en*
Give me a shave, please.	**Rasieren, bitte.**	*rah-ZEER-en BIT-eh*
I want a haircut, please.	**Haare schneiden, bitte.**	*HAAR-eh SHNEYED-en BIT-eh*
(Not too) short in back, long in front.	**(Nicht zu) kurz hinten, lang vorne.**	*(nikht tsoo) koorts HINT-en, lahng FORN-eh*
Take a little more off on top.	**Nehmen Sie oben ein bisschen mehr weg.**	*NAYM-en zee OHB-en eyen BISS-khen mayr vehk*
Nothing more on the sides.	**Nichts mehr an den Seiten.**	*nikhts mayr ahn dayn ZEYET-en*
That's enough.	**Das genügt.**	*dahs ge-NEWKT*
Just use the scissors, please.	**Nur mit der Schere, bitte.**	*noor mit dehr SHAYR-eh BIT-eh*

Don't use the machine.	**Keine Maschine, bitte.** *KEYEN-eh mah-SHEEN-eh BIT-eh*
Please, just a light trim.	**Bitte nur ausputzen.** *BIT-eh noor OWS-puts-en*
Please trim my ____.	**Bitte stutzen Sie mir ____.** *BIT-eh SHTUTS-en zee meer*
▓ beard	**den Bart** *dayn baart*
▓ moustache	**den Schnurrbart** *dayn SCHNOOR-baart*
▓ sideburns	**die Koteletten** *dee kot-eh-LEHT-en*
Please bring me a hand mirror.	**Bringen Sie mir bitte einen Handspiegel.** *BRING-en zee meer BIT-eh EYEN-en HAHNT-shpeeg-el*
How much do I owe you?	**Was schulde ich Ihnen?** *vahs SHULD-eh ikh EEN-en*
Is the service included?	**Ist die Bedienung inbegriffen?** *ist dee beh-DEEN-ung IN-beh-grif-en*

THE BEAUTY PARLOR

Is there a beauty parlor around here?	**Gibt es einen Damensalon hier in der Nähe?** *gipt ehs EYEN-en DAAM-en-zaa-long heer in dehr NAY-eh*
I'd like to make an appointment for today (tomorrow).	**Ich möchte mich für heute (morgen) anmelden.** *ikh MERKHT-eh mikh fewr HOYT-eh (MORG-en) AHN meld en*
I'd like ____.	**Ich möchte ____.** *ikh MERKHT-eh*
Can you give me ____?	**Können Sie mir ____ geben?** *KERN-en zee meer ____ GAYB-en*

■ a color rinse   **eine Farbspülung**   *EYEN-eh FAHRP-shpewl-ung*

■ a face pack   **eine Gesichtsmaske**   *EYEN-eh geh-ZIKHTS-mahsk-eh*

■ a manicure (pedicure)   **eine Maniküre (Pediküre)** *EYEN-eh MAHN-i-kewr-eh (PAYD-i-kewr-eh)*

■ a mudbath   **ein Schlammbad**   *eyen SHLAHM-baat*

■ a facial massage   **eine Gesichtsmassage**   *EYEN-eh geh-ZIKHTS-mah-sazh-eh*

■ a permanent   **eine Dauerwelle**   *EYEN-eh DOW-uh-vehl-eh*

■ a touch up   **eine Auffrischung**   *EYEN-eh OWF-frish-ung*

Just a shampoo and set, please.   **Nur Waschen und Legen, bitte.** *noor VAHSH-en unt LAYG-en BIT-eh*

No, don't cut it.   **Nein, nicht schneiden.**   *neyen, nikht SHNEYED-en*

I don't like the color anymore.   **Die Farbe gefällt mir nicht mehr.** *dee FAARB-eh geh-FEHLT meer nikht mayr*

This time I'm going to try ____.   **Diesmal versuche ich ____.** *DEES-maal fehr-ZOOKH-eh ikh*

■ auburn   **kastanienbraun**   *kahs-TAAN-yen-brown*

■ light blond   **hellblond**   *hel blont*

■ dark blond   **dunkelblond**   *DUNK-el blont*

■ brunette   **braun**   *brown*

■ a darker color   **eine dunklere Farbe**   *EYEN-eh DUNK-lehr-eh FAARB-eh*

■ a lighter color   **eine hellere Farbe**   *EYEN-eh HEL-ehr-eh FAARB-eh*

■ the same color	**dieselbe Farbe** *DEE-zehlb-eh FAARB-eh*
■ something exotic	**etwas Exotisches** *EHT-vahs eks-OHT-ish-es*
I'd like to look at the color chart again.	**Ich möchte mir nochmal die Farbtabelle ansehen.** *ikh MERKHT-eh meer NOKH-maal dee FAARP-tah-bel-eh AHN-zay-en*
Not too much hair spray.	**Nicht zu viel Haarspray.** *nikht tsoo feel HAAR-shpray*
No hair spray, please.	**Kein Haarspray, bitte.** *keyen HAAR-shpray BIT-eh*
More hair spray.	**Mehr Haarspray.** *mayr HAAR-shpray*
Do you carry wigs?	**Führen Sie Perücken?** *FEWR-en zee peh-REWK-en*
I want a new hairdo.	**Ich will eine neue Frisur.** *ikh vil EYEN-eh NOY-eh free-ZOOR*

Something striking.	**Etwas Auffallendes.** *EHT-vahs OWF-fahl-ehnd-es*
Something wild.	**Etwas ganz Tolles.** *EHT-vahs gahnts TOL-es*
With curls.	**Mit Löckchen.** *mit LERK-khen*
With waves.	**Mit Wellen.** *mit VEL-en*
In a bun on top or behind.	**In einem Knoten oben oder hinten.** *in EYEN-em KNOHT-en OHB-en OHD-uh HINT-en*
How about a page-boy style?	**Wie wär's mit einem Pagenschnitt?** *vee vayrs mit EYEN-em PAA-zhen-shnit*
Or a razor cut?	**Oder einen Messerschnitt?** *OHD-uh EYEN-em MESS-uh-shnit*
Or in bangs?	**Oder einer Ponyfrisur?** *OHD-uh EYEN-uh POHN-ee-free-zoor*
Please bring me a hand mirror.	**Bringen sie mir bitte einen Handspiegel.** *BRING-en zee meer BIT-eh EYEN-en HAHNT-shpee-gel*
What do I owe you?	**Was schulde ich Ihnen?** *vahs SHULD-eh ikh EEN-en*

SHOE REPAIRS

Can you fix these shoes (boots) right now?	**Können Sie gleich jetzt diese Schuhe (Stiefel) reparieren?** *KERN-en zee gleyekh yetst DEEZ-eh SHOO-eh (SHTEEF-el) reh-pah-REER-en*

They need new (half) soles and heels.	**Sie brauchen neue (Halb)sohlen und Absätze.** *zee BROWKH-en NOY-eh (hahlp)ZOHL-en unt AHP-zehts-eh*
I can come back in an hour.	**Ich kann in einer Stunde zurückkommen.** *ikh kahn in EYEN-uh SHTUND-eh tsoo-REWK-kom-en*
Please shine them also.	**Bitte putzen Sie sie auch.** *BIT-eh PUTS-en zee zee owkh*
Will they be ready by Friday?	**Sind sie bis Freitag fertig?** *zint zee bis FREYE-taak FEHRT-ikh*

LAUNDRY AND DRY CLEANING

Hotel signs in several languages will often inform you that it's strictly **verboten** to use electric heaters, wash clothes, etc. Yet, many people do wash out small items. Some hotels have laundry and dry-cleaning services, sometimes with multilingual lists. If not, ask:

Is there a laundry (dry cleaner's) nearby?	**Gibt es eine Wäscherei (chemische Reinigung) in der Nähe?** *gipt ehs EYEN-eh vehsh-eh-REYE (KHAY-mi-sheh REYE-ni-gung) in dehr NAY-eh?*
Can these clothes be washed (ironed, cleaned) for me?	**Kann man mir diese Kleider waschen (bügeln, reinigen)?** *kahn mahn meer DEEZ-eh KLEYED-uh VAHSH-en BEWG-eln, REYE-nig-en)*
Could I have it today (tomorrow, the day after tomorrow)?	**Könnte ich's schon heute (morgen, übermorgen) haben?** *KERNT-eh ikhs shon HOYT-eh (MORG-en, EWB-uh-morg-en) HAAB-en*

I absolutely must have it ____.	**Ich muss es unbedingt ____ haben.** *ikh muss ehs UN-beh-dingt ____ HAAB-en*

■ as soon as possible **so bald wie möglich** *zoh bahlt vee MERG-likh*

■ tonight **vor heute Abend** *for HOYT-eh AAB-ehnt*

■ tomorrow **vor morgen** *for MORG-en*

■ next week **vor nächste Woche** *for NAYKHST-eh VOKH-eh*

■ the day after tomorrow **vor übermorgen** *for EWB-uh-morg-en*

When will you bring it (them) back?	**Wann werden Sie es (sie) zurückbringen?** *vahn VEHRD-en zee ehs (zee) tsoo-REWK-bring-en*

When will it be ready?	**Wann wird es fertig sein?** *vahn virt ehs FEHR-tikh zeyen*

Here's the list:	**Hier ist die Liste:** *heer ist dee LIST-eh*

■ three shirts (men's) **drei Oberhemden** *dreye OBH-uh-hehmd-en*

■ twelve handkerchiefs **zwölf Taschentücher** *tsverlf TAHSH-en-tewkh-uh*

■ six pairs of socks **sechs Paar Socken** *zehks paar ZOK-en*

■ one blouse (nylon) **eine Nylonbluse** *EYEN-eh NEW-lon-blooz-eh*

■ four shorts **vier Unterhosen** *feer UNT-uh-hohz-en*

■ two pajamas **zwei Pyjama** *tsveye pid-ZHAAM-ah*

■ two suits **zwei Anzüge** *tsveye AHN-tsewg-eh*

■ three ties **drei Schlipse (Krawatten)** *dreye SHLIPS-eh (krah-VAHT-en)*

- two dresses (cotton) — **zwei Baumwollkleider** *tsveye BOWM-vol-kleyed-uh*
- two skirts — **zwei Röcke** *tsveye RERK-eh*
- one sweater (wool) — **ein Wollpullover** *eyen VOL-pul-oh-vuh*
- one pair of gloves — **ein Paar Handschuhe** *eyen paar HAHNT-shoo-eh*

Some hotels furnish mini sewing packets, no bigger than a match box. If they don't, say:

There's a button missing on this shirt (suit, dress). — **Es fehlt ein Knopf an diesem Hemd (Anzug, Kleid).** *ehs faylt eyen knopf ahn DEEZ-em hehmt (AHN-tsook, kleyet)*

Can you sew it on? — **Können Sie ihn annähen?** *KERN-en zee een AHN-nay-en*

Can you patch (mend) this hole? — **Können Sie dieses Loch flicken (aushessern)?** *KERN-en zee DEEZ-es lokh FLIK-en (OWSS-bess-ern)*

Here's a nasty spot, too. — **Hier ist auch ein verflixter Fleck.** *heer ist owkh eyen fehr-FLIKST-uh flek*

Can you remove it? — **Können Sie ihn entfernen?** *KERN-en zee een ehnt-FAYR-nen*

When will you bring it back? — **Wann können Sie es zurückbringen?** *vahn KERN-en zee ehs tsoo-REWK-bring-en*

When will it be ready? — **Wann wird es fertig sein?** *vahn virt ehs FEHR-tikh zeyen*

This isn't my laundry. — **Dies ist nicht meine Wäsche.** *dees ist nikht MEYEN-eh VEHSH-eh*

Proverb:

Er ist mit allen Wassern gewaschen. *ayr ist mit AHL-en VAASS-ehrn geh-VAHSH-en*

He's a sly one. (He's been washed with all waters.)

WATCH REPAIRS

I need ____.	**Ich brauche ____.** *ikh BROWKH-eh*
▓ a glass	**ein Glas** *eyen glaass*
▓ a stem	**ein Rad** *eyen raat*
▓ a battery	**eine Batterie** *EYEN-eh bah-teh-REE*
Please give me a receipt.	**Bitte geben Sie mir eine Quittung.** *BIT-eh GAYB-en zee meer EYEN-eh KVIT-ung*
Is it worth getting this watch fixed?	**Lohnt es sich diese Uhr reparieren zu lassen?** *lohnt ehs zikh DEEZ-eh oor reh-pah-REER-en tsoo LASS-en*
I dropped it.	**Ich habe sie fallen lassen.** *ikh HAAB-eh zee FAHL-en LASS-en*
It often stops.	**Sie bleibt oft stehen.** *zee bleyept oft SHTAY-en*
It's often fast (slow).	**Sie geht oft vor (nach).** *zee gayt oft fohr (nahkh)*
Maybe I'd do better to buy a new one.	**Vielleicht käufte ich lieber eine neue.** *fee-LEYEKHT KOYFT-eh ikh LEEB-uh EYEN-eh NOY-eh*
Then repair and clean the watch (clock).	**Dann reparieren und reinigen Sie die Uhr.** *dahn reh-pah-REER-en unt REYEN-ig-en zee dee oor*

How long do you need for that?	**Wie lange brauchen Sie dafür?** *vee LAHNG-eh BROWKH-en zee dah-FEWR*

CAMERA REPAIRS

Can you fix this (movie) camera?	**Können Sie diese (Film) Kamera reparieren?** *KERN-en zee DEEZ-eh (film) KAH-meh-raa reh-pah-REER-en*
How much would it cost to have this camera repaired?	**Wieviel würde es kosten, diese Kamera reparieren zu lassen?** *VEE-feel VEWRD-eh ehs KOST-en DEEZ-eh KAH-meh-raa reh-pah-REER-en tsoo LASS-en*
Would it take long?	**Würde es lange dauern?** *VEWRD-eh ehs LAHNG-eh DOW-ehrn*
The film doesn't advance.	**Der Film dreht sich nicht weiter.** *dayr film drayt zikh nikht VEYET-uh*
I think I need new batteries.	**Ich denke, ich brauche neue Batterien.** *ikh DEHNK-eh ikh BROWKH-eh NOY-eh bah-teh-REE-en*
May I have an estimate?	**Können Sie mir einen Kostenanschlag geben?** *KERN-en zee meer EYEN-en KOST-en-ahn-shlaak GAYB-en*
May I have a receipt?	**Darf ich eine Quittung haben?** *dahrf ikh EYEN-eh KVIT-ung HAAB-en*
When can I come and get it?	**Wann kann ich sie wieder abholen?** *vahn kahn ikh zee VEED-uh AHP-hohl-en*

I need it as soon as possible.	**Ich brauche sie sobald wie möglich.** *ikh BROWKH-eh zee zoh-BAHLT vee MERG-likh*

Travel Tips Hotels often levy a service charge for calls made from a guest room. To avoid paying too much, make all calls from a telephone booth and use a telephone company calling card for long distance.

MEDICAL CARE

AT THE PHARMACY

For prescription drugs, you need an **Apotheke** (pharmacy). For toilet articles, film, household articles, and patent medicines, go to a **Drogerie** (see pages 202–203). Many pharmacies also carry patent (nonprescription) medicines as well as herbal teas.

Where can I find the nearest (all-night) pharmacy?	**Wo finde ich die nächste Apotheke (mit Nachtdienst)?** *voh FIND-eh ikh dee NAYKST-eh ah-poh-TAYK-eh (mit NAHKHT-deenst)*
At what time does it open (close)?	**Um wieviel Uhr wird geöffnet (geschlossen)?** *um VEE-feel oor veert geh-ERF-net (geh-SHLOSS-en)*
I'm looking for something for ____.	**Ich suche etwas gegen ____.** *ikh ZOOKH-eh EHT-vahs GAYG-en*
▓ a cold	**eine Erkältung** *EYEN-eh ehr-KEHLT-ung*
▓ lack of appetite	**Appetitslosigkeit** *ah-peh-TEETS-loh-zikh-keyet*
▓ constipation	**Verstopfung** *fehr-SHTOPF-ung*
▓ a cough	**Husten** *HOOST-en*
▓ a fever	**Fieber** *FEEB-uh*
▓ diarrhea	**Durchfall** *DOORKH-fahl*
▓ a hangover	**Kater** *KAAT-uh*
▓ indigestion	**Magenverstimmung** *MAAG-en-fehr-shtim-ung*
▓ hay fever	**Heuschnupfen** *HOY-shnupf-en*
▓ headache	**Kopfschmerzen** *KOPF-shmehrts-en*

■ insomnia	**Schlaflosigkeit**	*SHLAAF-loh-zikh-keyet*
■ motion sickness	**Reisekrankheit**	*REYEZ-eh-krahnk-heyet*
■ insect bites	**Insektenstiche**	*in-ZEHKT-en-shtikh-eh*
■ prickly heat	**Hitzblattern**	*HITS-blaht-ehrn*
■ a blister	**eine Blase**	*EYEN-eh BLAAZ-eh*
■ a burn	**eine Brandwunde**	*EYEN-eh BRAHNT-vund-eh*
■ sunburn	**Sonnenbrand**	*ZON-en-brahnt*
■ a toothache	**Zahnschmerzen**	*TSAAN-shmehrts-en*

Must I have a prescription for the medicine? **Muss ich ein Rezept für das Medikament haben?** *muss ikh eyen reh-TSEPT fewr dahs may-di-kaa-MENT HAAB-en*

Is there a German equivalent for this medicine? **Gibt es ein deutsches Äquivalent für dieses Medikament?** *gipt ehs eyer DOYTSH-es ay-kvi-vah-LENT fewr DEEZ-es may-di-kaa-MENT*

Is there something similar? **Gibt es etwas Ähnliches?** *gipt ehs EHT-vahs AYN-likh-es*

Please look it up for me. **Bitte schlagen Sie es nach.** *BIT-eh SHLAAG-en zee ehs nahkh*

Can you fill this prescription for me now? **Können Sie mir dieses Rezept jetzt machen?** *KERN-en zee meer DEEZ-es reh-TSEPT yetst MAAKH-en*

It's urgent. **Es ist dringend.** *ehs ist DRING-ent*

How long will it take? **Wie lange wird's dauern?** *vee LAHNG-eh veerts DOW-ehrn*

I'll wait.	**Ich warte darauf.** *ikh VAART-eh dah-ROWF*
When can I pick it up?	**Wann kann ich's abholen?** *vahn kahn ikhs AHP-hohl-en*
I need ____.	**Ich brauche ____.** *ikh BROWKH-eh*
■ an antacid	**Magentabletten** *MAAG-en-tahb-leht-en*
■ an antiseptic	**ein Antiseptikum** *even ahn-tee-ZEP-ti-kum*
■ aspirin	**Aspirin** *ah-spee-REEN*
■ bandages	**Verbandzeug** *fehr-BAHNT-tsoyk*
■ Band Aids	**Heftpflaster** *HEHFT-pflahst-uh*
■ a contraceptive	**ein Verhütungsmittel** *eyen fehr-HEWT-ungs-mit-el*
■ corn plasters	**Hühneraugenpflaster** *HEWN-ehr-owg-en-pflahst-uh*
■ cotton balls	**Wattebäusche** *VAHT-eh-boysh-eh*
■ cough drops	**Hustenbonbons** *HOOST-en-bohn-BOHNS*
■ eardrops	**Ohrentropfen** *OHR-en-tropf-en*
■ eyedrops	**Augentropfen** *OWG-en-tropf-en*
■ herbal teas	**Kräutertees** *KROY-tehr-tayss*
■ first-aid kit	**einen Verbandkasten** *EYEN-en fehr BAHNT-kahst-en*
■ iodine	**Jod** *yoht*
■ an (herbal) laxative	**ein (Kräuter) Abführmittel** *eyen (KROYT-ehr) AHP-fewr-mit-el*
■ talcum powder	**Talkumpuder** *TAHLK-um-pood-uh*
■ a thermometer	**ein Thermometer** *eyen tehr-mo-MAYT-uh*
■ throat lozenges	**Halspastillen** *HAHLS-pahs-til-en*

- tranquilizers · **ein Beruhigungsmittel** *eyen beh-ROO-i-gungs-mit-el*
- vitamins · **Vitamine** *vee-taa-MEEN-eh*
- something for menstrual cramps · **etwas für Menstruationsbe-schwerden** *EHT-vahs fewr mehn-stroo-ah-TSYOHNS-beh-shvayrd-en*
- adhesive tape · **ein Leukoplast** *eyen LOY-ko-plahst*
- deodorant · **Desodorans** *dehs-oh-doh-RAHNS*

Modern homeopathy began in Germany with Hahnemann. You will see many homeopathic pharmacies.

Is there a homeopathic pharmacy here?	**Gibt's hier eine homöopathische Apotheke?** *gipts heer EYEN-eh homer-o-PAA-ti-sheh ah-po-TAYK-eh*
Do you have a book on medicinal herbs?	**Haben Sie ein Kräuterbuch?** *HAAB-en zee eyen KROYT-ehr-hookh*
Something about plant therapy (phytotherapy)?	**Etwas über die Pflanzenheilkunde (Phytotherapie)?** *EHT-vahs EWB-uh dee PFLAHNTS-en-heyel-kund-eh (PHEWT-oh-tay-rah-pee)*

WITH THE DOCTOR

We hope that you will not become ill. But if you do, we wish you **Gute Besserung** *(GOOT-eh BESS-eh-rung)*, a speedy recovery. Doctors' office hours in Germany are usually from 10 A.M. to 12 noon and from 4 to 6 P.M., except Wednesday, Saturday, and Sunday. For emergencies an **ärztlicher Notdienst** (medical emergency service) is listed in every telephone directory.

I don't feel well.	**Ich fühle mich nicht wohl.** *ikh FEWL-eh mikh nikht vohl*

I think I'm sick.	**Ich glaube, ich bin krank.** *ikh GLOWB-eh ikh bin krahnk*
I need a doctor.	**Ich brauche einen Arzt.** *ikh BROWKH-eh EYEN-en ahrtst*
Is there a doctor here who speaks English?	**Gibt's hier einen Arzt, der Englisch spricht?** *gipts heer EYEN-en ahrtst dehr EHNG-lish shprikht*
Where is his office?	**Wo ist seine Praxis?** *voh ist SEYEN-eh PRAHK-siss*
What are his office hours?	**Was sind seine Sprechstunden?** *vahs zint ZEYEN-eh SHPREKH-shtund-en*
Could the doctor come to me in my hotel?	**Könnte der Arzt zu mir ins Hotel kommen?** *KERNT-eh dehr ahrtst tsoo meer ins ho-TEL KOM-en*
I feel dizzy (nauseated).	**Mir ist schwindlig (übel).** *meer ist SHVIND-likh (EWB-el)*
I feel weak.	**Ich fühle mich schwach.** *ikh FEWL-eh mikh shvahkh*
I must sit (lie) down.	**Ich muss mich hinsetzen (hinlegen).** *ikh muss mikh HIN-zets-en (HIN-layg-en)*
I'm suffocating here.	**Ich ersticke hier.** *ikh ehr-STIK-eh heer*
I need air.	**Ich brauche Luft.** *ikh BROWKH-eh luft*
I think this wound is infected.	**Ich glaube diese Wunde ist infiziert.** *ikh GLOWB-eh DEEZ-eh VUND-eh ist in-fi-TSEERT*

Is there any danger of infection?	**Gibt es eine Ansteckungsgefahr?** *gipt ehs EYEN-eh AHN-steh-kungs-geh-faar*
Do I need an antibiotic?	**Brauche ich ein Antibiotikum?** *BROWKH-eh ikh eyen ahn-tee-bee-OH-tee-kum*
I'm (not) allergic to penicillin.	**Ich bin gegen Penizillin (nicht) allergisch.** *ikh bin GAYG-en peh-ni-tsi-LEEN (nikht) ah-LEHRG-ish*
My temperature is normal, I think.	**Meine Temperatur ist normal, glaube ich.** *MEYEN-eh tem-pay-raa-TOOR ist nor-MAAL GLOWB-eh ikh*

PARTS OF THE BODY

ankle	**der Knöchel** *dehr KNERKH-el*
appendix	**der Blinddarm** *dehr BLINT-dahrm*
arm	**der Arm** *dehr ahrm*
breast	**die Brust** *dee brust*
chest	**der Brustkorb** *dehr BRUST-korp*
ear	**das Ohr** *dahs ohr*
elbow	**der Ellbogen** *dehr EL-boh-gen*
eye	**das Auge** *dahs OWG-eh*
face	**das Gesicht** *dahs geh-ZIKHT*
foot	**der Fuß** *dehr fooss*
hand	**die Hand** *dee hahnt*
head	**der Kopf** *dehr kopf*

heart	**das Herz**	*dahs hehrts*
hip	**die Hüfte**	*dee HEWFT-eh*
knee	**das Knie**	*dahs knee*
leg	**das Bein**	*dahs beyen*
liver	**die Leber**	*dee LAYB-uh*
mouth	**der Mund**	*dehr munt*
neck	**der Nacken**	*dehr NAHK-en*
nose	**die Nase**	*dee NAAZ-eh*
shoulder	**die Schulter**	*dee SHULT-uh*
skin	**die Haut**	*dee howt*
throat	**der Hals**	*dehr hahls*
tooth	**der Zahn**	*dehr tsaan*
wrist	**das Handgelenk**	*dahs HAHNT-geh-lenk*
I have ____.	**Ich habe ____.**	*ikh HAAB-eh*
■ an abscess	**einen Abszess**	*EYEN-en ahps-TSESS*
■ a broken leg	**einen Beinbruch**	*EYEN-en BEYEN-brukh*
■ a bruise	**eine Quetschung**	*EYEN-eh KVETSH-ung*
■ a burn	**eine Brandwunde**	*EYEN-eh BRAHNT-vund-eh*
■ a cold	**eine Erkältung**	*EYEN-eh ehr-KEHLT-ung*
■ constipation	**Verstopfung**	*fehr-SHTOPF-ung*
■ cramps	**Krämpfe**	*KREHMPF-eh*

▓ a cut	**eine Schnittwunde** *EYEN-eh SHNIT-vund-eh*
▓ diarrhea	**Durchfall** *DOORKH-fahl*
▓ dysentery	**Ruhr** *roor*
▓ fever	**Fieber** *FEEB-uh*
▓ a fracture	**einen Bruch** *EYEN-en brookh*
▓ an eye inflammation	**eine Augenentzündung** *EYEN-eh OWG-en-ehnt-tsewnd-ung*
▓ a lump	**eine Beule** *EYEN-eh BOYL-eh*
▓ a sore throat	**Halsschmerzen** *HAHLS-shmehrts-en*
▓ a skin disease	**eine Hautkrankheit** *EYEN-eh HOWT-krahnk-heyet*
▓ a stomach ulcer	**ein Magengeschwür** *eyen MAAG-en-geh-shvewr*
▓ a sty	**einen Augenliderbrand** *EYEN-en OWG-en-leed-ehr-brahnt*
▓ a swelling	**eine Schwellung** *EYEN-eh SHVEL-ung*
▓ a wound	**eine Wunde** *EYEN-eh VUND-eh*
▓ a venereal disease	**eine Geschlechtskrankheit** *EYEN-eh geh-SHLEKHTS-krahnk-heyet*
▓ a head (back) ache	**Kopf (Rücken) schmerzen** *kopf (REWK-en) SHMERTS-en*
I have chills.	**Mich fröstelt.** *mikh FRERST-elt*
It hurts me here.	**Hier tut es weh.** *heer toot ehs vay*
I hurt all over.	**Es tut mir überall weh.** *ehs toot meer EWB-ehr-ahl vay*
My _____ hurts (hurt).	**Mein(e) _____ tut (tun) mir weh.** *meyen(eh) _____ toot (toon) meer vay*
▓ my ankle	**mein Knöchel** *meyen KNERKH-el*

■ my arm   **mein Arm**   *meyen ahrm*

■ my ear   **mein Ohr**   *meyen ohr*

■ my eye   **mein Auge**   *meyen OWG-eh*

■ my face   **mein Gesicht**   *meyen geh-ZIKHT*

■ my finger   **mein Finger**   *meyen FING-uh*

■ my foot   **mein Fuß**   *meyen fooss*

■ my glands   **meine Drüsen**   *MEYEN-eh DREWZ-en*

■ my hand   **meine Hand**   *MEYEN-eh hahnt*

■ my hip joint   **mein Hüftgelenk**   *meyen HEWFT-geh-lehnk*

■ my heel   **meine Ferse**   *MEYEN-eh FEHRZ-eh*

■ my leg   **mein Bein**   *meyen beyen*

■ my nose   **meine Nase**   *MEYEN-eh NAAZ-eh*

■ my ribs   **meine Rippen**   *MEYEN-eh RIP-en*

■ my shoulder   **meine Schulter**   *MEYEN-eh SHULT-uh*

■ my stomach   **mein Magen**   *meyen MAAG-en*

■ my toe   **meine Zehe**   *MEYEN-eh TSAY-eh*

■ my wrist   **mein Handgelenk**   *meyen HAHNT-geh-lenk*

I've had this pain since yesterday.	**Seit gestern habe ich diese Schmerzen.** *zeyet GEHST-ehrn HAAB-eh ikh DEEZ-eh SHMEHRTS-en*
I've been suffering from this disease for some time.	**Seit einiger Zeit leide ich an dieser Krankheit.** *zeyet EYE-ni-guh tseyet LEYED-eh ikh ahn DEEZ-uh KRAHNK-heyet*
I'm close to a nervous breakdown.	**Ich bin einem Nervenzusammen-bruch nahe.** *ikh bin EYEN-em NERV-en-tsoo-ZAHM-en-brukh NAA-eh*

| Can you prescribe sleeping pills for me? | **Können Sie mir Schlaftabletten verschreiben?** *KERN-en zee meer SHLAAF-tah-blet-en fehr-SHREYEB-en* |
| Can you recommend ____? | **Können Sie ____ empfehlen?** *KERN-en zee ____ ehm-PFAYL-en* |

- a specialist   **einen Facharzt** *EYEN-en FAHKH-ahrtst*

- an ophthalmologist   **einen Augenarzt** *EYEN-en OWG-en-ahrtst*

- a gynecologist   **einen Frauenarzt** *EYEN-en FROW-en-ahrtst*

I have heart trouble.	**Ich bin herzkrank.** *ikh bin HEHRTS-krahnk*
Two years ago I had a heart attack.	**Vor zwei Jahren erlitt ich einen Herzanfall.** *for tsveye YAAR-en ehr-LIT ikh EYEN-en HEHRTS-ahn-fahl*
I often have palpitations.	**Ich habe oft Herzklopfen.** *ikh HAAB-eh oft HEHRTS-klopf-en*

I also suffer from circulatory problems.	**Ich leide auch an Kreislaufstörung-en.** *ikh LEYED-eh owk ahn KREYES-lowf-shter-rung-en*
I am a diabetic and take insulin.	**Ich bin Diabetiker und nehme Insulin.** *ikh bin dee-ah-BEH-tik-uh unt NAYM-eh in-zoo-LEEN*
The dosage must be checked.	**Die Dosis muss kontrolliert werden.** *dee DOH-ziss muss kon-tro-LEERT VAYRD-en*
I often have to throw up in the morning.	**Morgens muss ich oft brechen.** *MORG-ens muss ikh oft BREKH-en*
Perhaps I'm pregnant.	**Vielleicht bin ich schwanger.** *fee-LEYEKHT bin ikh SHVAHNG-uh*
I feel better (worse) now.	**Es geht mir jetzt besser (schlecht-er).** *ehs gayt meer yehtst BESS-uh (SHLEHKHT-uh)*
I hope it's nothing serious.	**Hoffentlich ist es nichts Ernstes.** *HOF-ehnt-likh ist ehs nikhts EHRNST-es*
Could it be ____?	**Ist es vielleicht ____?** *ist ehs fee-LEYEKHT*
■ appendicitis	**eine Blinddarmentzündung** *EYEN-eh BLINT-dahrm-ehn-tsewnd-ung*
■ the flu	**die Grippe** *dee GRIP-eh*
■ pneumonia	**eine Lungenentzündung** *EYEN-eh LUNG-en-ehn-tswend-ung*
■ tonsillitis	**eine Mandelentzündung** *EYEN-eh MAHND-el-ehn-tsewnd-ung*
Do I have to go to the hospital?	**Muss ich ins Krankenhaus?** *muss ikh ins KRAHNK-en-howss*

When can I continue my trip?	**Wann kann ich meine Reise fort-setzen?** *vahn kahn ikh MEYEN-eh REYEZ-eh FORT-zets-en*
Are you going to give me a prescription for it?	**Verschreiben Sie mir etwas dafür?** *fehr-SHREYEB-en zee meer EHT-vahs dah-FEWR*
How often must I take this medicine (these pills)?	**Wie oft muss ich dieses Medikament (diese Pillen) nehmen?** *vee oft muss ikh DEEZ-es may-di-kah-MENT (DEEZ-eh PIL-en) NAYM-en*
Must I stay in bed? How long?	**Muss ich im Bett bleiben? Wie lange?** *muss ikh im bet BLEYEB-en vee LAHNG-eh*
Thank you for everything, doctor.	**Ich danke Ihnen vielmals, Herr (Frau) Doktor.** *ikh DAHNK-eh EEN-en FEEL-maals hehr (frow) DOK-tor*
How much do I owe you for your services?	**Wieviel bin ich Ihnen schuldig?** *vee-FEEL bin ikh EEN-en SHULD-ikh*

NOTE: Often both a Germanic and a Latin or Greek derivative exist for the same thing. Pneumonia, for example, is both **Lungenentzündung** and **Pneumonie.** Use the medical term you know, and chances are the doctor will recognize it.

IN THE HOSPITAL

Help me, quick!	**Helfen Sie mir, schnell!** *HELF-en zee meer shnel*
It's urgent.	**Es ist dringend.** *ehs ist DRING-ehnt*
Call a doctor immediately.	**Rufen Sie sofort einen Arzt.** *ROOF-en zee zoh-FORT EYEN-en ahrtst*

Get an ambulance.	**Holen Sie einen Krankenwagen.** *HOHL-en zee EYEN-en KRAHNK-en-vaag-en*
Take me (him) to the hospital.	**Bringen Sie mich (ihn) ins Krankenhaus.** *BRING-en zee mikh (een) ins KRAHNK-en-howss*
I need first aid.	**Ich brauche erste Hilfe.** *ikh BROWKH-eh EHRST-eh HILF-eh*
I'm bleeding.	**Ich blute.** *ikh BLOOT-eh*
I've (he's) lost a lot of blood.	**Ich habe (er hat) viel Blut verloren.** *ikh HAAB-eh (ehr haht) feel bloot fehr-LOHR-en*
I think something is broken (dislocated).	**Ich glaube, es ist etwas gebrochen (verrenkt).** *ikh GLOWB-eh ehs ist EHT-vahs geh-BROKH-en (fehr-REHNKT)*
I can't move the elbow (arm, knee, leg).	**Ich kann den Ellbogen (Arm, Knie, Bein) nicht bewegen.** *ikh kahn dayn EHL-bohg-en (ahrm, knee, beyen) nikht beh-VAYG-en*
How long will I have to stay in the hospital?	**Wie lange werde ich im Krankenhaus bleiben müssen?** *vee LAHNG-eh vayrd ikh im KRAHNK-en-howss BLEYEB-en MEWSS-en*

SPECIAL NEEDS

Where can I get ____?	**Wo bekomme ich ____?** *voh beh-KOM-eh ikh*
■ a cane	**einen Stock** *EYEN-en shtok*
■ crutches	**Krücken** *KREWK-en*

■ a hearing aid   **ein Hörgerät** *eyen HEWR-geh-RAYT*

■ a walker   **einen Laufstuhl** *EYEN-en LOWF-shtool*

■ a wheelchair   **einen Rollstuhl** *EYEN-en ROL-shtool*

What services are available for the handicapped?	**Welche Dienstleistungen gibt es für Behinderte?** *VELKH-eh DEENST-leyest-ung-en gipt ehs fewr beh-HIND-ehr-teh*
I need a wheelchair for me/my mother/my father.	**Ich brauche einen Rollstuhl für mich/meine Mutter/meinen Vater.** *ikh BROWKH-eh EYEN-en ROL-shtool fewr mikh/MEYEN-eh MUT-uh/ MEYEN-en FAAT-uh*
Does the hotel/the room/the restaurant have facilities for the handicapped?	**Ist das Hotel/das Zimmer/das Restaurant behindertengerecht?** *ist dahs hoh-TEL/dahs TSIM-uh/dahs res-tow-RAHNG beh-HIN-dehr-ten-geh-REKHT*
Is there a toilet for disabled persons?	**Gibt es ein WC für Behinderte?** *gipt ehs eyen vay-tsay fewr beh-HIN-dehrt-eh*
Is the building/the theater/the place/ the bus/the train also easily accessible to the handicapped?	**Ist das Gebäude/das Theater/ das Lokal/der Bus/der Zug auch für Behinderte leicht zugänglich?** *ist dahs geh-BOY-duh/dahs tay-AAT-uh/dahs loh-KAAL/dehr bus/dehr tsook owkh fewr beh-HIN-dehrt-eh leyekht TSOO-geng-likh*
Is there a ramp/an elevator for people in wheelchairs?	**Gibt es eine Rampe/einen Aufzug für Rollstuhlfahrer?** *gipt ehs EYEN-eh RAHM-peh/EYEN-eh OWF-tsook fewr ROL-shtool-FAAR-uh*

Where can I buy a cane/orthopedic shoes here?	**Wo kann ich hier einen Stock/ orthopädische Schuhe kaufen?** *voh kahn ikh heer EYEN-en shtok/or- toh-PAY-dish-eh SHOO-eh KOWF-en*

AT THE DENTIST

Unfortunately, I must go to the dentist.	**Leider muss ich zum Zahnarzt.** *LEYED-uh muss ikh tsoom TSAAN- ahrtst*
Do you know a good one?	**Kennen Sie einen guten?** *KEN-en zee EYEN-en GOOT-en*
I have a toothache that's driving me crazy.	**Ich habe wahnsinnige Zahnschmerzen.** *ikh hahp VAAN-zi- nig-eh TSAAN-shmehrts-en*
I've lost a filling (crown).	**Ich habe eine Plombe (Krone) verloren.** *ikh hahp EYEN-eh PLOMB- eh (KROHN-eh) fehr-LOHR-en*
I broke a tooth on hard nuts.	**Ich habe mir an harten Nüssen ein- en Zahn ausgebissen.** *ikh hahp meer ahn HAHRT-en NEWSS-en EYEN-en tsaan OWSS-geh-biss-en*
I can't chew.	**Ich kann nicht kauen.** *ikh kahn nikht KOW-en*
My gums are bleeding.	**Das Zahnfleisch blutet.** *dahs TSAAN-fleyesh BLOOT-et*
Do I have an abscess?	**Habe ich einen Abszess?** *hahb ikh EYEN-en ahps-TSESS*
Can the tooth be saved?	**Ist der Zahn noch zu retten?** *ist dehr tsaan nokh tsoo RET-en*

I won't have it pulled.	**Ich will ihn nicht ziehen lassen.** *ikh vil een nikht TSEE-en LAHSS-en*
I will wait and ask my dentist at home.	**Ich warte, und frage meinen Zahnarzt zu Hause.** *ikh VAART-eh unt FRAAG-eh MEYEN-en TSAAN-ahrtst tsoo HOWZ-eh*
I just want a temporary filling (treatment).	**Ich möchte nur eine provisorische Füllung (Behandlung).** *ikh MERKHT-eh noor EYEN-eh pro-vee-ZOR-ish-eh FEWL-ung (beh-HANT-lung)*
Not in gold. Something less expensive.	**Nicht in Gold. Etwas, was weniger kostet.** *nikht in golt EHT-vahs vahs VAYN-ig-uh KOST-et*
Can you fix ____?	**Können Sie ____ reparieren?** *KERN-en zee ____ reh-pah-REER-en*
■ this denture	**dieses Gebiss** *DEEZ-es geh-BISS*
■ these false teeth	**diesen Zahnersatz** *DEEZ-en TSAAN-ehr-zahts*
Can you recommend a toothbrush (toothpaste)?	**Können Sie mir eine Zahnbürste (Zahnpasta) empfehlen?** *KERN-en zee meer EYEN-eh TSAAN-bewrst-eh (TSAAN-pahs-tah) ehmp-FAYL-en*
How much do I owe you for your services?	**Wieviel bin ich Ihnen schuldig?** *VEE-feel bin ikh EEN-en SHULD-ikh*

WITH THE OPTICIAN

I'd like to get these glasses repaired.	**Diese Brille möchte ich reparieren lassen.** *DEEZ-eh BRIL-eh MERKHT-eh ikh reh-pah-REER-en LAHSS-en*

Can you put in a new lens for the broken one?	**Können Sie das gebrochene Glas auswechseln?** *KERN-en zee dahs geh-BROKH-en-eh glaas OWSS-vehks-eln*
The screw must be replaced.	**Die Schraube muss ersetzt werden.** *dee SHROWB-eh muss ehr-ZETST VAYRD-en*
It fell out.	**Sie ist herausgefallen.** *zee ist hehr-OWSS-geh-fahl-en*
Could you repair them right away?	**Können Sie sie gleich jetzt reparieren?** *KERN-en zee zee gleyekh yetst reh-pah-REER-en*
I can wait.	**Ich kann warten.** *ikh kahn VAART-en*
I need them.	**Ich brauche sie.** *ikh BROWKH-eh zee*
I have no others.	**Ich habe keine andere.** *ikh hahp KEYEN-eh AHN-deh-reh*
I may try contact lenses.	**Ich werde vielleicht Kontaktlinsen (Haftschalen) versuchen.** *ikh VAYRD-eh fee-LEYEKHT kon-TAHKT-linz-en (HAHFT-shaal-en) fehr-ZOOKH-en*
These sunglasses are prescription glasses.	**Diese Sonnenbrille ist eine optische Brille.** *DEEZ-eh ZON-en-bril-eh ist EYEN-eh OP-tish-eh BRIL-eh*
What kind of sun-glasses do you have?	**Was für Sonnenbrillen haben Sie?** *vahs fewr ZON-en-brill-en HAAB-en zee*
How much do these cost?	**Was kostet diese?** *vahs KOST-et DEEZ-eh*

Travel Tips   There was a time when buying an airline ticket was simple. Since the airline industry was deregulated, however, travelers must shop and compare prices, buy charter or discount tickets far in advance and join frequent flier clubs to become eligible for free tickets. Read the fine print in ads and ask questions when making reservations. Often, discount fare tickets cannot be exchanged for cash or another ticket if travel plans must be changed. If you must change plans en route, talk to an airline ticket agent. Sometimes they have soft hearts!

COMMUNICATIONS

POST OFFICE

In Germany post office hours are usually 8 A.M. to 6 P.M., Monday through Friday, and 8 A.M. to 12 noon on Saturday. In some towns the post offices will close between the hours of 12 noon and 2 P.M. Post offices in railway terminals in large cities stay open till late in the evening on weekdays. Mailboxes in German-speaking countries are usually painted yellow (sometimes blue in Austria). In order to pick up your mail at the general delivery window, you will need your passport or identity card.

I must mail some letters.	**Ich muss einige Briefe auf die Post tragen.** *ikh muss EYE-ni-geh BREEF-eh owf dee post TRAAG-en*
I want to send (mail) these postcards home.	**Ich will diese Postkarten mit der Post nach Hause schicken.** *ikh vil DEEZ-eh POST-kart-en mit dehr post nahkh HOWZ-eh SHIK-en*
I want to mail these packages home.	**Ich möchte diese Pakete mit der Post nach Hause schicken.** *ikh MERKHT-eh DEEZ-eh pah-KAYT-eh mit dehr post nahkh HOWZ-eh SHIK-en*
Where is the post office?	**Wo ist das Postamt?** *voh ist dahs POST-ahmt*
Where can I find a mailbox?	**Wo finde ich einen Briefkasten?** *voh FIND-eh ikh EYEN-en BREEF-kahst-en*
What is the postage on ____ to the U.S. (England, Canada, Australia)?	**Was kostet ____ nach USA (England, Kanada, Australien)?** *vahs KOST-et ____ nahkh oo-ess-aa (EHNG-lahnt, KAA-naa-dah, owss-TRAAL-yen)*

■ a letter	**ein Brief** *eyen breef*
■ an airmail letter	**ein Luftpostbrief** *eyen LUFT-post-breef*
■ a registered letter	**ein Einschreibebrief** *eyen EYEN-shreyeb-eh-breef*
■ a special delivery letter	**ein Eilbrief** *eyen EYEL-breef*
■ a postcard	**eine Postkarte** *EYEN-eh POST-kaart-eh*
■ this package	**dieses Paket** *DEEZ-es pah-KAYT*
Can I have this letter (this package) insured?	**Kann ich diesen Brief (dieses Paket) versichern lassen?** *kahn ikh DEEZ-en breef (DEEZ-es pah-KAYT) fehr-ZIKH-ehrn LAHSS-en*
When will it arrive?	**Wann wird's ankommen?** *vahn veerts AHN-kom-en*
Where is the ____ window?	**Wo ist der Schalter für ____?** *voh ist dehr SHAHLT-uh fewr*
■ general delivery	**postlagernde Sendungen** *POST-laa-gehrnd-eh ZEHND-ung-en*
■ money orders	**Postanweisungen** *POST-ahn-veyez-ung-en*
■ philately	**Briefmarkensammler** *BREEF-mahrk-en-zahm-luh*
■ stamps	**Briefmarken** *BREEF-mahrk-en*
Are there any stamp dealers in this town?	**Gibt es Briefmarkenhändler in dieser Stadt?** *gipt ehs BREEF-mahrk-en-hehnt-luh in DEEZ-uh shtaht*
Please let me have ____.	**Geben Sie mir bitte ____.** *GAYB-en zee meer BIT-eh*
■ eight envelopes	**acht Umschläge** *ahkht UM-shlayg-eh*

■ twelve postcards   **zwölf Postkarten**   *tsverlf POST-kaart-en*

■ twenty (air mail) stamps   **zwanzig (Luftpost) Briefmarken** *TSVAHN-tsikh (LUFT-post) BREEF-mahrk-en*

At what window can I mail this package?   **An welchem Schalter kann ich dieses Paket aufgeben?** *ahn VELKH-em SHAHLT-uh kahn ikh DEEZ-es pah-KAYT OWF-gayb-en*

Are there any letters for me?   **Ist Post für mich da?** *ist post fewr mikh daa*

My name is ____.   **Ich heiße ____.** *ikh HEYESS-eh*

FAX

Do you have a fax machine?   **Haben Sie ein Faxgerät?** *HAAB-en zee eyen FAHKS-geh-RAYT*

What is your fax number?   **Wie ist Ihre Faxnummer?** *vee ist EER-eh FAHKS-noom-uh*

I want to send a fax.   **Ich will ein Fax senden.** *ikh vil eyen fahks SEHND-en*

May I fax this, please?   **Darf ich dies bitte faxen?** *dahrf ikh dees BIT-eh FAHKS-en*

May I fax this letter (document) to you?   **Darf ich Ihnen diesen Brief (dieses Dokument) faxen?** *dahrf ikh EEN-en DEEZ-en breef (DEEZ-ehs dok-oo-MENT) FAHKS-en*

Fax it to me.   **Faxen Sie es mir.** *FAHKS-en zee ehs meer*

I didn't get your fax.   **Ihr Fax hab ich nicht bekommen.** *eer fahks haab ikh nikht beh-KOM-en*

Did you receive my fax?	**Haben Sie mein Fax bekommen?** *HAAB-en zee meyen fahks beh-KOM-en*
Your fax is illegible.	**Ihr Fax ist unleserlich.** *eer fahks ist un-LAYZ-uh-likh*
Please send it again.	**Bitte senden Sie es wieder.** *BIT-eh ZEND-en zee ehs VEED-uh*

COMPUTERS

To get information on the internet:

1. Go to the location box in your net browser
2. Type *http://www.altavista.digital.com* or *www.hotbot.com*
3. Click *Enter*
4. You will see a search screen. Click on *Any Language*
5. Select *German*
6. You can search for any subject.

Do you have ____?	**Haben Sie ____?** *Haab-en zee*
■ a Macintosh computer	**einen Macintosh Computer** *EYEN-en MEHK-in-tosh com-PYOOT-uh*
■ a PC	**einen PC** *EYEN-en pay-tsay*
What operating system are you using?	**Welches Betriebssystem benutzen Sie?** *VELKH-es beh-TREEPS-sewss-TAYM beh-nutz-en zee*
What word processing program are you using?	**Welches Textverarbeitungs-programm benutzen Sie?** *VELKH-es text-fehr-AHR-beyet-ungs-proh-grahm beh-NUTZ-en zee*
What spreadsheet program are you using?	**Welches Tabellenkalkulationspro-gramm benutzen Sie?** *VELKH-es tah-BEL-en-kahl-koo-lahts-yohns-proh-grahm beh-NUTZ-en zee*

What peripherals do you have?	**Welche Peripheriegeräte haben Sie?** *VELKH-eh peh-rif-eh-REE-geh-RAYT-eh HAAB-en zee*
Are our systems compatible?	**Sind unser Systeme kompatibel?** *zint UNZ-ehr-eh sewss-TAYM-eh kom-pah-TEE-bel*
What is your e-mail address?	**Wie ist Ihre E-Mail Adresse?** *vee ist EER-eh ee-mayl ah-DREHSS-eh*
My laptop is broken/ having problems.	**Mein Laptop ist kaputt/gestört.** *meyen laptop ist kap-PUT/geh-SHTEWRT*
Where can I have it repaired?	**Wo kann ich ihn reparieren lassen?** *voh kahn ikh een reh-pah-REER-en LAHSS-en*

COMPUTER MINI-DICTIONARY

access	**der Zugriff** *dehr TSOO-grif*
backup disk	**die Sicherungsplatte** *die ZIKH-her-ungs-plaht-eh*
byte	**das Byte** *dahs BEWT-eh*
cable	**das Kabel** *dahs KAAB-el*
CD-ROM disk	**die CD-ROM-Platte** *dee tsay-day rom PLAHT-eh*
chip	**das Chip** *dahs chip*
(to) click	**clicken** *KLIK-en*
clipboard	**das Klemmbrett** *dahs KLEM-bret*
CPU	**die Zentraleinheit** *dee tsen-TRAAL-eyen-heyet*

computer programmer	**der (die) Programmierer(in)** *dehr (dee) proh-grahm-EER-ehr(in)*
computer science	**die Informatik** *dee in-fohr-MAH-teek*
computer scientist	**der (die) Informatiker(in)** *dehr (dee) in-fohr-MAH-teek-ehr(in)*
(to) copy	**kopieren** *ko-PEER-en*
cursor	**der Cursor** *dehr KERS-uh*
(to) cut	**schneiden** *SHENEYED-en*
database	**die Databank** *dee DAA-tah-bahnk*
disk	**die Diskette** *dee dis-KEHT-eh*
disk drive	**das Diskettenlaufwerk** *dahs dis-KEHT-en-LOWF-vehrk*
diskette	**die Diskette** *dee dis-KEHT-eh*
document	**das Dokument** *dahs dok-oo-MENT*
DOS	**das DOS** *dahs doss*
(to) download	**runterladen** *ROONT-ehr-LAAD-en*
e-mail	**die E-Mail** *dee EE-mayl*
file	**die Datei** *dee daa-TEYE*
floppy disk	**die Floppydisk** *dee FLOP-ee-disk*
font	**die Schrift** *dee shrift*
graphics	**die Grafik** *die GRAAF-ik*
hardware	**die Hardware** *dee hahrd-wayr*

icon	**das Ikon** *dahs ee-KOHN*
inkjet printer	**der Tintenstrahldrucker** *dehr TINT-en-shtrahl-druk-uh*
the internet	**das Internet** *dahs in-tehr-net*
joystick	**der Joystick** *dehr JOY-stik*
key	**die Taste** *dee TAHST-eh*
keyboard	**die Tastatur** *dee tahst-ah-TOOR*
(to) keyboard	**eingeben** *EYEN-gayb-en*
laptop	**der Laptop** *dehr laptop*
laser printer	**der Laserdrucker** *dehr LAYZ-ehr-druk-uh*
memory	**der Speicher** *dehr SHPEYEKH-uh*
modem	**der Modem** *dehr MOHD-em*
monitor	**der Monitor** *dehr MOHN-ee-tohr*
motherboard	**die Hauptplatine** *dee HOWPT-plaa-teen-eh*
mouse	**die Maus** *dee mowss*
network	**das Netzwrk** *dahs NETS-vehrk*
on-line service	**der Onlinedienst** *dehr ahn-leyen-DEENST*
(to) paste	**einfügen** *EYEN-fewg-en*
program	**das Programm** *dahs proh-GRAHM*
(to) save	**sichern** *ZIKH-ehrn*

scanner	**der Scanner** *dehr scanner*
screen	**der Bildschirm** *dehr BILT-sheerm*
search engine	**der Suchlaufmotor** *dehr ZOOKH-lowf-moh-tohr*
site	**die Site** *dee seyet*
software	**die Software** *dee software*
speed	**die Schnelligkeit** *dee SHNEL-ikh-keyet*
spell checker	**die Rechtschreibprüfung** *dee REKHT-schreib-prewf-ung*
symbol	**das Symbol** *das zewm-BOHL*
thesaurus	**der Thesaurus** *der teh-ZOW-rus*
website	**die Website** *dee website*
zip disk	**die Zipdiskette** *dee ZIP-disk-eht-eh*
zip drive	**das Ziplaufwerk** *dahs ZIP-lowf-vehrk*

TELEPHONES

You may also go to the post office for telephone calls abroad, since it is considerably cheaper than from hotels. **Fernsprecher** *(FEHRN-shprehkh-uh)*, the Germanic word for "telephone," is often used, but less frequently than **Telefon.**

There are public telephone booths, similar in appearance to those in the United States, on the streets in Germany. You must insert a coin into the slot before dialing. There are multilingual instructions on each instrument on how to use the phone. Local calls are 30 **Pfennig.** For long-distance calls, pay phones make change. The newer instruments indicate when you have used up all but 10-Pfennig worth of time. Be sure to check the indicator and insert more change, or you will be cut off. Large bars and restaurants will have coin-operated phones, but in the smaller ones you may have to ask the proprietor if you may use the phone.

I'm looking for ____. **Ich suche ____.** *ikh ZOOKH-eh*

■ a telephone booth **eine Telefonzelle** *EYEN-eh tay-leh-FOHN-tsel-eh*

■ a telephone directory **ein Telefonbuch** *eyen tay-leh-FOHN-bookh*

May I use your phone? **Darf ich Ihr Telefon benutzen?** *dahrf ikh eer tay-leh-FOHN beh-NUTS-en*

Here is the number. **Hier ist die Nummer.** *heer ist dee NUM-uh*

I don't know the area code. **Ich weiss die Vorwahlnummer nicht.** *ikh veyes dee FOHR-vaal-num-uh nikht.*

Can you help me? **Können Sie mir helfen?** *KERN-en zee meer HELF-en*

It's a local call. **Es ist ein Ortsgespräch.** *ehs ist eyen ORTS-geh-shpraykh*

■ a long-distance call **ein Ferngespräch** *eyen FEHRN-geh-shpraykh*

Where can I buy a telephone card? **Wo kann ich eine Telefonkarte kaufen?** *voh kahn ikh EYEN-eh TAY-leh-FOHN-kaart-eh KOWF-en*

Do you sell telephone cards? **Verkaufen Sie Telefonkarten?** *fehr-KOWF-en zee TAH-leh-FOHN-kaart-en*

How many units is it good for?	**Wie viele Einheiten sind darauf?** *vee FEEL-eh EYEN-heyet-en zint dah-ROWF*
How much does this card cost?	**Was kosten diese Karte?** *vahss KOST-en DEEZ-eh KAART-eh*
■ a person-to-person call	**ein Gespräch mit Voranmeldung** *eyen geh-SHPRAYKH mit FOHR-ahn-mehld-ung*
■ a collect call	**ein R-Gespräch** *eyen ehr-geh-SHPRAYKH*
May I speak to Mr. (Mrs., Miss) ___?	**Darf ich bitte Herrn (Frau, Fräulein) ___ sprechen?** *dahrf ikh BIT-eh hehrn (frow, FROY-leyen) SHPREHKH-en*
Speaking.	**Am Apparat.** *ahm ah-pah-RAAT*
Hello.	**Hallo.** *hah-LOH*

This is ____.	**Hier ist ____.** *heer ist*
Speak louder (more slowly).	**Sprechen Sie lauter (langsamer).** *SHPREHKH-en zee LOWT-uh (LAHNG-zaam-uh)*
Don't hang up.	**Bleiben Sie am Apparat.** *BLEYEB-en zee ahm ah-pah-RAAT*
There's no answer.	**Es meldet sich niemand.** *ehss MEHLD-et zikh NEE-mahnt*
The line is busy.	**Die Leitung ist besetzt.** *dee LEYET-ung ist beh-ZEHTST*
You gave me the wrong number.	**Sie haben mich falsch verbunden.** *zee HAAB-en mikh fahlsh fehr-BUND-en*
I'll call again later.	**Später rufe ich noch einmal an.** *SHPAYT-uh roof ikh nokh EYEN-maal ahn*
I'd like to leave a message.	**Ich möchte etwas ausrichten lassen.** *ikh merkht EHT-vahs OWSS-rikht-en LAHSS-en*

TELEGRAMS

Telegrams are sent from post offices.

I'd like to send a telegram to ____.	**Ich möchte ein Telegramm nach ____ aufgeben.** *ikh MERKHT-eh eyen tay-leh-GRAHM nakh ____ OWF-gayb-en*
How much is it per word?	**Was kostet es pro Wort?** *vahs KOST-et ehs proh vort*

Please let me have a form.

Geben Sie mir bitte ein Formular.
GAYB-en zee meer BIT-eh eyen for-mu-LAAR

Travel Tips Before departing for a foreign country, exchange about $50 into its currency for telephone calls, taxis, or other expenses you will have upon arrival. Carry little cash. Travelers' checks are safe but paying by credit cards usually guarantees the best exchange rate.

GENERAL
INFORMATION

TELLING TIME

What time is it?	**Wieviel Uhr ist es?** *VEE-feel oor ist ehs*
■ hour	**Stunde** *SHTUND-eh*
■ minute	**Minute** *mi-NOOT-eh*
■ second	**Sekunde** *zeh-KUN-deh*
■ half an hour	**eine halbe Stunde** *EYEN-eh HAHLB-eh SHTUND-eh*
■ an hour and a half	**anderthalb Stunden** *AHN-dehrt-haalp SHTUND-en*
At what time shall we meet?	**Um wieviel Uhr treffen wir uns?** *um VEE-feel oor TREHF-en veer uns*

Telling time in conversation is done as in English.

We'll eat at eight (o'clock).	**Wir essen um acht (Uhr).** *veer ESS-en um ahkht (oor)*

12:20 can be expressed as

twenty after twelve	**zwanzig nach zwölf** *TSVAHNTS-ikh nahkh tsverlf*
or	
twelve twenty	**zwölf Uhr zwanzig** *tsverlf oor TSVAHNTS-ikh*

1:30 is either

one-thirty	**ein Uhr dreissig**	*eyen oor DREYSS-ikh*
or		
half an hour (30 minutes) to two	**halb zwei**	*hahlp tsveye*

German usually focuses not on the hour completed but on the hour coming up.

4:30 (half an hour to five)	**halb fünf**	*hahlp fewnf*
7:30 (half an hour to eight)	**halb acht**	*hahlp ahkht*

The easiest way for you to tell the time in German is to state the hour (**ein Uhr, zwei Uhr, drei Uhr,** etc.) and then the minutes (from 1 to 60).

9:37	**neun Uhr siebenunddreißig**	*noyn oor ZEEB-en-unt-dreyess-ikh*

Nach (after) and **vor** (to, before) are not difficult either.

eight to three (2:52)	**acht vor drei**	*ahkht for drey*
five to seven (6:55)	**fünf vor sieben**	*fewnf for ZEEB-en*
nine after four (4:09)	**neun nach vier**	*noyn nahkh feer*

| a quarter after three (3:15) | **viertel nach drei** *FEERT-el nahkh dreye* |

Timetables use the 24-hour clock, so that the next hour after 12 noon is 13 (1:00 P.M.). Thus 2:00 P.M. is **vierzehn Uhr,** and so on.

| My train leaves at 8:20 P.M. | **Mein Zug fährt um zwanzig Uhr zwanzig.** *meyen tsook fayrt um TSVAHN-tsikh oor TSVAHN-tsikh* |

DAYS OF THE WEEK

Today is ___.	**Heute ist ___.** *HOYT-eh ist*
■ Monday	**Montag** *MOHN-taak*
■ Tuesday	**Dienstag** *DEENS-taak*
■ Wednesday	**Mittwoch** *MIT-vokh*
■ Thursday	**Donnerstag** *DON-ehrs-taak*
■ Friday	**Freitag** *FREYE-taak*
■ Saturday	**Samstag/Sonnabend** *ZAHMS-taak/ ZON-aab-ent*
■ Sunday	**Sonntag** *ZON-taak*

yesterday	**gestern** *GEST-ehrn*
the day before yesterday	**vorgestern** *FOHR-gest-ehrn*
tomorrow	**morgen** *MORG-en*
the day after tomorrow	**übermorgen** *EWB-ehr-morg-en*
in the morning (afternoon, evening)	**am Morgen (Nachmittag, Abend)** *ahm MORG-en (NAHKH-mit-taak, AAB-ent)*
mornings	**morgens** *MORG-ens*
evenings	**abends** *AAB-ents*
all day	**den ganzen Tag** *dayn GAHNTS-en taak*
tonight	**heute Abend** *HOYT-eh AAB-ent*
this afternoon	**heute nachmittag** *HOYT-eh NAHKH-mit-taak*
every day	**jeden Tag** *YAYD-en taak*

Proverb:
Man soll den Tag nicht vor dem Abend loben.

Don't praise the day before the evening, i.e., don't count your chickens before they're hatched.

MONTHS OF THE YEAR

January	**Januar/Jänner** (Austria) *YAA-noo-aar/YEH-nehr*
February	**Februar** *FAY-broo-aar*

March	**März** *mehrts*	
April	**April** *ah-PRIL*	
May	**Mai** *meye*	
June	**Juni** *YOON-ee*	
July	**Juli** *YOOL-ee*	
August	**August** *ow-GUST*	
September	**September** *zep-TEHM-buh*	
October	**Oktober** *ok-TOH-buh*	
November	**November** *no-VEHM-buh*	
December	**Dezember** *deh-TSEHM-buh*	
What is today's date?	**Der Wievielte ist heute?** *dehr VEE-feelt-eh ist HOYT-eh*	
Today is May 3.	**Heute ist der 3. Mai.** *HOYT-eh ist dehr DRIT-eh meye*	
■ March 8	**der 8. März** *dehr AHKHT-eh mehrts*	
monthly	**monatlich** *MOHN aat-likh*	
this month	**in diesem Monat** *in DEEZ-em MOHN-aat*	
next month	**im nächsten Monat** *im NAYKHST-en MOHN-aat*	
last month	**im letzten Monat** *im LETST-en MOHN-aat*	
two months ago	**vor zwei Monaten** *for tsveye MOHN-aaten*	

THE FOUR SEASONS

spring	**der Frühling**	*dehr FREW-ling*
summer	**der Sommer**	*dehr ZOM-uh*
autumn	**der Herbst**	*dehr hehrpst*
winter	**der Winter**	*dehr VINT-uh*
during the spring	**während des Frühlings**	*VEHR-ent dehs FREW-lings*
every summer	**jeden Sommer**	*YAYD-en ZOM-uh*
in the winter	**im Winter**	*im VINT-uh*

THE WEATHER

How is the weather today?	**Wie ist das Wetter heute?** *vee ist dahs VEHT-uh HOYT-eh*
The weather is good (bad).	**Es ist gutes (schlechtes) Wetter.** *ehs ist GOOT-es (SHLEHKHT-es) VEHT-uh*
What splendid (horrible) weather!	**Was für ein herrliches (scheußliches) Wetter!** *vahs fewr eyen HEHR-likh-es (SHOYSS-likh-es) VEHT-uh*

It is ____.   **Es ist ____.** *ehs ist*

- hot   **heiss** *heyess*
- warm   **warm** *vaarm*
- cold   **kalt** *kahlt*
- cool   **kühl** *kewl*
- sunny   **sonnig** *ZON-ikh*

■ windy **windig** *VIND-ikh*

It's raining (snowing). **Es regnet (schneit).** *ehs RAYG-net (shneyet)*

The English say "It's raining cats and dogs." Germans say **Das ist ein Hundewetter (Sauwetter)** (That's a dog's [sow's] weather) when the weather's really foul.

TEMPERATURE CONVERSIONS

To change degrees Fahrenheit to Centigrade, subtract 32 and multiply by 5/9.

To change degrees Centigrade to Fahrenheit, multiply by 9/5 and add 32.

Grad

Celsius   **Fahrenheit**

Thermometer

OFFICIAL PUBLIC HOLIDAYS IN GERMANY, AUSTRIA, AND SWITZERLAND

███████

Our list begins with New Year's Day, although most celebrating is done on New Year's Eve **(Silvesterabend)**. St. Sylvester's history is about as shaky and uncertain as most of the resolutions made on his holiday.

Jan. 1	New Year's Day	**Neujahr**
April	Easter Monday	**Ostermontag**
May	Ascension Thursday	**Christi Himmelfahrt**
May or June	Pentecost (Whit Monday)	**Pfingstmontag**
Dec. 25	Christmas Day	**Erster Weihnachtstag**
Dec. 26	St. Stephen's Day	**Zweiter Weihnachstag**

Germany and Austria celebrate Labor Day **(Tag der Arbeit)** on May 1. Good Friday **(Karfreitag)** is also a public holiday in Germany and in most cantons of Switzerland. Some Swiss cantons also celebrate National Day **(Nationalfeiertag)** on August 1. October 3 is celebrated as National Unity Day **(Tag der Deutschen Einheit)**.

In addition to the above, Austria also observes the following official holidays:

Jan. 6	Epiphany	**Heiligedreikönigstag**
June 15	Corpus Christi Day	**Fronleichnam**

August 15	Assumption Day	**Mariä Himmelfahrt**
Oct. 26	Flag Day	**Nationalfeiertag**
Nov. 1	All Saints' Day	**Allerheiligen**
Dec. 8	Immaculate Conception	**Unbefleckte Empfängnis**

Visiting Austria in 1983, the Pope complained of that country's declining church attendance. Nevertheless, Austria's Catholic background is reflected in many of the holidays. The Hapsburgs were not only **kaiserlich und königlich** (imperial and royal) but also **apostolisch** (apostolic) majesties.

Better known than some of the official holidays are popular festivals, such as Munich's **Oktoberfest** (which begins in late September) and the famed pre-Lenten festivities **(Karneval, Fasching)** in the Rhineland and southern areas. In addition, great numbers of local festivities are celebrated, such as **Schützenfeste** (marksmanship festivals), and colorful historical pageants, such as Rothenburg's **Der Meistertrunk** (the Master Draught). Ask at the Tourist Office.

Merry Christmas!	**Fröhliche Weihnachten!**	*FRER-likh-eh VEYE-nahkht-en*
Happy New Year!	**Glückliches Neujahr**	*GLEWK-likh-es NOY-yaar*
Happy Birthday!	**Herzlichen Geburtstag!**	*HEHRTS-likh-en geh-BOORTS-taak*

COUNTRIES

My homeland is:	**Mein Heimatland ist:**	*meyen HEYE-maat-lahnt ist*
Africa	**Afrika**	*AAF-ree-kah*

Argentina	**Argentinien**	*ahr-gehn-TEEN-yen*
Australia	**Australien**	*ows-TRAAL-yen*
Austria	**Österreich**	*ERST-eh-reyekh*
Belgium	**Belgien**	*BELG-yen*
Brazil	**Brasilien**	*brah-ZEEL-yen*
Canada	**Kanada**	*KAH-nah-dah*
China	**China**	*KHEE-nah*
Croatia	**Kroatien**	*Kroh-ah-tsee-en*
Czech Republic	**Tschechien**	*TSCHEHKH-ee-en*
Denmark	**Dänemark**	*DAYN-eh-mahrk*
Egypt	**Ägypten**	*ay-GEWPT-en*
England	**England**	*EHNG-lahnt*
Estonia	**Estland**	*EST-lahnt*
Europe	**Europa**	*oy-ROH-pah*
France	**Frankreich**	*FRAHNK-reyekh*
Germany	**Deutschland**	*DOYTSH-lahnt*
The Federal Republic of Germany	**die Bundesrepublik Deutschland**	*dee BUND-es-reh-poob-leek DOYTSH-lahnt*
Great Britain	**Grossbritannien**	*GROHS-bri-tahn-yen*
Greece	**Griechenland**	*GREEKH-en-lahnd*

Hungary	**Ungarn**	*UN-gahrn*
India	**Indien**	*IN-dyen*
Ireland	**Irland**	*EER-lahnt*
Italy	**Italien**	*ee-TAAL-yen*
Japan	**Japan**	*YAA-pahn*
Korea	**Korea**	*COR-ay-ah*
Latvia	**Lettland**	*LET-lahnt*
Liechtenstein	**Liechtenstein**	*LEEKHT-en-shteyen*
Lithuania	**Litauen**	*LIT-ow-en*
Luxembourg	**Luxemburg**	*LUKS-ehm-boork*
Mongolia	**die Mongolei**	*dee MON-go-leye*
the Netherlands	**die Niederlande**	*dee NEED-uh-lahnd-eh*
New Zealand	**Neuseeland**	*noy-ZAY-lahnt*
Norway	**Norwegen**	*NOR-vayg-en*
Poland	**Polen**	*POHL-en*
Russia	**Russland**	*RUSS-lahnt*
Scotland	**Schottland**	*SHOT-lahnt*
Slovakia	**die Slowakei**	*dee SLO-vah-keye*
Slovenia	**Slowenien**	*SLO-vayn-yen*
South Africa	**Südafrika**	*ZEWT-aaf-ree-kah*

Spain	**Spanien**	*SHPAAN-yen*
Sweden	**Schweden**	*SHVAYD-en*
Switzerland	**die Schweiz**	*dee shveyets*
Ukraine	**die Ukraine**	*die OOK-reyen-eh*
the United States	**die Vereinigten Staaten**	*dee fehr-EYEN-ikh-ten SHTAAT-en*
the Universe (cosmos)	**Das Weltall**	*dahs VELT-ahl*

GERMANY REUNITED

The Berlin Wall was toppled, with much emotion and enthusiasm, in November of 1989. The disappearance of the Soviet Union at the end of 1991 was preceded by the Federal Republic of Germany's absorption, on October 3, 1990, of the German Democratic Republic (known to most as "East Germany" but still "Central Germany" to nationalists and some historians). The present single German state exists in the frontiers created by the Allies at the end of World War II. Germany is committed to the European Community and, despite the discontent of expellee organizations, has renounced claims to former German areas.

In Russia, Saint Petersburg is no longer "Leningrad" and in Germany, the Saxon city Chemnitz again bears that name after an interlude as "Karl-Marx-Stadt." More name changes may occur.

IMPORTANT SIGNS

Abfahrten	Departures
Achtung	Attention
Angebot	Featured item (in a sale)

Aufzug	Elevator
Ausfahrt	Highway exit
Ausgang	Exit
Auskunft	Information
Ausverkauf	Clearance sale
Ausverkauft	Sold out
Baden verboten	No swimming
Belegt	Filled up
Besetzt	Occupied
Betreten des Rasens verboten	Keep off the grass
Damentoilette	Ladies' room
Drücken	Push
Einfahrt	Highway entrance
Eingang	Entrance
Eintritt frei	No admission charge
Frei	Vacant
Für Unbefugte verboten	No trespassing
Gefahr	Danger
Geöffnet von ____ bis ____	Open from ____ to ____

Geschlossen	Closed
Geschlossene Gesellschaft	Private party
Heiß	Hot
Kalt	Cold
Herrentoilette	Men's room
Kasse	Cashier
Kein Zutritt	No entry
Lebensgefahr	Mortal danger
Lift	Elevator
Nicht berühren	Do not touch
Nichtraucher	Nonsmoking compartment (section)
Notausgang	Emergency exit
Privatstrand	Private beach
Privatweg	Private road
Rauchen verboten	No smoking
Raucher	Smoking compartment
Reserviert	Reserved
Schlussverkauf	Final sale
Unbefugtes Betreten verboten	No trespassing

____ verboten	____ prohibited
Vorsicht	Caution
Vorsicht, Bissiger Hund	Beware of the dog
Ziehen	Pull
Zimmer frei	Room(s) to let
Zu den Bahnsteigen	To the railroad platforms

EMERGENCY TELEPHONE NUMBERS

Police	110 (Germany)
	133 (Austria)
	117 (Switzerland)
Fire	112 (Germany)
	122 (Austria)
	118 (Switzerland)

COMMON ABBREVIATIONS

Abt.	**Abteilung**	compartment
ACS	**Automobil-Club der Schweiz**	Automobile Association of Switzerland
ADAC	**Allgemeiner Deutscher Automobil Club**	General Automobile Association of Germany
Bhf	**Bahnhof**	railway station

BRD	**Bundesrepublik Deutschland**	Federal Republic of Germany
CDU	**Christlich-Demokratische Union**	Christian Democratic Union
DB	**Deutsche Bahn**	German Rail
DP	**Deutsche Post**	German Postal Service
DZT	**Deutsche Zentrale für Tourismus**	German National Tourist Board
d.h.	**das heißt**	that is (i.e.)
e.V.	**eingetragener Verein**	registered association (corporation)
FKK	**Freikörperkultur**	Free Physical Culture (nudism)
Frl.	**Fräulein**	Miss
GmbH	**Gesellschaft mit beschränkter Haftung**	limited-liability corporation
Hr.	**Herr**	Mr.
JH	**Jugendherberge**	youth hostel
km	**Kilometer**	kilometer
KG	**Kommandit-gesellschaft**	limited partnership
LKW	**Lastkraftwagen**	truck

Mill.	**Million**	million
ÖAMTC	**Österreichischer Automobil-Motorrad- und Touring- Club**	Austrian Automobile, Motorcycle, and Touring Association
ÖBB	**Österreichische Bundesbahnen**	Austrian Federal Railroad
PKW	**Personenkraftwagen**	passenger car
PTT	**Post, Telefon, Telegraph**	Postal, Telephone, and Telegraph Office
SBB	**Schweizerische Bundesbahnen**	Swiss Federal Railways
SPD	**Sozialdemokrat-ische Partei Deutschlands**	Social Democratic Party of Germany
Str.	**Straβe**	street
TCS	**Touring-Club der Schweiz**	Swiss Touring Association
usf/usw.	**und so fort/und so weiter**	et cetera (etc.)
Ztg.	**Zeitung**	newspaper
z.Z.	**zur Zeit**	at the present time

CENTIMETERS/INCHES

It is usually unnecessary to make exact conversions from your customary inches to the metric system used in German-speaking Europe, but to give you an approximate idea of how they compare, we give you the following guide.

Centimeter

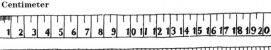

Zollen

To convert centimeters into inches, multiply by 0.39.
To convert inches into centimeters, multiply by 2.54.

METERS/FEET

1 meter (Meter) = 39.37 inches   1 foot = 0.3 meters
3.28 feet   1 yard = 0.9 meters
1.09 yards

How tall are you in meters? See for yourself.

WHEN YOU WEIGH YOURSELF

1 kilogram (kilo) = 2.2 pounds
1 pound = 0.45 kilograms

LIQUID MEASURES

1 liter = 1.06 quarts
4 liters = 1.06 gallons

For quick approximate conversions, multiply the number
of gallons by 4 to get liters. Divide the number of liters by 4 to
get gallons.

MINI-DICTIONARY FOR BUSINESS TRAVELERS

For other commercial terms, see Banking (pages 26–30) and Common Abbreviations (pages 260–262).

amount	**Betrag**	*beh-TRAAK*
appraise	**schätzen**	*SHEHTS-en*
authorize	**bevollmächtigen**	*beh-FOL-mekht-ig-en*
■ authorized edition	**Lizenzausgabe**	*li-TSEHNTS-ows-gaab-eh*
bill	**Rechnung**	*REHKH-nung*
■ bill of exchange	**Wechsel**	*VEHK-sel*
■ bill of lading	**Frachtbrief**	*FRAHKHT-breef*
■ bill of sale	**Kaufbrief**	*KOWF-breef*
business operations	**Betriebe**	*beh-TREEB-eh*
cash	**Bargeld**	*BAAR-gehlt*
■ to buy, sell for cash	**gegen Barzahlung kaufen, verkaufen**	*GAY-gen BAAR-tsaal-ung KOWF-en, fehr-KOWF-en*
cash a check	**einen Scheck einlösen**	*EYEN-en shehk EYEN-lerz-en*
certified check	**beglaubigter Scheck**	*beh-GLOWB-ig-tuh shehk*
Chamber of Commerce	**Handelskammer**	*HAHND-ehls-kahm-uh*
compensation for damage	**Schadenersatz**	*SHAAD-en-ehr-zahts*

competition	**Wettbewerb** *VEHT-beh-vehrp*
competitive price	**konkurrenzfähiger Preis** *kon-koo-REHNTS-fay-ig-uh preyess*
contract	**Vertrag** *fehr-TRAAK*
contractual obligation	**vertragsmäßige Verpflichtung** *fehr-TRAAKS-mayss-ig-eh fehr-PFLIKHT-ung*
controlling interest	**Aktienmehrheit** *AHKTS-yen-mayr-heyet*
co-owner	**Miteigentümer** *MIT-eye-gen-tewm-uh*
co-partner	**Mitteilhaber** *MIT-teyel-haab-uh*
down payment	**Anzahlung** *AHN-tsaal-ung*
due	**fällig** *FEH-likh*
enterprise	**Unternehmen** *UN-tehr-naym-en*
expedite delivery	**die Lieferung beschleunigen** *dee LEE-fehr-ung beh-SHLOY-nig-en*
expenses	**Kosten, Spesen** *KOST-en, SHPAYZ-en*
goods	**Waren** *VAAR-en*
infringement of patent rights	**Verletzung von Patentrechten** *fehr-LEHTS-ung fon pah-TEHNT-rehkht-en*
insurance against all risks	**Versicherung gegen jede Gefahr** *febr-ZIKH-uh-rung GAYG-en YAYD-eh geh-FAAR*

international law	**Völkerrecht** *FERLK-uh-rehkht*
lawful possessor	**rechtsmäßiger Besitzer** *REHKHTS-mayss-ig-uh beh-ZITS-uh*
lawsuit	**Prozess** *proh-TSEHSS*
lawyer	**Rechtsanwalt** *REHKHTS-ahn-vahlt*
mail-order business	**Postversandgeschäft** *POST-fehr-zahnt-geh-shehft*
manager	**Geschäftsleiter, Betriebsleiter** *geh-SHEHFTS-leyet-uh, beh-TREEPS-leyet-uh*
market value	**Marktwert** *MAARKT-vehrt*
payment	**Zahlung** *TSAAL-ung*
■ partial payment	**Teilzahlung** *TEYEL-tsaal-ung*
past due	**überfällig** *EWB-uh-feh-likh*
post office box	**Postschließfach** *POST-shleess-fahkh*
property	**Eigentum** *EYEG-en-toom*
purchasing agent	**Einkaufsvertreter** *EYEN-kowfs-fehr-trayt-uh*
put on the American market	**in den amerikanischen Handel bringen** *in dayn ah-meh-ri-KAA-nish-en HAHND-el BRING-en*
sale	**Verkauf** *fehr-KOWF*
(to) sell	**verkaufen** *fehr-KOWF-en*
(to) send	**senden, schicken, versenden** *ZEHND-en, SHIK-en, fehr-ZEHND-en*

■ send back	**zurücksenden** *tsoo-REWK-zehnd-en*	
■ send C.O.D.	**per Nachnahme senden** *pehr NAHKH-naam-eh ZEHND-en*	
shipment	**Sendung** *ZEHND-ung*	
tax	**Steuer** *SHTOY-uh*	
■ tax exempt	**steuerfrei** *SHTOY-uh-freye*	
■ sales tax	**Umsatzsteuer** *UM-zahts-shtoy-uh*	
■ value-added tax	**Mehrwertsteuer** *MAYR-vehrt-shtoy-uh*	
trade	**Handel** *HAHND-el*	
transact business	**Geschäfte machen** *geh-SHEHFT-eh MAHKH-en*	
transfer	**übertragen** *EWB-uh-traag-en*	
transportation charges	**Beförderungskosten** *beh-FERD-eh-rungs-kost-en*	
via	**über, via** *EWB-uh, VEE-ah*	
yield a profit	**einen Gewinn bringen** *EYEN-en geh-VIN BRING-en*	

Travel Tips   There are many theories and much research on how to survive jet lag—the adjustment to a long trip into a different time zone. Some multinational corporations take jet lag so seriously that they do not allow employees to make business decisions on the first day abroad. Most experts agree on several techniques: avoid alcohol but drink plenty of other fluids while flying to avoid dehydration; take frequent strolls around the plane to keep your blood circulating; if possible, get some rest on the flight; ear plugs, an eye mask and an inflatable neck collar make sleep easier; if you arrive early in the morning, take an after-lunch nap, get up for some exercise and dinner, then go to bed at the regular new time; if you arrive at your destination in the afternoon or later, skip the nap and sleep late the next morning; in countries where massage or saunas are standard hotel service, indulge yourself on the evening of arrival to help you sleep soundly that night.

QUICK GRAMMAR GUIDE

NOUNS AND THE DEFINITE ARTICLE

All German nouns start with a capital and are either masculine, feminine, or neuter. In the subject (nominative case), the definite article *(the)* is either **der, die,** or **das.** All three genders use **die** for the plural.

MASCULINE	FEMININE	NEUTER
der Zug the train	**die Autobahn** the highway	**das Schiff** the ship
der Bruder the brother	**die Schwester** the sister	**das Kind** the child
der Wagen the car	**die Milch** the milk	**das Bier** the beer
der Wein the wine	**die Liebe** (the) love	**das Theater** the theater

PLURALS

Plural nouns may show a variety of changes, such as an umlaut or the endings *-e*, *-en*, *-er*, or even *-s*. Sometimes the noun remains unchanged. Here are the plurals of some of the nouns listed above:

die Züge, Brüder, Wagen, Weine, Autobahnen, Schwestern, Schiffe, Kinder, Biere, Theater

DECLENSIONS

German nouns, and the articles *(the, an)* and adjectives that accompany them, have cases. Case is determined by the noun's function in a sentence. There are four cases: the subject (nominative), possessive (genitive), indirect object (dative), and direct object (accusative).

MASCULINE		
SINGULAR		
Subj.	**der nächste Zug**	the next train
Poss.	**des nächsten Zuges**	of the next train (the next train's)
Ind. obj.	**dem nächsten Zug**	to the next train
Dir. obj.	**den nächsten Zug**	the next train
PLURAL		
Subj.	**die nächsten Züge**	the next trains
Poss.	**der nächsten Züge**	of the next trains
Ind. obj.	**den nächsten Zügen**	to (for) the next trains
Dir. obj.	**die nächsten Züge**	the next trains

FEMININE		
SINGULAR		
Sub.	**die neue Autobahn**	the new highway
Poss.	**der neuen Autobahn**	of the new highway
Ind. obj.	**der neuen Autobahn**	to (for) the new highway
Dir. obj.	**die neue Autobahn**	the new highway
PLURAL		
Subj.	**die neuen Autobahnen**	the new highways
Poss.	**der neuen Autobahnen**	of the new highways
Ind. obj.	**den neuen Autobahnen**	to (for) the new highways
Dir. obj.	**die neuen Autobahnen**	the new highways

NEUTER		
SINGULAR		
Subj.	**das schöne Schiff**	the beautiful ship
Poss.	**des schönen Schiffes**	of the beautiful ship (the beautiful ship's)
Ind. obj.	**dem schönen Schiff**	to (for) the beautiful ships
Dir. obj.	**das schöne Schiff**	the beautiful ship
PLURAL		
Subj.	**die schönen Schiffe**	the beautiful ships
Poss.	**der schönen Schiffe**	of the beautiful ships
Ind. obj.	**den schönen Schiffen**	to (for) the beautiful ships
Dir. obj.	**die schönen Schiffe**	the beautiful ships

THE INDEFINITE ARTICLE

A or *an* is **ein** in German. The masculine subject and the neuter subject and direct object use **ein** with no additional ending. The other masculine and neuter cases and the entire feminine gender are declined like the definite article *(the)* and use the same endings.

	MASCULINE	FEMININE	NEUTER
Subj.	**ein** Zug	**eine** Autobahn	**ein** Schiff
Poss.	**eines** Zuges	**einer** Autobahn	**eines** Schiffes
Ind. obj.	**einem** Zug	**einer** Autobahn	**einem** Schiff
Dir. obj.	**einen** Zug	**eine** Autobahn	**ein** Schiff

Ein has no plural, but the negative **kein** and the possessive adjectives (**mein, dein,** etc.) do.

	MASCULINE	FEMININE	NEUTER
Subj.	**keine** Züge	**keine** Autobahnen	**keine** Schiffe
Poss.	**keiner** Züge	**keiner** Autobahnen	**keiner** Schiffe
Ind. obj.	**keinen** Zügen	**keinen** Autobahnen	**keinen** Schiffen
Dir. obj.	**keine** Züge	**keine** Autobahnen	**keine** Schiffe

ADJECTIVES

All descriptive adjectives, like the definite and indefinite
articles, agree with the nouns they modify in number, gender,
and case.

DEMONSTRATIVE ADJECTIVES

The demonstrative adjective **dies** and the question word
welch- have the same endings as the declined forms of **der,**
die, and **das,** given above.

Welcher Bruder? **Welche Autobahn?** **Welches Schiff?**
Which brother?   What highway?   What ship?

Welchen Mann meinen Sie? **Diesen.**
Which man do you mean?   This one.

Mit welchem Zug fahren Sie? **Mit diesem.**
On what train are you traveling?   On this one.

POSSESSIVE ADJECTIVES

Possessive adjectives agree in gender and number with the
noun they modify. Therefore, the same speaker, male or female,
will say **mein Bruder** (my brother) or **meine Schwester**
(my sister). Here is a complete list of the possessive adjectives
(sometimes called "**ein** words," because they are declined
like **ein**).

my	**mein**	our	**unser**
your (familiar)	**dein**	your (familiar)	**euer**
his	**sein**	your (formal)	**Ihr**
her	**ihr**	their	**ihr**

A WORD ABOUT THE DECLENSION OF ARTICLES AND ADJECTIVES

It is certainly not our aim to encourage you to speak incorrect German. Nevertheless, if quick communication is essential, do not struggle over the correct case forms in the preceding tables. For forms of the definite article *(the)*, merely say **de** in all cases. It is incorrect, but many speakers of **Plattdeutsch** in Northern Germany use **de** everywhere, as do the Flemings and the Dutch. The English *the* is related to this North German **de,** and there are many other German-English cognates, such as **durch** (through), **danken** (to thank), **denken** (to think), **dick und dünn** (thick and thin), **Dieb** (thief), and **Daumen** (thumb). As for the indefinite article *(a, an)*, just be sure to remember that it is **ein** even if you aren't sure of the ending. If you are studying or plan to study German, you must not be cavalier about endings. But if you want to get your meaning across quickly and simply, you can temporarily sacrifice grammatical correctness. German sensibilities will not be too offended, since most speakers of German, like most Italians and Spaniards, are flattered when foreigners try to speak their language, and are therefore patient and helpful to neophytes. Most of the time, the endings on adjectives are not essential to comprehension.

PRONOUNS

These, too, are declined. German distinguishes between the familiar forms (**du** and its plural **ihr**) for *you* and the polite form **Sie,** which is both singular and plural. To differentiate between **sie** *(they)* and **Sie** *(you)*, the *s* is capitalized. The same is true of all polite forms, such as **Ihnen** *(to you)*, as

distinct from **ihnen** *(to them)*, as well as the possessive
adjective **Ihr** *(your)*. **Du** and **ihr** are used when addressing
friends, relatives, children, gods, animals, or inanimate objects.
Young people tend to use the **du** form among themselves
even though they may not be well acquainted. For travelers,
the most important form of *you* is **Sie**.

PERSONAL PRONOUNS		
SINGULAR		
Subj.	**ich** (I)	**du** (you)	**er, sie, es** (he, she, it)
Poss.	**meiner** (of me)	**deiner** (of you)	**seiner, ihrer, seiner** (of him, her, it)
Ind. obj.	**mir** (to me)	**dir** (to you)	**ihm, ihr, ihm** (to him, her, it)
Dir. obj.	**mich** (me)	**dich** (you)	**ihn, sie, es** (him, her, it)
PLURAL		
Subj.	**wir** (we)	**ihr** (you)	**sie, Sie** (they, you)
Poss.	**unser** (of us)	**euer** (of you)	**ihrer, Ihrer** (of them, you)
Ind. obj.	**uns** (to us)	**euch** (to you)	**ihnen, Ihnen** (to them, you)
Dir. obj.	**uns** (us)	**euch** (you)	**sie, Sie** (them, you)

The possessive forms are given here for the sake of
completeness. However, they are not commonly used.

VERBS

The great majority of German infinitives end in *-en*. The
first and third person plural of the present tense are the same
as the infinitive [exception: **sein** *(to be)*]. In addition, many

infinitives are used as verbal nouns. Such nouns are always capitalized (like all nouns). They are neuter and are usually translated by a final -*ing* in English.

das Rauchen (smoking)   **das Reisen** (traveling)

das Tanzen (dancing)

The present tense is the tense you will use most frequently. The endings for the present tense shown here have been separated from the verbal stem of **gehen** (to go) by a hyphen.

ich geh-e	I go (am going, do go)
du geh-st	you go (are going, do go)
er, sie, es geh-t	he, she, it goes (is going, does go)
wir geh-en	we go (are going, do go)
ihr geh-t	you go (are going, do go)
sie, Sie geh-en	they, you go (are going, do go)

As in English, the present tense can be used with a future implication.

Ich reise morgen ab.
I leave (will leave) tomorrow.

Der Zug kommt um 10 Uhr 30 an.
The train arrives (will arrive) at 10:30 A.M.

Both German and English have regular and irregular verbs. Compare the following and note that many German past participles begin with *ge-*.

REGULAR VERBS		
INFINITIVE	PAST TENSE	PAST PARTICIPLE
learnen (to learn)	**lernte** (learned)	**gelernt** (learned)
sagen (to say)	**sagte** (said)	**gesagt** (said)
kochen (to cook)	**kochte** (cooked)	**gekochte** (cooked)
lieben (to love)	**leibte** (loved)	**geliebt** (loved)
leben (to live)	**lebte** (lived)	**gelebt** (lived)

IRREGULAR VERBS		
INFINITIVE	PAST TENSE	PAST PARTICIPLE
kommen (to come)	**kam** (came)	**gekommen** (come)
fallen (to fall)	**fiel** (fell)	**gefallen** (fallen)
beginnen (to begin)	**begann** (began)	**begonnen** (begun)
trinkin (to drink)	**trank** (drank)	**getrunken** (drunk)
essen (to eat)	**aβ** (ate)	**gegessen** (eaten)

The verbs **sein** (to be), **haben** (to have), and **werden** (to become) are frequently used alone and also to form compound tenses and special constructions.

SEIN	
SINGULAR	PLURAL
ich bin I am	**wir sind** we are
du bist you are	**ihr seid** you are
er, sie, es ist he, she, it is	**sie, Sie sind** they, you are

HABEN	
SINGULAR	PLURAL
ich habe I have	**wir haben** we have
du hast you have	**ihr habt** you have
er, sie, es hat he, she, it has	**sie, Sie haben** they, you have

WERDEN	
SINGULAR	PLURAL
ich werde I become	**wir werden** we become
du wirst you become	**ihr werdet** you become
er, sie, es wird he, she, it becomes	**sie, Sie werden** they, you become

WORD ORDER

You may have heard about the complexities of German sentences. Nevertheless, verbs certainly don't always go "at the end." In questions and commands, they even come first! In most sentences the verb is the *second* element and comes just after the subject, which may be one word or several words, as in English.

Emmy reist viel.
Emmy travels a lot.

Emmy, Hans und die ganze Familie reisen viel.
Emmy, Hans, and the whole family travel a lot.

There is certainly no need to be intimidated by sentences like:

Otto trinkt Bier.
Otto drinks beer.

Ernst trinkt Wein.
Ernest drinks wine.

The verb remains the *second* element or unit if the sentence begins with some sentence unit other than the subject (for instance, a prepositional phrase).

Um 8 Uhr 45 kommt unser Flugzeug an.
At 8:45 A.M. our plane arrives.

In Amerika haben wir das nicht.
In America we don't have that.

The verb *does* go at the end in subordinate clauses. These are clauses introduced by subordinating conjunctions, such as **dass,** or by a relative pronoun.

Ich hoffe, dass der Zug bald ankommt.
I hope that the train arrives soon.

Der Zug, der jetzt ankommt, fährt nach Köln.
The train that is now arriving is going to Cologne.

QUESTIONS

In questions, the subject follows the verb.

Sprechen Sie Deutsch?
Do you speak German?

Fahren Sie nach Europa?
Are you traveling to Europe?

Gehen Sie ins Kino?
Are you going to the movies?

Trinken Sie Bier oder Wein?
Do you drink beer or wine?

COMMANDS

In commands or imperatives, the verb comes first and is followed by the personal pronoun. An exclamation point (!) is placed at the end of the sentence.

Trinken Sie mit mir!
Drink with me.

Trinken wir ein Glas Wein!
Let's drink a glass of wine.

Sprechen Sie Deutsch!
Speak German.

Fahren Sie nach Europa!
Travel to Europe.

NEGATIVES

A sentence can be made negative by **nicht** or **kein** (negative of the indefinite article **ein**).

Emmy liebt Hans nicht.
Emmy doesn't love Hans.

Das Baby will nicht essen.
The baby doesn't want to eat.

Sie trinkt keinen Kaffee.
She doesn't drink coffee.
(She drinks no coffee.)

Ich habe kein deutsches Geld.
I have no German money.

SEPARABLE PREFIXES

German verbs are often combined with prefixes. The verb **steigen** (to climb) may form **einsteigen** (to get into a vehicle), **aussteigen** (to get out of a vehicle), or **umsteigen** (to transfer from one bus or train to another). In the imperative, and sometimes elsewhere, the prefix is at the end of the sentence.

Steigen Sie sofort ein!
Get on board right away.

Steigen Sie in Frankfurt um!
Transfer in Frankfurt.

Steigen Sie bitte hier aus!
Please get off here.

Travel Tips Simple toiletries such as toothpaste and shaving cream can be purchased easily when you arrive at your destination, but prescription medicines should be brought from home.

ENGLISH-GERMAN DICTIONARY

Nouns are followed by the abbreviations *m.* (masculine), *f.* (feminine), *n.* (neuter), or *pl.* (plural). The first letter of nouns is always capitalized. Infinitives of German verbs end in *-en*. You can thus easily distinguish between **Tanz** (m.) (the dance) and **tanzen** (to dance). The *to* of the English infinitive has been omitted.

A

a, an   ein(e) *eyen(eh)*
abbey   Kloster (*n.*) *KLOHST-uh*
(be) able   kann *kahn*, können *KERN-en*
abscess   Abszess (*m.*) *ahps-TSESS*
absolutely   unbedingt *UN-beh-dinkt*
accept   annehmen *AHN-naym-en*
accident   Unfall (*m.*) *UN-fahl*
accompany   begleiten *beh-GLEYET-en*
account   Konto (*n.*) *KONT-oh*
ace   As (*n.*) *ahs*
actor   Schauspieler (*m.*) *SHOW-shpeel-uh*
actress   Schauspielerin (*f.*) *SHOW-shpeel-ehr-in*
adhesive tape   Heftpflaster (*n.*) *HEFT-pflahst-uh*
admission   Eintritt (*m.*) *EYEN-trit*
adults   Erwachsene (*pl.*) *ehr-VAHKS-ehn-eh*
adventure   Abenteuer (*n.*) *AH-ben-toy-uh*
advise   raten *RAAT-en*
Africa   Afrika (*n.*) *AAF-ree-kah*
after   nach *nahkh*
afternoon   Nachmittag (*m.*) *NAHKH-mit-aak*

again   wieder *VEED-uh*, noch einmal *nokh EYEN-maal*
against   gegen *GAYG-en*
age   Alter (*n.*) *AHLT-uh*
air   Luft (*f.*) *luft*
air-conditioned   luftgekühlt *LUFT-geh-kewlt*
air conditioner   Klimaanlage (*f.*) *KLEE-mah-ahn-laag-eh*
(by) airmail   (mit) Luftpost (*f.*) *(mit) LUFT-post*
airplane   Flugzeug (*n.*) *FLOOK-tsoyk*
airport   Flughafen (*m.*) *FLOOK-haaf-en*
Aix-la-Chapelle   Aachen *AAKH-en*
alcohol   Alkohol (*m.*) *AHL-koh-hol*, Schnaps (*m.*) *shnahps*, Spirituosen (*pl.*) *spee-ree-too-OHZ-en*
All aboard!   Einsteigen! *EYEN-shteyeg-en*
allowed   erlaubt *ehr-LOWPT*
almonds   Mandeln (*pl.*) *MAHND-eln*
alone   allein *ah-LEYEN*
alongside   bei *beye*
already   schon *shon*
also   auch *owkh*
alter   ändern *EHND-ehrn*
alterations   Änderungen (*pl.*) *EHND-eh-rung-en*
always   immer *IM-uh*

am bin *bin*

amber Bernstein (*m.*) *BEHRN-shteyen*

ambulance Krankenwagen (*m.*) *KRAHNK-en-vaag-en*

amethyst Amethyst (*m.*) *ah-meh-TEWST*

amount Betrag (*m.*) *beh-TRAHK*

amplifiers Verstärker (*pl.*) *fehr-SHTEHRK-uh*

amusement park Vergnügungspark (*m.*) *fehr-GNEWG-unks-pahrk*

ancestors Vorfahren (*pl.*) *FOR-faar-en*

and und *unt*

angel Engel (*m.*) *EHNG-el*

angry zornig *TSORN-ikh*

animal Tier (*n.*) *teer*

ankle Knöchel (*m.*) *KNERKH-el*

answer antworten *AHNT-vort-en*, Antwort (*f.*) *AHNT-vort*

antacid Magentabletten (*pl.*) *MAAG-en-tahb-let-en*

antiques Antiquitäten (*pl.*) *ahn-tik-vi-TAYT-en*

antiseptic Antiseptikum (*n.*) *ahn-tee-ZEHP-tik-um*

apartment Wohnung (*f.*) *VOHN-ung*

appendicitis Blinddarment-zündung (*f.*) *BLINT-dahrm-ent-tsewnd-ung*

appetizer Vorspeise (*f.*) *FOR-shpeyez-eh*

appliance Apparat (*m.*) *ah-pah-RAAT*, Gerät (*n.*) *ge-RAYT*

appointment Verabredung (*f.*) *fehr-ahp-RAYD-ung*

approximately ungefähr *UN-geh-fayr*

are sind *zint*

area Gegend (*f.*) *GAY-gent*

area code Vorwahlnummer (*f.*) *FOR-vaal-num-uh*

Argentina Argentinien (*n.*) *ahr-gen-TEEN-yen*

arm Arm (*m.*) *ahrm*

armchair Sessel (*m.*) *ZESS-el*

around um *um*

arrival Ankunft (*f.*) *AHN-kunft*

arrive ankommen *AHN-kom-en*, eintreffen *EYEN-trehf-en*

art Kunst (*f.*) *kunst*

artificial künstlich *KEWNST-likh*

artificial skating rink Kunsteisbahn (*f.*) *KUNST-eyess-baan*

artist Künstler *KEWNST-luh*

artists' quarter Künstlerviertel (*n.*) *KEWNST-luh-feert-el*

ashtray Aschenbecher (*m.*) *AHSH-en-bekh-uh*

Asia Asien (*n.*) *AAZ-yen*

ask fragen *FRAAG-en*, bitten *BIT-en*

association Verein (*m.*) *feh-REYEN*

at bei *beye*, zu *tsoo*; **at what time?** Um wieviel Uhr? *um VEE-feel oor*

attack Anfall (*m.*) *AHN-fahl*

attention Achtung (*f.*) *AHKHT-ung*

auburn kastanienbraun *kahs-TAAN-yen-brown*

Australia Australien (*n.*) *owss-TRAAL-yen*

Austria (*n.*) Österreich *ERST-eh-reyekh*

author Autor (*m.*) *OWT-or*

auto lights Beleuchtung (*f.*) *beh-LOYKHT-ung*

automatic automatisch *ow-toh-MAAT-ish*

automobile Auto (*n.*) *OW-toh*, Wagen (*m.*) *VAAG-en*

avenue Allee (*f.*) *ah-LAY*

away weg *vek*, fort *fort*

awful scheußlich *SHOYSS-likh*

B

back zurück *tsoo-REWK*, Rücken (*m.*) *REWK-en*

backache Rückenschmerzen (*pl.*) *REWK-en-shmehrts-en*

bacon Speck (*m.*) *shpehk*

bad schlecht *shlehkht*

bag Tüte (*f.*) *TEWT-eh*

baggage Gepäck (*n.*) *geh-PEHK*

baggage checkroom Gepäckaufbewahrung (*f.*) *geh-PEHK-owf-beh-vaar-ung*

bake backen *BAHK-en*

bakery Bäckerei (*f.*) *BEHK-eh-reye*

bald kahl *kaal*

bald pate Glatze (*f.*) *GLAHTS-eh*

ballet Ballett (*n.*) *bah-LET*

bandages Verbandzeug (*n.*) *fehr-BAHNT-tsoyk*

bangs Ponyfrisur (*f.*) *POH-nee-free-zoor*

bank Bank (*f.*) *bahnk*

barber Friseur (*m.*) *free-ZEWR*

bark bellen *BEL-en*

bat Fledermaus (*f.*) *FLAYD-uh-mowss*

bathe baden *BAAD-en*

bathing suit Badeanzug (*m.*) *BAAD-eh-ahn-tsook*

bathroom Bad (*n.*) *baat*, Toilette (*f.*) *toy-LET-eh*

baths Bäder (*pl.*) *BAYD-uh*

bathtub Badewanne (*f.*) *BAAD-eh-vahn-eh*

battery Batterie (*f.*) *bat-teh-REE*

Bavaria Bayern (*n.*) *BEYE-ehrn*

be sein *zeyen*, werden (passive) *VEHRD-en*

bean Bohne (*f.*) *BOHN-eh*

beard Bart (*m.*) *bahrt*

beat schlagen *SHLAAG-en*

beautiful schön *shern*

beauty Schönheit (*f.*) *SHERN-heyet*

beauty parlor Damensalon (*m.*) *DAAM-en-zah-lon*, Kosmetiksalon (*m.*) *kos-MAY-tik-zah-lon*

because weil *veyel*

become werden *VEHRD-en*

becomes wird *veert*

bed Bett (*n.*) *bet*

bedroom Schlafzimmer (*n.*) *SHLAAF-tsim-uh*

beef Rindfleisch (*n.*) *RINT-fleyesh*

beer Bier (*n.*) *beer*

beer garden Biergarten (*m.*) *BEER-gahrt-en*

beer stein Bierkrug (*m.*) *BEER-krook*

begin beginnen *beh-GIN-en*, anfangen *ahn-FAHNG-en*

behavior Benehmen (*n.*) *beh-NAYM-en*

behind hinten *HINT-en*

behold anschauen *ahn-SHOW-en*

Belgium Belgien (*n.*) *BEHLG-yen*

believe glauben *GLOWB-en*

bell Glocke (*f.*) *GLOK-eh*

bellboy Hotelpage (*m.*) *ho-TEL-paazh-eh*

belt Gürtel (*m.*) *GEWRT-el*

better besser *BESS-uh*

bicycle Fahrrad (*n.*) *FAAR-raat*

big groβ *grohss*

bigger groβer *GRERSS-uh*

bilingual zweisprachig *TSVEYE-shprahkh-ikh*

bill Rechnung (*f.*) *REKH-nung*

bills (currency) Scheine (*pl.*) *SHEYEN-eh*

bird Vogel (*m.*) *FOHG-el*

bishop (chess) Läufer (*m.*) *LOYF-uh*

bite beiβen *BEYESS-en*

black schwarz *shvahrts*

blanket Decke (f.) *DEHK-eh*

bleed bluten *BLOOT-en*

blender Mixer (m.) *MIKS-uh*

blister Blase (f.) *BLAAZ-eh*

blond blond *blont*

blood Blut (n.) *bloot*

blood sausage Blutwurst (f.) *BLOOT-voorst*

blouse Bluse (f.) *BLOOZ-eh*

blue blau *blow*

bluish bläulich *BLOY-likh*

boardinghouse Pension (f.) *pehn-ZYOHN*; Fremdenheim (n.) *FREHMD-en-heymi*

boat Boot (n.) *boht*; **boat tour of the harbor** Hafenrundfahrt (f.) *HAAF-en-runt-faart*

body Körper (m.) *KERP-uh*

boiled gekocht *geh-KOKHT*

bone Knochen (m.) *KNOKH-en*; **fishbone** Gräte (f.) *GRAYT-eh*

book Buch (n.) *bookh*

bookstore Buchhandlung (f.) *BOOKH-hahnt-lung*

boots Stiefel (pl.) *SHTEEF-el*

botanical garden Botanischer Garten (m.) *bo-TAAN-ish-ehr GAHRT-en*

bottle Flasche (f.) *FLAHSH-eh*

bowl Schüssel (f.) *SHEWSS-el*

bowl kegeln *KAYG-eln*

bowling alley Kegelbahn (f.) *KAYG-el-baan*

bracelet Armband (n.) *AHRM-bahnt*

brakes Bremsen (pl.) *BREHMZ-en*

brand Marke (f.) *MAHRK-eh*

brass-band music Blasmusik (f.) *BLAASS-moo-zeek*

brassiere Büstenhalter (m.) *BEWST-en-hahlt-uh*; **bra** BH *bay-hah*

Brazil Brasilien (n.) *brah-ZEEL-yen*

bread Brot (n.) *broht*

break brechen *BREHKH-en*

breakdown Zusammenbruch (m.) *tsoo-ZAHM-en-brukh*; (**mechanical**) Panne (f.) *PAHN-eh*

breakfast Frühstück (n.) *FREW-shtewk*; (**Swiss**) Zmorge (n.) *TSMORG-eh*

breakfast room Frühstückszimmer (n.) *FREW-shtewks-tsim-uh*

breast Brust (f.) *brust*

breath Atem (m.) *AAT-em*

breathe atmen *AAT-men*

breed Rasse (f.) *RAHSS-eh*

bridge Brücke (f.) *BREWK-eh*

briefcase Aktentasche (f.) *AHKT-en-tahsh-eh*

bring bringen *BRING-en*

broken gebrochen *geh-BROKH-en*, kaputt *kah-PUT*

bronzes Bronzen (pl.) *BRONTS-en*

brooch Brosche (f.) *BROHSH-eh*

brook Bach (m.) *bahkh*

brown braun *brown*

browse sich umsehen *zikh UM-zayen*

brunette braun *brown*

Brunswick Braunschweig (n.) *BROWN-shveyek*

brush Bürste (f.) *BEWRST-eh*

burn brennen *BREN-en*

burn Brandwunde (f.) *BRAHNT-vund-eh*

bus Bus (m.) *buss*; **bus stop** Bushaltestelle (f.) *BUSS-hahlt-eh-shtehl-eh*; **bus tour of the city** Stadtrundfahrt (f.) *SHTAHT-runt-faart*

business Geschäft (n.) *geh-SHEHFT*

business trip Geschäftsreise (f.) *geh-SHEHFTS-reyez-eh*

busy (**telephone**) besetzt *beh-ZEHTZT*

but aber *AAB-uh*

butcher Fleischer (*m.*) *FLEYESH-uh*, Metzger (*m.*) *METS-guh*

butter Butter (*f.*) *BUT-uh*

button Knopf (*m.*) *knopf*

buy kaufen *KOWF-en*

by durch *durkh*, von *fon*

C

cabin Kabine (*f.*) *kah-BEEN-eh*

cable-car railway Seilbahn (*f.*) *ZEYEL-baan*

cake Kuchen (*m.*) *KOOKH-en*

calculate rechnen *REHKH-nen*

call rufen *ROOF-en*

camera Kamera (*f.*) *KAH-meh-raa*

camping site Campingplatz (*m.*) *KEHMP-ing-plahts*

can (be able) kann *kahn*, können *KERN-en*

can Dose (*n.*) *DOHZ-eh*, Büchse (*f.*) *BEWKS-eh*; **can opener** Büchsenöffner (*m.*) *BEWKS-en-erfn-uh*

Canada Kanada (*n.*) *KAH-nah-dah*

canal Kanal (*m.*) *kah-NAAL*

candle Kerze (*f.*) *KERTS-eh*

candy Konfekt (*n.*) *kon-FEHKT*

cap Mütze (*f.*) *MEWTS-eh*

car Wagen (*m.*) *VAAG-en*, Auto (*n.*) *OW-toh*

carat Karat (*n.*) *kah-RAAT*

carburetor Vergaser (*m.*) *fehr-GAAZ-uh*

card Karte (*f.*) *KAART-eh*; **card tricks** Kartenkunststücke (*pl.*) *KAART-en-kunst-shtewk-eh*

Careful! Vorsicht! *FOUR-zikht*

(be) careful aufpassen *OWF-pahss-en*

carry tragen *TRAAG-en*; **have in stock** führen *FEWR-en*

carry-on luggage Handgepäck (*n.*) *HAHNT-geh-pehk*

carton Stange (*f.*) *SHTAHNG-eh*

carvings Schnitzereien (*pl.*) *SHNITS-eh-reye-en*

cash einlösen *EYEN-lerz-en*

cash Bargeld (*n.*) *BAAR-gelt*

cash desk Kasse (*f.*) *KAHSS-eh*

cassette Kassette (*f.*) *kah-SET-eh*

castle Schloss (*n.*) *shloss*, Burg (*f.*) *boork*

castle hotel Schlosshotel (*n.*) *SHLOSS-ho-tel*

cat Katze (*f.*) *KAHTS-eh*

catch fangen *FAHNG-en*

cathedral Dom (*m.*) *dohm*, Kathedrale (*f.*) *kah-teh-DRAAL-eh*

Catholic katholisch *kah-TOHL-ish*

caution Vorsicht (*f.*) *FOHR-zikht*

celebrate feiern *FEYE-ehrn*

cemetery Friedhof (*m.*) *FREET-hohf*

chain Kette (*f.*) *KEHT-eh*

chair Stuhl (*m.*) *shtool*

chambermaid Zimmermädchen (*n.*) *TSIM-uh-mayd-khen*

chamber music Kammermusik (*f.*) *KAHM-uh-moo-zeek*

champagne Sekt (*m.*) *zehkt*

change wechseln *VEHKS-eln*; **change trains**, etc. umsteigen *UM-shteyg-en*

change Kleingeld (*n.*) *KLEYEN-gelt*

charge Gebühr (*f.*) *geh-BEWR*

chart Tabelle (*f.*) *tah-BEL-eh*

chauffeur Fahrer (*m.*) *FAHR-uh*

cheap billig *BIL-ikh*

check kontrollieren *kon-tro-LEER-en*, prüfen *PREWF-en*

check Scheck (*m.*) *shehk*

checkers Dame (*f.*) *DAAM-eh*

checkmate schachmatt *SHAHKH-maht*

check out (depart) abreisen *AHP-reyez-en*

checkroom Garderobe (*f.*) *gahr-deh-ROHB-eh*

cheerful heiter *HEYET-uh*, munter *MUNT-uh*

Cheers! Prost! *prohst*

cheese Käse (*m.*) *KAYZ-eh*

chess Schach (*n.*) *shahkh*

chew kauern *KOW-ehrn*

chewing tobacco Kautabak (*m.*) *KOW-taa-bahk*

chic (elegant) schick *shik*

chicken Huhn (*n.*) *hoon*

child Kind (*n.*) *kint*

(be) chilled frösteln *FRERST-eln*

china Porzellan (*n.*) *por-tseh-LAAN*

China China (*n.*) *KHEE-nah*

chocolate Schokolade (*f.*) *shok-o-LAAD-eh*

chopped meat Hackfleisch (*n.*) *HAHK-fleyesh*

church Kirche (*f.*) *KIRKH-eh*

cigar Zigarre (*f.*) *tsi-GAHR-eh*

cigarette Zigarette (*f.*) *tsi-gah-RET-eh*

cigarette holder Zigaretten-spitze (*f.*) *tsi-gah-RET-en-shpits-eh*

cigarette lighter Feuerzeug (*n.*) *FOY-uh-tsoyk*

cinema Kino (*n.*) *KEEN-oh*

circulation Kreislauf (*m.*) *KREYES-lowf*

citizen Bürger (*m.*) *BEWRG-uh*; **citizen of the cosmos** Weltallbürger (*m.*) *VELT-ahl-bewrg-uh*; **citizen of the world** Weltbürger (*m.*) *VELT-bewrg-uh*

city Stadt (*f.*) *shtaht*

city center Stadtmitte (*f.*) *SHTAHT-mit-eh*, Zentrum (*n.*) *TSEHNT-rum*

city hall Rathaus (*n.*) *RAAT-howss*

class Klasse (*f.*) *KLAHSS-eh*

classical music klassische Musik (*f.*) *KLAHSS-ish-eh moo-ZEEK*

clean (*verb*) reinigen *REYEN-ig-en*

clean (*adjective*) rein *reyen*, sauber *ZOWB-uh*

cleansing cream Reinigungs-creme (*f.*) *REYEN-ig-ungs-kraym*

climb steigen *SHTEYEG-en*

clogged verstopft *fehr-SHTOPFT*

close schließen *SHLEESS-en*, zumachen *TSOO-mahkh-en*

close (near) nahe *NAA-eh*

closed geschlossen *geh-SHLOSS-en*, zu *tsoo*

clothes Kleidungsstücke (*pl.*) *KLEYED-ungs-shtewk-eh*, Kleider (*pl.*) *KLEYED-uh*

clothing store Bekleidungsge-schäft (*n.*) *beh-KLEYED-ungs-geh-shehft*

clubs (cards) Kreuz (*n.*) *kroyts*

coat Mantel (*m.*) *MAHNT-el*

coffee Kaffee (*m.*) *KAH-feh*

coffeehouse Kaffeehaus (*n.*) *kah-FAY hows*

cogwheel railroad Zahnrad-bahn (*f.*) *TSAAN-raat-baan*

cold kalt *kahlt*

(a) cold Erkältung (*f.*) *ehr-KEHLT-ung*

cold cuts Kalter Aufschnitt (*m.*) *KAHLT-uh OWF-shnit*

collect sammeln *ZAHM-eln*

collect call R-Gespräch (*n.*) *ehr-geh-SHPRAYKH*

cologne Kölnisch Wasser (*n.*) *KERLN-ish VAHSS-uh*

color Farbe (*f.*) *FAHRB-eh*

color chart Farbtabelle (*f.*) *FAHRP-tah-behl-eh*

color rinse Farbspülung (f.) *FAHRP-shpewl-ung*

comb kämmen *KEHM-en*

comb Kamm (m.) *kahm*

comedy Komödie (f.) *kom-ERD-yeh*, Lustspiel (n.) *LUST-shpeel*

comfort Komfort (m.) *kom-FOR*

comfortable bequemlich *beh-KVAYM-likh*

command befehlen *beh-FAYL-en*

commerce Handel (m.) *HAHND-el*

commercial geschäftlich *geh-SHEHFT-likh*

commission Gebühr (f.) *geh-BEWR*

compare vergleichen *fehr-GLEYEKH-en*

compartment Abteil (n.) *AHP-teyel*

compensation Schadenersatz (m.) *SHAAD-en-ehr-zahts*

concert Konzert (n.) *kon-TSEHRT*

conduct (an orchestra) dirigieren *di-ri-GEER-en*

connect anschließen *AHN-shleess-en*, verbinden *fehr-BIND-en*

constipation Verstopfung (f.) *fehr-SHTOPF-ung*

contact lenses Kontaktlinsen (pl.) *kon-TAHKT-linz-en*, Haftschalen (pl.) *HAHFT-shaal-en*

contain behalten *beh-HAHLT-en*

continue fortsetzen *FORT-zets-en*, weiter *VEYET-eh*

contraceptive Verhütungsmittel (n.) *fehr-HEWT-ungs-mit-el*

convenient praktisch *PRAHKT-ish*

conversation Gespräch (n.) *geh-SHPRAYKH*

cook kochen *KOKH-en*

cook Koch (m.) *kokh*, Köchin (f.) *KERKH-in*

cookies Kekse (pl.) *KAYKS-eh*

cool kühl *kewl*

copper Kupfer (n.) *KUPF-uh*

copy Exemplar (n.) *eks-ehm-PLAAR*

cordial herzlich *HEHRTS-likh*

corner Ecke (f.) *EK-eh*

corn plasters Hühneraugen-pflaster (pl.) *HEWN-ehr-owg-en-pflahst-uh*

cost kosten *KOST-en*

cotton Baumwolle (f.) *BOWM-vol-eh*

cough husten *HOOST-en*

cough drops Hustenbonbons (pl.) *HUST-en-bons-bons*

could könnte(n) *KERNT-eh(n)*

count zählen *TSAYL-en*

count (title) Graf (m.) *graaf*

countess Gräfin (f.) *GRAYF-in*

country Land (n.) *lahnt*

courtyard Hof (m.) *hohf*

cover decken *DEK-en*

cramp Krampf (m.) *krahmpf*

crazy verrückt *fehr-REWKT*, wahnsinnig *VAHN-zin-ikh*

cream Sahne (f.) *ZAAN-eh*

croissants Hörnchen (pl.) *HERN-khyen*, Kipfel (pl.) *KIPF-el*

crown Krone (f.) *KROHN-eh*

crumbs Brocken (pl.) *BROK-en*

cuckoo clock Kuckucksuhr (f.) *KUK-uks-oor*

cuff links Manschettenknöpfe (pl.) *mahn-SHEHT-en-knerpf-eh*

cup Tasse (f.) *TAHSS-eh*

curls Locken (pl.) *LOK-en*

curtains Vorhänge (pl.) *FOR-hehng-eh*

curves Windungen (pl.) *VIND-ung-en*

customs Zoll (m.) *tsol*

customs official Zollbeamte (*m.*) *TSOL-beh-ahmt-eh*

cut schneiden *SHNEYED-en*

cut (cards) abheben *ahp-HAYB-en*

cutlery Essbesteck (*n.*) *ESS-beh-shtek*

D

damage beschädigen *beh-SHAYD-ig-en*, schaden *SHAAD-en*

dance (*verb*) tanzen *TAHNTS-en*

dance (*noun*) Tanz (*m.*) *tahnts*

dancing shoes Tanzschuhe (*pl.*) *TAHNTS-shoo-eh*

danger Gefahr (*f.*) *geh-FAAR*, Lebensgefahr (*f.*) *LAY-bens-geh-faar*

dangerous gefährlich *geh-FAYR-likh*

dark dunkel *DUNK-el*

daughter Tochter (*f.*) *TOKHT-uh*

day Tag (*m.*) *taak*

dealer Händler (*m.*) *HEHNT-luh*

deed Tat (*f.*) *taat*

deep tief *teef*

defective defekt *deh-FEHKT*

delay Verspätung (*f.*) *fehr-SHPAYT-ung*

delicatessen Delikatessengeschäft (*n.*) *deh-li-kah-TESS-en-geh-shehft*

delicious lecker *LEK-uh*

demand verlangen *fehr-LAHNG-en*

Denmark Dänemark (*n.*) *DAYN-eh-mahrk*

dentist Zahnarzt (*m.*) *TSAAN-ahrtst*

dentures Gebiss (*n.*) *geh-BISS*

deodorant Desodorans (*n.*) *dehz-odor-AHNS*

department store Warenhaus (*n.*) *VAAR-en-howss*

departure Abfahrt (*f.*) *AHP-faart*, Abreise (*f.*) *AHP-reyez-eh*; **(by plane)** Abflug (*m.*) *AHP-flook*

despite trotz *trots*

dessert Nachtisch (*m.*) *NAHKH-tish*

determine feststellen *FEHST-shtehl-en*

detour Umleitung (*f.*) *UM-leyet-ung*

develop entwickeln *ent-VIK-eln*

diabetes Zuckerkrankheit (*f.*) *TSUK-uh-krahnk-heyet*

diabetic Diabetiker (*m.*) *dee-ah-BAYT-ik-uh*

dial wählen *VAYL-en*

dial direct durchwählen *DOORKH-vayl-en*

diamond Diamant (*m.*) *dee-ah-MAHNT*

diamonds (cards) Karo (*n.*) *KAAR-oh*

diapers Windeln (*pl.*) *VIND-eln*

diarrhea Durchfall (*m.*) *DOORKH-fahl*

dictionary Wörterbuch (*n.*) *VER-tehr-bookh*

difficult schwer *shvayr*

dining car Speisewagen (*m.*) *SHPEYEZ-eh-vaag-en*

dining room Esszimmer (*n.*) *ESS-tsim-uh*, Speisesaal (*m.*) *SHPEYEZ-eh-zaal*

dinner Abendessen (*n.*) *AAB-ehnt-ess-en*

direct direkt *dee-REHKT*

direction Richtung (*f.*) *RIKHT-ung*

dirty schmutzig *SHMUTS-ikh*, dreckig *DREK-ikh*

discotheque Diskothek (*f.*) *dis-koh-TAYK*

discover entdecken *ehnt-DECK-en*

disgusting ekelhaft *AYK-el-hahft*

dislocated verrenkt *fehr-REHNKT*

disposable wegwerfbar *VEHK-vehrf-bahr*

disturb stören *SHTERR-en*

dive tauchen *TOWKH-en*

divine göttlich *GERT-likh*

dizzy schwindlich *SHVINT-likh*

do tun *toon*

docks Hafenanlagen (*pl.*) *HAAF-en-ahn-laag-en*

doctor Arzt (*m.*) *ahrtst*

dog Hund (*m.*) *hunt*, Hündin (*f.*) *HEWND-in*

dog biscuits Hundekuchen (*pl.*) *HUND-eh-kookh-en*

doll Puppe (*f.*) *PUP-eh*

door Tür (*f.*) *tewr*

dosage Dosis (*f.*) *DOH-ziss*

double bed Doppelbett (*n.*) *DOP-el-beht*, französisches Bett (*n.*) *frahn-TSER-zish-ehs bet*

double room Doppelzimmer (*n.*) *DOP-el-tsim-uh*

down unten *UNT-en*

downtown Zentrum (*n.*) *TSEHNT-rum*

dozen Dutzend (*n.*) *DUTS-ehnt*

draw zeichnen *TSEYEKH-nen*

drawing Zeichnung (*f.*) *TSEYEKH-nung*

dream Traum (*m.*) *trowm*

dreamy träumerisch *TROY-mehrish*

dress Kleid (*n.*) *kleyet*

drink trinken *TRINK-en*

drink Getränk (*n.*) *geh-TREHNK*

drinkable trinkbar *TRINK-bahr*

drinking water Trinkwasser (*n.*) *TRINK-vahss-uh*

drive fahren *FAAR-en*

drive-in movie Auto-Kino *OW-toh-kee-noh*

driver's license Füherschein (*m.*) *FEWR-ehr-sheyen*

drops Tropfen (*pl.*) *TROPF-en*

drugstore Drogerie (*f.*) *dro-geh-REE*, Apotheke (*f.*) *ah-poh-TAYK-eh*

dry trocken *TROK-en*

dry cleaning chemische Reinigung (*f.*) *KHAYM-ish-eh REYEN-ig-ung*

duck Ente (*f.*) *ENT-eh*

due fällig *FEHL-ikh*

dumpling Kloss (*m.*) *kloss*

duty Pflicht (*f.*) *pflikht*

duty-free zollfrei *TSOL-freye*

E

ear Ohr (*n.*) *ohr*

ear drops Ohrentropfen (*pl.*) *OHR-en-tropf-en*

early früh *frew*

earring Ohrring (*m.*) *OHR-ring*

earth Erde (*f.*) *EHRD-eh*

east Osten (*m.*) *OST-en*

easy leicht *leyekht*

easy-care pflegeleicht *PFLAYG-eh-leyekht*

eat essen *EHS-en*

edible essbar *EHS-bahr*

edition Ausgabe (*f.*) *OWSS-gaab-eh*

eggs Eier (*pl.*) *EYE-uh*

elbow Ellbogen (*m.*) *EL-bohg-en*

elegant elegant *eh-lay-GAHNT*

elevator Aufzug (*m.*) *OWF-tsook*

elevator operator Liftjunge (*m.*) *LIFT-yung-eh*

embroidered articles Stickereien (*pl.*) *SHTICK-eh-reye-en*

emeralds Smaragde (*pl.*) *smah-RAHKT-eh*

emergency Notfall (*m.*) *NOHT-fahl*

emergency exit Notausgang
(*m.*) *NOHT-owss-gahng*
emperor Kaiser (*m.*) *KEYEZ-uh*
empire Reich (*n.*) *reyekh*
empty leer *layr*
end Ende (*n.*) *END-eh*
engagement ring Verlobungsring (*m.*) *fehr-LOHB-ungs-
ring*
England England (*n.*) *EHNG-
lahnt*
English-speaking englischsprachig *EHNG-lish-
shprahkh-ikh*
engraving Stich (*m.*) *shtikh*
enjoy genießen *geh-NEESS-en*
enlarge vergrößern *fehr-
GRERSS-ehrn*
enlargement Vergrößerung
(*f.*) *fehr-GRERSS-ehr-ung*
ennoble veredeln *fehr-AYD-len*
enough genug *geh-NOOK*
enrich bereichern *beh-
REYEKH-ehrn*
entitled berechtigt *beh-
REHKHT-ikht*
entrance Eingang (*m.*) *EYEN-
gahng*, Eintritt (*m.*) *EYEN-
trit*; **(to the highway)**
Einfahrt (*f.*) *EYEN-faart*
envelope Umschlag (*m.*) *UM-
shlahk*
equipment Ausrüstung (*f.*)
OWSS-rewst-ung
equivalent Äquivalent (*n.*) *ay-
kvi-vah-LEHNT*
eraser Radiergummi (*m.*) *rah-
DEER-gum-ee*
especially besonders *beh-
ZOND-ehrs*
eternal ewig *AYV-ikh*
Europe Europa (*n.*) *oy-ROH-
pah*
even selbst *zelpst*
evening Abend (*m.*) *AAB-ehnt*
evening dress Abendgarderobe
(*f.*) *AAB-ehnt-gahr-deh-rohb-
eh*

evening gown Abendkleid (*n.*)
AAB-ehnt-kleyet
every jed- *yayd*
everyone jeder *YAYD-uh*
everything alles *AHL-ehss*
everywhere überall *EWB-ehr-
ahl*
excellent ausgezeichnet
OWSS-geh-tseyekh-net
except außer *OWSS-uh*
exchange (rate of) Wechselkurs (*m.*) *VEHKS-el-koorss*
exchange (*verb*) auswechseln
OWSS-vehk-seln
excursion Ausflug (*m.*) *OWS-
flook*
excuse entschuldigen *ehnt-
SHULD-ig-en*
exit Ausgang (*m.*) *OWS-gahng*,
Ausfahrt (*f.*) *OWS-faart*
exotic exotisch *eks-OHT-ish*
expect erwarten *ehr-VAART-en*
expenses Kosten (*pl.*) *KOST-en*
expensive teuer *TOY-uh*
explain erklären *ehr-KLAYR-en*
express Express (*m.*) *eks-
PREHS*, Fernschnellzug (*m.*)
FEHRN-shnel-tsook
extra extra *EKS-traa*,
zusätzlich *TSOO-zehts-likh*
eye Auge (*n.*) *OWG-eh*
eyebrow pencil Augenbrauenstift (*m.*) *OWG-en-brow-en-
shtift*
eyeglasses Brille (*f.*) *BRIL-eh*
eyeliner Lidstift (*m.*) *LEET-
shtift*
eye shadow Lidschatten (*m.*)
LEET-shaht-en

F

face Gesicht (*n.*) *geh-ZIKHT*
face pack Gesichtsmaske (*f.*)
geh-ZIKHTS-mahsk-eh
fairy tale Märchen (*n.*)
MAYRKH-en
faith Glaube (*m.*) *GLOWB-eh*

fall fallen *FAHL-en;* **autumn** Herbst (*m.*) *hehrpst*

falling rocks Steinschlag (*m.*) *SHTEYEN-shlahk*

false falsch *fahlsh*

false teeth Zahnersatz (*m.*) *TSAAN-ehr-zahts*

family Familie (*f.*) *fah-MEEL-yeh*

famous berühmt *beh-REWMT*

fan Ventilator (*m.*) *vehn-ti-LAAT-ohr*

fantastic fabelhaft *FAAB-el-hahft*

far weit *veyet*

farm Bauernhof (*m.*) *BOW-ehrn-hohf*

farmer Bauer (*m.*) *BOW-uh*

fat Fett (*n.*) *feht,* dick *dik*

favorable günstig *GEWNST-ikh*

fear Angst (*f.*) *ahngst*

fear Angst haben *ahngst HAAB-en*

Federal Republic Bundesrepublik (*n.*) *BUND-ehs-reh-pub-leek*

feel fühlen *FEWL-en*

ferry Fähre (*f.*) *FAYR-eh*

festival Fest (*n.*) *fehst*

festival performance Festspiel (*n.*) *FEST-shpeel*

fever Fieber (*m.*) *FEEB-uh*

fiber Faser (*f.*) *FAAZ-uh*

field Feld (*n.*) *fehlt*

file Feile (*f.*) *FEYEL-eh*

fill füllen *FEWL-en*

filled up (hotels) belegt *beh-LAYKT*

filling Füllung (*f.*) *FEWL-ung*

film Film (*m.*) *film*

filter Filter (*m.*) *FILT-uh*

final sale Schlussverkauf (*m.*) *SHLUSS-fehr-kowf*

find finden *FIND-en*

fine fein *feyen*

finger Finger (*m.*) *FING-uh*

finished fertig *FEHRT-ikh*

fire Feuer (*n.*) *FOY-uh*

first erst *ehrst*

first-aid kit Verbandkasten (*m.*) *fehr-BAHNT-kahst-en*

fish Fisch (*m.*) *fish*

fish bone Gräte (*f.*) *GRAYT-eh*

fishing Angeln (*n.*) *AHNG-eln*

fishing license Angelschein (*m.*) *AHNG-el-sheyen*

fit passen *PAHSS-en*

fix reparieren *reh-paa-REER-en*

flea market Flohmarkt (*m.*) *FLOH-mahrkt*

flight Flug (*m.*) *flook*

flint Feuerstein (*m.*) *FOY-uh-shteyen*

floor Etage (*f.*) *ay-TAAZH-eh,* Stock (*m.*) *shtok*

flour Mehl (*n.*) *mayl*

flow fließen *FLEESS-en*

flower Blume (*f.*) *BLOOM-eh*

flu Grippe (*f.*) *GRIP-eh*

fly fliegen *FLEEG-en*

folk dances Volkstänze (*pl.*) *FOLKS-tehnts-eh*

folk music Volksmusik (*f.*) *FOLKS-moo-zeek*

folk songs Volkslieder (*pl.*) *FOLKS-leed-uh*

food Essen (*n.*) *ESS-en,* Speise (*f.*) *SHPEYEZ-eh;* **animal fodder** Futter (*n.*) *FUT-uh*

foot Fuß (*n.*) *fooss*

football Fußball (*m.*) *FOOSS-bahl*

foot powder Fußpuder (*m.*) *FOOSS-pood-uh*

for für *fewr,* denn *den*

forbidden verboten *fehr-BOHT-en*

foreign fremd *frehmt*

foreigner Ausländer *OWSS-lehnd-uh*

forest Wald (*m.*) *vahlt*

forget vergessen *fehr-GEHSS-en*

forgive verzeihen *fehr-TSEYE-en*

fork Gabel (f.) *GAAB-el*

form Form (f.) *form*

format Format (n.) *for-MAAT*

fortress Burg (f.) *boork*, Festung (f.) *FEST-ung*

fortune Venmögen (n.) *fehr-MERG-en*

fountain Brunnen (m.) *BRUN-en*

fracture Bruch (m.) *brookh*

frame Rahmen (m.) *RAAM-en*; **(eyeglasses)** Fassung (f.) *FASS-ung*

France Frankreich (n.) *FRAHNK-reyekh*

Franconia Franken (n.) *FRAHNK-en*

free *(adjective)* frei *freye*, kostenlos *KOSTEN-lohss*

free *(verb)* befreien *beh-FREYE-en*

freeze frieren *FREER-en*

French französisch *frahn-TSER-zish*

fresh frisch *frish*

Friday Freitag (m.) *FREYE-taak*

fried brat *braat*

fried eggs Spiegeleier (pl.) *SHPEE-gel-eye-uh*

friend Freund (m.) *froynt*, Freundin (f.) *FROYND-in*

friendly freundlich *FROYNT-likh*

from von *fon*, aus *owss*

frontier Grenze (f.) *GREHNTS-eh*

frost Frost (m.) *frost*

frozen gefroren *geh-FROH-ren*

fruit Frucht (f.) *frukht*, Obst (n.) *ohpst*

frying pan Bratpfanne (f.) *BRAAT-pfahn-eh*

full voll *foll*; **full room and board** Vollverpflegung (f.) *FOLL-fehr-pflayg-ung*

function funktionieren *funkts-yon-NEER-en*

furniture Möbel (pl.) *MERB-el*

furrier Kürschner (m.) *KEWRSH-nehr*

furs Pelze (pl.) *PELTS-eh*

further weiter *VEYET-uh*

G

gambling casino Spielkasino (n.) *SHPEEL-kah-zee-noh*

game Spiel (n.) *shpeel*; **wild game** Wild (n.) *vilt*

garage Garage (f.) *gah-RAA-zheh*

gardener Gärtner (m.) *GEHRT-nuh*

gardens Gärten (pl.) *GEHRT-en*, Grünanlagen (pl.) *GREWN-ahn-lahg-en*

gas Benzin (n.) *ben-TSEEN*

gas station Tankstelle (f.) *TAHNK-shtehl-eh*

general delivery postlagernd *POST-laag-ehrnt*

genuine echt *ehkht*

German deutsch *doytsh*

Germany Deutschland (n.) *DOYTSH-lahnt*

get (fetch) holen *HOHL-en*

get (obtain) bekommen *beh-KOM-en*; **get gas** tanken *TAHNK-en*; **get into a vehicle** einsteigen *EYEN-shteyeg-en*; **get out of a vehicle** aussteigen *OWSS-shteyeg-en*; **get on (vehicle, ship)** besteigen *beh-SHTEYEG-en*

gift Geschenk (n.) *geh-SHEHNK*

gin rummy Rommé (n.) *ROM-may*

gipsy Zigeuner (m.) *tsi-GOYN-uh*

girl Mädchen (n.) *MAYT-khen*

give geben *GAYB-en*

gladly gern *gehrn*

glands Drüsen (pl.) *DREWZ-en*

gloomy düster *DEWST-uh*

glossy finish Hochglanz (*m.*) *HOHKH-glahnts*

gloves Handshuhe (pl.) *HAHNT-shoo-eh*

glow glühen *GLEW-en*

glue Leim (*m.*) *leyem*

go gehen *GAY-en*

goblet Becher (*m.*) *BEHKH-uh*

god Gott (*m.*) *got*

gods Götter (*pl.*) *GERT-uh*

gold Gold (*n.*) *golt*

gold plate vergoldet *fehr-GOLD-et*

golf clubs Golfschläger (*pl.*) *GOLF-shlayg-uh*

golf course Golfplatz (*pl.*) *GOLF-plahts*

good gut *goot*

good-bye auf Wiedersehen *owf VEED-uh-zayen*, auf Wiederschauen *owf VEED-uh-show-en*

goodness Güte (*f.*) *GEWT-eh*

goose Gans (*f.*) *gahns*

gourmet Feinshmecker (*m.*) *FEYEN-shmehk-uh*

gourmet foods Feinkost (*f.*) *FEYEN-kost*

grace Gnade (*f.*) *GNAAD-eh*

gracious gnädig *GNAYD-ikh*

grammar Grammatik (*f.*) *grah-MAHT-ik*

gray grau *grow*

Great Britain Großbritannien (*n.*) *gross-bri-TAHN-yen*

Greece Griechenland (*n.*) *GREEKH-en-lahnt*

green grün *grewn*

greenish grünlich *GREWN-likh*

greet grüßen *GREWSS-en*

grilled gegrillt *geh-GRILLT*

grocery store Lebensmittel-geschäft *LAYB-ens-mi-tehl-geh-shehft*

grooves (in road) Spurrillen (*pl.*) *SHPOOR-ril-en*

grow wachsen *VAHKS-en*

guidebook Reiseführer (*m.*) *REYEZ-eh-fewr-uh*

guided tour Führung (*f.*) *FEWR-ung*

guilt Schuld (*f.*) *shult*

gums Zahnfleisch (*n.*) *TSAAN-fleyesh*

gymnasium Turnhalle (*f.*) *TURN-hahl-eh*

gynecologist Frauenarzt (*m.*) *FROW-en-ahrtst*

H

habit Gewohnheit (*f.*) *geh-VOHN-heyet*

had hatte *HAHT-eh*

hair Haar (*n.*) *haar*

hair bun Knoten (*m.*) *KNOHT-en*

hairdo Frisur (*f.*) *FREEZ-oor*

hair dryer Haartrockner (*m.*) *HAAR-trok-nuh*

hair spray Haarspray (*m.*) *HAAR-shpray*

hair tonic Haarwasser (*n.*) *HAAR-vahss-uh*

half Hälfte (*f.*) *HEHLFT-eh*, halb *hahlp*

half-board Halbpension (*f.*) *HAHLP-pen-zee-ohn*

hall Halle (*f.*) *HAHL-eh*

hand Hand (*f.*) *hahnt*

hand carved handgeschnitzt *HAHNT-geh-shnitst*

hand mirror Handspiegel (*m.*) *HAHNT-shpeeg-el*

hand painted handgemalt *HAHNT-geh-maalt*

hang hängen *HEHNG-en*

hangers (clothes) Kleiderbügel (*pl.*) *KLEYED-uh-bewg-el*

hangover Kater (*m.*) *KAAT-uh*

happy glücklich *GLEWK-likh*

hard hart *hahrt*

hard-boiled hartgekocht *HAHRT-geh-kokht*

hardware store Eisenwaren-handlung (f.) *EYEZ-en-vaar-en-hahnt-lung*

harmful schädlich *SHAYT-likh*

has hat *haht*

haste Eile (f.) *EYEL-eh*

hat Hut (m.) *hoot*

have haben *HAAB-en*

hay fever Heuschnupfen (m.) *HOY-shnup-fen*

he er *ehr*

head Kopf (m.) *kopf*

headache Kopfschmerzen (pl.) *KOPF-shmehrts-en*

heal heilen *HEYEL-en*

health Gesundheit (f.) *geh-ZUNT-heyet*

health-food store Reformhaus (n.) *reh-FORM-howss*

healthy gesund *geh-ZUNT*

hear hören *HER-en*

heart Herz (n.) *hehrts*

heart trouble herzkrankheit *HEHRTS-krahnk-heyet*

heat Hitze (f.) *HITS-eh*, Heizung (f.) *HEYETS-ung*

heater Heizapparat (m.) *HEYETS-ah-pah-raat*

heath Heide (f.) *HEYED-eh*

heaven Himmel (m.) *HIM-el*

heavy traffic starker Verkehr (m.) *SHTAHRK-uh fehr-KAYR*

heel Ferse (f.) *FEHRZ-eh*

helicopter Hubschrauber (m.) *HOOP-shrowb-uh*

hell Hölle (f.) *HERL-eh*

help helfen *HELF-en*

help Hilfe (f.) *HILF-eh*; **help oneself** sich bedienen *zikh beh-DEEN-en*

hematite Blutstein (m.) *BLOOT-shteyen*

her sie *zee*, ihr *eer*

herb Kraut (n.) *krowt*

herbal liqueur Kräuterlikör (m.) *KROY-tehr-li-kehr*

herbal tea Kräutertee (m.) *KROY-tehr-tay*

here hier *heer*

high hoch *hohkh*

high tide Flut (f.) *floot*

highway Autobahn (f.) *OW-toh-baan*

hike wandern *VAHND-ehrn*

hiking trails Wanderwege (pl.) *VAHND-uh-vayg-eh*

hill Hügel (m.) *HEWG-el*

him ihn *een*, ihm *eem*

hip Hüfte (f.) *HEWFT-eh*

hire out vermieten *fehr-MEET-en*

hits (musical) Schlager (pl.) *SHLAAG-uh*

hold halten *HAHLT-en*

hole Loch (n.) *lokh*

holy heilig *HEYEL-ikh*

home Heim (n.) *heyem*

(at) home zu Hause *tsoo HOWZ-eh*

homeland Heimat (f.) *HEYEM-aat*, Heimatland (n.) *HEYEM-aat-lahnt*

honey Honig (m.) *HOHN-ikh*

honk (car) hupen *HOOP-en*

honor ehren *AYR-en*

hope hoffen *HOF-en*; **hopefully** hoffentlich *hof-en-likh*

horrible schrecklich *SHREHK-likh*

horse Pferd (n.) *pfayrt*

hospital Krankenhaus *KRAHNK-en-howss*

hospitality Gastfreundlichkeit (f.) *GAHST-froynt-likh-keyet*

hot heiß *heyess*

hotel Hotel (n.) *ho-TEL*

hour Stunde (f.) *SHTUND-eh*

house Haus (n.) *howss*

how wie *vee*; **how much?** wieviel? *VEE-feel*

human being Mensch (m.) *mehnsh*

Hungary Ungarn (n.) *UN-gahrn*

hunger Hunger (m.) *HUNG-uh*

hungry hungrig *HUNG-rikh*

hunt jagen *YAAG-en*

hunt Jagd (f.) *yahkt*
hurry eilen *EYEL-en*
hurry Eile (f.) *EYEL-eh*
hurt weh tun *vay toon*,
schmerzen *SHMEHRTS-en*
husband Mann (m.) *mahn*
hut Hütte (f.) *HEWT-eh*
hydrofoil Luftkissenboot (n.)
LUFT-kiss-en-boht

I

I ich *ikh*
ice Eis (n.) *eyess*
ice cream Eis (n.) *eyess*
ice cubes Eiswürfel (pl.)
EYESS-vewrf-el
if wern *vehn*, ob *op*
ignite anzünden *AHN-tsewnd-en*
ignition system Zündung (f.)
TSEWND-ung
immediately sofort *zoh-FORT*, gleich *gleykh*
immersible heater Tauchsieder (m.) *TOWKH-zeed-uh*
imperial kaiserlich *KEYEZ-ehr-likh*
in back hinten *HINT-en*
included einbegriffen *EYEN-beh-grif-en*
India Indien (n.) *IND-yen*
indigestion Verdauungsstörung (f.) *fehr-DOW-ungs-shterr-ung*
inexpensive billig *BIL-ikh*,
preiswert *PREYESS-vehrt*
information Auskunft (f.)
OWSS-kunft
in front vorne *FORN-eh*
injection Spritze (f.)
SHPRITS-eh
inn Gasthaus (n.) *GAHST-howss*,
Gasthof (m.) *GAHST-hohf*
in order (OK) in Ordnung *in ORT-nung*
inscription Inschrift (f.) *IN-shrift*

insect bites Insektenstiche
(pl.) *in-ZEHKT-en-shtikh-eh*
insomnia Schlaflosigkeit (f.)
SHLAAF-loh-zikh-keyet
institution Anstalt (f.) *AHN-shtahlt*
instruction Unterricht (m.)
UNT-ehr-rikht
insurance Versicherung (f.)
fehr-ZIKH-ehr-ung
(be) interested in sich
interessieren für *zikh in-teh-reh-SEER-en fewr*
introduce vorstellen *FOR-shtel-en*
invite einladen *EYEN-laad-en*
iodine Jod (n.) *yoht*
Ireland Irland (n.) *EER-lahnt*
iron bügeln *BEWG-eln*
iron Bügeleisen (n.) *BEWG-el-eyez-en*
is ist *ist*; **(passive)** wird *veert*
island Insel (f.) *INZ-el*
Italy Italien (n.) *i-TAAL-yen*
ivory Elfenbein (n.) *ELF-en-beyen*

J

jack (cards) Bube (m.)
BOOB-eh
jacket Jacke (f.) *YAHK-eh*
jam Marmelade (f.) *mahr-meh-LAAD-eh*
jeweler Juwelier (m.) *yoov-eh-LEER*
jewels Schmuck (m.) *shmuk*
join beitreten *BEYE-trayt-en*
joint Gelenk (n.) *geh-LENK*
joy Freude (f.) *FROYD-eh*,
Lust (f.) *lust*
juice Saft (m.) *zahft*

K

key Schlüssel (m.) *SHLEWSS-el*
kidneys Nieren (pl.) *NEER-en*

kilometer Kilometer (*m.*) *ki-lo-MAYT-uh*

kind (type) Sorte (*f.*) *ZORT-eh*; **(good)** gütig *GEWT-ikh*

kindness Güte (*f.*) *GEWT-eh*

king König (*m.*) *KERN-ikh*

kiss küssen *KEWSS-en*

kiss Kuss (*m.*) *kuss*

kitchen Küche (*f.*) *KEWKH-eh*

knee Knie (*n.*) *knee*

knife Messer (*n.*) *MESS-uh*

knight Ritter (*m.*) *RIT-uh*; **(chess)** Springer (*m.*) *SHPRING-uh*

knitwear Stricksachen (*f.*) *SHTRIK-zah-khen*

know kennen *KEN-en*, wissen *VISS-en*

L

label Etikette (*f.*) *eh-tee-KEHT-eh*

(be) lacking fehlen *FAYL-en*

ladies' hairdresser Damenfriseur (*m.*) *DAAM-en-free-zewr*

ladies' room Damentoilette (*f.*) *DAAM-en-toy-let-eh*

lake See (*m.*) *zay*

lamb Lammfleisch (*n.*) *LAHM-fleyesh*

lamp Lampe (*f.*) *LAHMP-eh*

land Land (*n.*) *lahnt*

land landen *LAHND-en*

landscape Landschaft (*f.*) *LAHNT-shahft*

lane Gasse (*f.*) *GAHSS-eh*

last (*adjective*) letzt *lehtst*

last (*verb*) dauern *DOW-ehrn*; **last stop** Endstation (*f.*) *EHNT-shtah-tsyohn*

late spät *shpayt*

later später *SHPAYT-uh·*

launder waschen *VAHSH-en*

laundry Wäscherei (*f.*) *veh-sheh-REYE*

law Recht (*n.*) *rekht*

lawsuit Prozess (*m.*) *pro-TSESS*

lawyer Rechtsanwalt (*m.*) *REHKHTS-ahn-vahlt*

lawn Rasen (*m.*) *RAAZ-en*

laxative Abführmittel (*n.*) *AHP-fewr-mit-el*

lay legen *LAYG-en*

lazy faul *fowl*

lead führen *FEWR-en*

leading role Hauptrolle (*f.*) *HOWPT-rol-eh*

lean mager *MAAG-uh*

learn lernen *LEHRN-en*

leather Leder (*n.*) *LAYD-eh*

leather goods Lederwaren (*pl.*) *LAYD-uh-vaar-en*

leave lassen *LAHSS-en*, verlassen *fehr-LAHSS-en*, abreisen *AHP-reyez-en*; **leave a deposit** etwas hinterlegen *EHT-vaas HINT-ehr-layg-en*

left links *links*

leg Bein (*n.*) *beyen*

lemon Zitrone (*f.*) *tsi-TROHN-eh*

letter Brief (*m.*) *breef*

library Bibliothek (*f.*) *bib-lee-oh-TAYK*

lick lecken *LEK-en*

lie (be situated) liegen *LEEG-en*; **(prevaricate)** lügen *LEWG-en*

lie down sich hinlegen *zikh HIN-layg-en*

life Leben (*n.*) *LAYB-en*

light Licht (*n.*) *likht*; **light in color** hell *hell*

like gern haben *gehrn HAAB-en*, mögen *MERG-en*, gefallen *geh-FAHL-en*

line Linie (*f.*) *LEEN-yeh*; **telephone line** Leitung (*f.*) *LEYET-ung*

linen goods Leinenzeug (*n.*) *LEYEN-en tsoyk*

lingerie Damenunterwäsche (*f.*) *DAAM-en-un-tehr-vehsh-eh*

lip Lippe (f.) *LIP-eh*

lipstick Lippenstift (m.) *LIP-en-shtift*

liqueur Likör (m.) *li-KERR*

liquor store Spirituosenhandlung (f.) *spee-ree-tu-OHZ-en-hahnt-lung*

little wenig *VAYN-ikh*; **a little** ein bisschen *eyen BISS-khen*; **a little more** etwas mehr *EHT-vahss mayr*

live (be alive) leben *LAYB-en*; **(reside)** wohnen *VOHN-en*

lively lebhaft *LAYB-hahft*

liver Leber (f.) *LAYB-uh*

living room Wohnzimmer (n.) *VOHN-tsim-uh*

local call Ortsgespräch (n.) *ORTS-geh-shpraykh*

local train Personenzug (m.) *pehr-ZOHN-en-tsook*

lock abschließen *AHP-shleess-en*

locker Schließfach (n.) *SHLEESS-fahkh*

long lang *lahng*

long-distance call Ferngespräch (n.) *FEHRN-geh-shpraykh*

long-playing record Langspielplatte (f.) *LAHNG-shpeel-plaht-eh*

look at ansehen *AHN-zay-en*, schauen *SHOW-en*

look for suchen *ZOOKH-en*

look up (reference) nachschlagen *NAHKH-shlaag-en*

loose los *lohs*

lose verlieren *fehr-LEER-en*

lost verloren *fehr-LOHR-en*; **(while driving)** verfahren *fehr-FAAR-en*; **(while walking)** verlaufen *fehr-LOWF-en*

lost and found Fundbüro (n.) *FUNT-bew-roh*

loud laut *lowt*

love lieben *LEEB-en*

love Liebe (f.) *LEEB-eh*

lovely lieblich *LEEP-likh*

loyal treu *troy*

low niedrig *NEED-rikh*

low tide Ebbe (f.) *EHB-uh*

luck Glück (n.) *glewk*

luggage Gepäck (n.) *geh-PEHK*

luggage carts Kofferkuhlis (pl.) *KOF-uh-koo-lees*

luggage locker Schließfach (n.) *SHLEESS-fahkh*

lunch Mittagessen (n.) *MIT-taak-ess-en*

Luxembourg Luxemburg (n.) *LUKS-em-boork*

luxury Luxus (m.) *LUKS-uss*

M

machine Maschine (f.) *mah-SHEEN-eh*

magazine Illustrierte (f.) *i-lus-TREERT-eh*, Zeitschrift (f.) *TSEYET-shrift*

magic Zauber (m.) *TSOWB-uh*

mail Post (f.) *post*

mail auf die Post tragen *owf dee post TRAAG-en*

mailbox Briefkasten (m.) *BREEF-kahst-en*

main railroad station Hauptbahnhof (m.) *HOWPT-baan-hohf*

make machen *MAHKH-en*

man Mann (m.) *mahn*

manager Geschäftsführer (m.) *geh-SHEHFTS-fewr-uh*

manicure Maniküre (f.) *MAH-ni-kewr-eh*

map Karte (f.) *KAART-eh*; **map of the city** Stadtplan (m.) *SHTAHT-plaan*

March Marz (m.) *mehrts*

market Markt (m.) *mahrkt*

married verheiratet *fehr-HEYE-raat-et*

marry heiraten *HEYE-raat-en*

mass (ritual) Messe (f.) MES-eh

massage Massage (f.) mah-SAA-zheh

master Meister (m.) MEYES-tuh

matches Streichhölzer (pl.) SHTREYEKH-hert-tsuh

material Stoff (m.) shtoff

matte finish matt maht

matter Sache (f.) ZAHKH-eh

may darf dahrf, dürfen DEWRF-en

May Mai (m.) meye

maybe vielleicht fee-LEYEKHT

me mich mikh, mir meer

meadow Wiese (f.) VEEZ-eh

meal Mahlzeit (f.) MAAL-tseyet

mean bedeuten beh-DOYT-en, heißen HEYESS-en

meaning Bedeutung (f.) beh-DOYT-ung

measure Maß (n.) maass

measure messen MESS-en

meat Fleisch (n.) fleyesh

mechanic Mechaniker (m.) meh-KHAAN-ik-ehr

medical ärzlich EHRTS-likh

medicine Medikament (n.) may-di-kah-MENT

medium mittel MIT-el

medium-boiled wachsweich-gekocht VAHKS-veyekh-geh-kokht

meet treffen TREF-en

memento Andenken (n.) ahn-DENK-en

mend ausbessern OWSS-behss-ehrn

men's room Herrentoilette (f.) HEHR-en-toy-let-eh

menu Speisekarte (f.) SHPEYEZ-eh-kaart-eh

merry froh froh, fröhlich FRERL-ikh

message Nachricht (f.) NAHKH-rikht

middle Mitte (f.) MIT-eh

middle-class bügerlich BEWRG-ehr-likh

midnight Mitternacht (f.) MIT-ehr-nahkht

mild mild milt

milk Milch (f.) milkh

mineral water Mineralwasser (n.) min-eh-RAAL-vahss-uh

minimum charge Mindestge-bühr (f.) MIND-est-geh-bewr

minister (clergyman) Pfarrer (m.) PFAHR-uh

mink coat Nerzmantel (m.) NEHRTS-mahnt-el

mirror Spiegel (m.) SHPEEG-el

miscalculate verrechnen fehr-REHKH-nen

Miss Fräulein (n.) FROY-leyen

miss versäumen fehr-ZOYM-en, verpassen fehr-PASS-en

Mister Herr (m.) hehr

mixture Mischung (f.) MISH-ung

modern modern mo-DEHRN

modest bescheiden beh-SHEYED-en

moist towelettes Erfrisch-ungstücher (pl.) ehr-FRISH-ungs-tewkh-uh

moment Augenblick (m.) OWG-en-blik

monastery Kloster (n.) KLOHST-uh

Monday Montag (m.) MOHN-taak

money Geld (n.) gelt

money order Postanweisung (f.) POST-ahn-veyez-ung

month Monat (m.) MOHN-aat

monthly monatlich MOHN-att-likh

monument Denkmal (n.) DEHNK-maal

more mehr mayr

morning Morgen (m.) MORG-en

mosque Moschee (f.) mo-SHAY

motion sickness Reisekrankheit (f.) *REYEZ-eh-krahnk-heyet*

motorcycle Motorrad (n.) *moh-TOHR-raat*

mountain Berg (m.) *behrk*

mountain pass Pass (m.) *pahss*

mountain railway Bergbahn (f.) *BEHRK-baan*

mountains Gebirge (n.) *geh-BEERG-eh*

moustache Schnurbart (m.) *SCHNOOR-bahrt*

mouth Mund (m.) *munt*

move bewegen *beh-VAYG-en*

movie Film (m.) *film*

movie theater Kino (n.) *KEEN-oh*

Mrs. Frau *frow*

much viel *feel*

mulled wine Glühwein (m.) *GLEW-veyen*

municipal theater Stadttheater (n.) *SHTAHT-toy-aat-uh*

museum Museum (n.) *moo-ZAY-um*

music Musik (f.) *moo-ZEEK*

must (have to) muss *mus*, müssen *MEWSS-en*

mustard Senf (m.) *zehnf*

my mein(e) *meyen(eh)*

mystery Geheimnis (n.) *geh-HEYEM-nis*

mystery story Krimi (m.) *KREEM-ee*

N

nail Nagel (m.) *NAAG-el*

nail polish Nagellack (m.) *NAAG-el-lahk*

naked nackt *nahkt*

name Name (m.) *NAAM-eh*

(be) named heißen *HEYESS-en*

narrow eng *ehng*

nasty verflixt *fehr-FLIKST*

native einheimisch *EYEN-heyem-ish*

natural natürlich *nah-TEWR-likh*

nature Natur (f.) *nah-TOOR*

nauseous übel *EWB-el*

near nah *naa*

nearby in der Nähe *in dehr NAY-eh*

necessary nötig *NERT-ikh*

necessity Not (f.) *noht*

neck Nacken (m.) *NAHK-en*, Hals (m.) *hahls*

necklace Halskette (f.) *HAHLS-keht-eh*

need brauchen *BROWKH-en*

needle Nadel (f.) *NAAD-el*

nerves Nerven (pl.) *NEHRF-en*

Netherlands Niederlande (n.) *NEED-uh-lahnd-eh*

never nie *nee*

nevertheless doch *dokh*

new neu *noy*

newspaper Zeitung (f.) *TSEYET-ung*

newsstand Zeitungsstand (m.) *TSEYET-ungs-shtahnt*

New Zealand Neuseeland (n.) *noy-ZAY-lahnt*

next nächst *naykst*

nice nett *neht*, schön *shern*

night Nacht (f.) *nahkht*

nightclub Nachtlokal (n.) *NAHKHT-loh-kaal*

no nein *neyen*

no, none, not kein(e) *keyen(eh)*

nobody niemand *NEE-mahnt*

noise Lärm (m.) *lehrm*

nonprescription rezeptfrei *reh-TSEPT-freye*

nonsmoking Nichtraucher *nikht-ROWKH-uh*

noodle Nudel (f.) *NOOD-el*

noon Mittag (m.) *MIT-aak*

north Nord (m.) *nort*

Norway Norwegen (n.) *NOR-vay-gen*

nose Nase (f.) *NAAZ-eh*
not nicht *nikht*
notebook Notizheft (n.) *no-TEETS-hehft*
nothing nichts *nikhts*
notice Bekanntmachung (f.) *beh-KAHNT-mahkh-ung*
novel Roman (m.) *roh-MAAN*
now jetzt *yetst*
number Nummer (f.) *NUM-uh*
nurse Krankenpflegerin (f.) *KRAHNK-en-pflay-gehr-in*
nuts Nüsse (pl.) *NEWSS-eh*

O

obtain erhalten *ehr-HAHLT-en*, bekommen *beh-KOM-en*
occupied besetzt *beh-ZEHTST*
o'clock Uhr (f.) *oor*
of von *fon*
of course selbstverständlich *ZEHLPST-fehr-shtehnt-likh*
office Amt (n.) *ahmt*, Büro (n.) *bew-ROH*
office hours Sprechstunden (pl.) *SHPREHKH-shtund-en*
oil Öl (n.) *erl*
old alt *ahlt*; **old part of town** Altstadt (f.) *AHLT-shtaht*
omelette Omelette (f.) *om-eh-LET-eh*
omit weglassen *VEHK-lahss-en*
on auf *owf*, an *ahn*
one (number) eins *eyens*
one-way einfach *EYEN-fahkh*
one-way street Einbahnstraße (f.) *EYEN-baan-shtraass-eh*
only nur *noor*
open aufmachen *OWF-mahkh-en*, öffnen *ERF-nen*
open(ed) geöffnet *geh-ERF-net*, offen *OFF-en*
open-air museum Freilichtmuseum (n.) *FREYE-likht-moo-zay-um*
opera Oper (f.) *OH-pehr*

opera highlights Opernquerschnitt (m.) *OH-pehrn-kvehr-shnit*
operetta Operette (f.) *opeh-RET-eh*
ophthalmologist Augenarzt (m.) *OWG-en-ahrtst*
optical optisch *OP-tish*
optician Optiker (m.) *OP-tik-uh*
or oder *OHD-uh*
orange Orange (f.) *o-RAHNZH-eh*
orange juice Apfelsinensaft (m.) *ahp-fel-ZEEN-en-zahft*
orchestra Orchester (n.) *or-KHEST-uh*; (theater) Parkett (n.) *pahr-KEHT*
order bestellen *beh-SHTEL-en*
organization Verein (m.) *fehr-EYEN*
other ander *AHND-ehr*
otherwise sonst *zonst*
ought (should) soll *zoll*, sollen *ZOLL-en*
our unser(e) *UNZ-ehr(eh)*
out aus *owss*
outdoor pool Freibad (n.) *FREYE-baat*
outside of außerhalb *OWSS-ehr-hahlp*
oven Ofen (m.) *OHF-en*
over (across) über *EWB-eh*; (finished) zu Ende *tsoo EHND-eh*
overrun überlaufen *EWB-ehr-lowfen*
owe schulden *SHULD-en*
oysters Austern (pl.) *OWSS-tehrn*

P

pack packen *PAHK-en*
pack Paket (n.) *pah-KAYT*, Schachtel (f.) *SHAHKHT-el*
package Paket (n.) *pah-KAYT*
page Seite (f.) *ZEYET-eh*

pageboy haircut Pagenschnitt (m.) *PAHZH-en-shnit*

pain Schmerzen (pl.) *SHMEHRTS-en*, Weh (n.) *vay*

paint malen *MAAL-en*

painter Maler (m.) *MAAL-uh*

painting Gemhälde (n.) *geh-MAYLD-eh*

pair Paar (n.) *paar*

palace Palais (n.) *pah-LAY*, Palast (m.) *pah-LAHST*, Schloss (n.) *shloss*

palatinate Pfalz (f.) *pfahlts*

palpitations Herzklopfen (n.) *HEHRTS-klopf-en*

panties Schlüpfer (m.) *SHLEWPF-uh*

pants Hose (f.) *HOHZ-eh*

panty hose Strumpfhose (f.) *SHTRUMPF-hohz-eh*

pardon Entschuldigung (f.) *ehnt-SHUL-dee-gung*, Verzeihung (f.) *fehr-TSEYE-ung*

parents Eltern (pl.) *EHLT-ehrn*

park parken *PAHRK-en*

park Park (m.) *pahrk*

parking place Parkplatz (m.) *PAHRK-plahts*

part Teil (m.) *teyel*

passport Pass (m.) *pahss*

pastry shop Konditorei (f.) *kon-dee-toh-REYE*

patch flicken *FLIK-en*

path Pfad (m.) *pfaat*

pawn (chess) Bauer (m.) *BOW-uh*

pay zahlen *TSAAL-en*, bezahlen *beh-TSAAL-en*

peace Friede (m.) *FREED-eh*

peaceful friedlich *FREET-likh*

pearl Perle (f.) *PEHRL-eh*

peasant costumes Trachten (pl.) *TRAHKHT-en*

peasant dress (Alpine) Dirndlkleid (n.) *DEERNDL-kleyet*

pedestrian Fußgänger (m.) *FOOS-gehng-uh*

pediatrician Kinderarzt (m.) *KIND-uh-ahrtst*

pen (ball point) Kugelschreiber (m.) *KOOG-el-shreyeb-uh*

pencil Bleistift (m.) *BLEYE-shtift*

peninsula Halbinsel (f.) *HAHLP-inz-el*

penny (Ger.) Pfennig (m.) *PFEN-ikh*; **(Aust.)** Groschen (m.) *GROSH-en*; **(Switz.)** Rappen (m.) *RAHP-en*

people Leute (pl.) *LOYT-eh*, Menschen (pl.) *MENSH-en*, Volk (n.) *folk*

per pro *proh*

performance Vorstellung (f.) *FOHR-shtel-ung*

performance schedule Spielplan (m.) *SHPEEL-plaan*

periodical Zeitschrift (f.) *TSEYET-shrift*

permanent wave Dauerwelle (f.) *DOW-uh-vel-eh*

person Person (f.) *pehr-ZOHN*; **person-to-person call** Gespräch mit Voranmeldung *geh-SHPRAYKH mit FOHR-ahn-meld-ung*

personal check Barscheck (m.) *BAAR-shek*

pharmacy Apotheke (f.) *ah-poh-TAYK-eh*

photo Foto (n.) *FOH-toh*, Aufnahme (f.) *OWF-naam-eh*

photograph fotografieren *foh-toh-grah-FEER-en*, knipsen *KNIPS-en*

piano Klavier (n.) *klah-VEER*

pick up abholen *AHP-hohl-en*

picture Bild (n.) *bilt*

piece Stück (n.) *shtewk*

pill Pille (f.) *PIL-eh*

pillow Kopfkissen (n.) *KOPF-kiss-en*

pin Anstecknadel (f.) *AHN-shtehk-naad-el*

pinch drücken *DREWK-en*

pink rosa *ROH-zaa*

pipe Pfeife (f.) *PFEYEF-eh*

pirates Seeräuber (pl.) *ZAY-royb-eh*

place Platz (m.) *plahts*, Ort (m.) *ort*,

place legen *LAYG-en*, stellen *SHTEHL-en*

plant Pflanze (f.) *PFLAANTS-eh*

plant therapy Pflanzenheilkunde (f.) *PFLAANTS-en-heyel-kund-eh*

plate Teller (m.) *TEL-uh*

platform Bahnsteig (m.) *BAAN-shteyek*

platinum Platin (n.) *plah-TEEN*

play spielen *SHPEEL-en*

play Stück (n.) *shtewk*

playing cards Spielkarten (pl.) *SHPEEL-kaart-en*

playing field Sportplatz (m.) *SHPORT-plahts*

pleasant angenehm *AHN-geh-naym*

please bitte *BIT-eh*

pleased erfreut *ehr-FROYT*

plug Steckdose (f.) *SHTEHK-dohz-eh*

pneumonia Lungenentzündung (f.) *LUNG-en-ehnt-tsewnd-ung*, Pneumonie (f.) *pnoy-moh-nee*

pocket Tasche (f.) *TAHSH-eh*

poem Gedicht (n.) *geh-DIKHT*

poet Dichter (m.) *DICHT-uh*

Poland Polen (n.) *POHL-en*

police Polizei (f.) *po-lits-EYE*

pond Teich (m.) *teykh*

poor arm *ahrm*

porcelain Porzellan (n.) *por-tseh-LAAN*

pork Schweinefleisch (n.) *SHVEYEN-eh-fleyesh*

port Hafen (m.) *HAAF-en*

portable tragbar *TRAAK-baar*

porter Gepäckträger (m.) *geh-PEHK-trayg-uh*; **hotel porter** Hausdiener (m.) *HOWSS-deen-uh*

possible möglich *MERG-likh*

postcards Postkarten (pl.) *POST-kaart-en*

post office Postamt (n.) *POST-ahmt*

potatoes Kartoffeln (pl.) *kahr-TOF-ehln*

poultry Geflügel (n.) *geh-FLEWG-el*

pour einschenken *EYEN-shehnk-en*

powder Puder (m.) *POOD-uh*

power Macht (f.) *mahkht*

powerful kräftig *KREHFT-ikh*

praise loben *LOHB-en*

precious stones Edelsteine (pl.) *AYD-el-shteyen-eh*

pregnant schwanger *SHVAHNG-uh*

prepare vorbereiten *FOR-beh-reyet-en*

prescribe verschreiben *fehr-SHREYEB-en*

prescription Rezept (n.) *reh-TSEHPT*

press drücken *DREWK-en*

pressure Druck (m.) *druk*

price Preis (m.) *preyess*

prickly heat Hitzblattern (pl.) *HITS-blaht-ehrn*

priest Priester (m.) *PREEST-uh*

print drucken *DRUK-en*

print Abzug (m.) *AHP-tsook*

printed matter Drucksachen (pl.) *DRUK-zahkh-en*

private bath Privatbad (n.) *pri-VAAT-baat*

private beach Privatstrand (m.) *pri-VAAT-shtrahnt*

profession Beruf (m.) *beh-ROOF*

prohibited verboten *fehr-BOHT-en*

property Grundstück (*n.*) *GRUNT-shtewk*

Protestant evangelisch *ay-fahn-GAYL-ish*

proud stolz *shtolts*

proverb Sprichwort (*n.*) *SHPRIKH-vort*

Prussia Preußen (*n.*) *PROYSS-en*

public öffentlich *ERF-ehnt-likh*

pull ziehen *TSEE-en*

puppy Hündchen (*n.*) *HEWNT-khen*

purchases Einkäufe (*pl.*) *EYEN-koyf-eh*

pure rein *reyen*

purse Handtasche (*f.*) *HAHNT-tahsh-eh*

push drücken *DREWK-en*

put stellen *SHTEHL-en*, legen *LAYG-en*

Q

queen Königin (*f.*) *KERN-ig-in*; **(games)** Dame (*f.*) *DAAM-eh*

question Frage (*f.*) *FRAAG-eh*

quick schnell *shnel*

quiet ruhig *ROO-ikh*

R

rabbi Rabbiner (*m.*) *rah-BEEN-uh*

rabbit Hase (*m.*) *HAAZ-eh*

rabies Tollwut (*f.*) *TOL-voot*

race (run) rennen *REHN-en*

racetrack Rennbahn (*f.*) *REHN-baan*

radio Radio (*n.*) *RAAD-ee-oo*

rage wüten *VEWT-en*

railroad Eisenbahn (*f.*) *EYEZ-en-baan*

railroad station Bahnhof (*m.*) *BAAN-hohf*

rain Regen (*m.*) *RAYG-en*

raincoat Regenmantel (*m.*) *RAYG-en-mahnt-el*

raisins Rosinen (*pl.*) *rah-ZEEN-en*

ramparts Stadtmauer (*f.*) *SHTAHT-mow-uh*

rare selten *ZEHLT-en*; **(meat)** blutig *BLOOT-ikh*

rather lieber *LEEB-uh*; **(somewhat)** ziemlich *TSEEM-likh*

razor Rasierapparat (*m.*) *rah-ZEER-ah-pah-raat*

razor blades Rasierklingen (*pl.*) *rah-ZEER-kling-en*

razor cut Messerschnitt (*m.*) *MEHSS-uh-shnit*

reach erreichen *ehr-REYEKH-en*

read lesen *LAYZ-en*

ready bereit *beh-REYET*

real wirklich *VIRK-likh*

receipt Quittung (*f.*) *KVIT-ung*; **give a receipt** quittieren *kvit-EER-en*

receive bekommen *beh-KOM-en*, erhalten *ehr-HAHLT-en*

reclining chair Liegestuhl (*m.*) *LEEG-eh-shtool*

recognize erkennen *ehr-KEHN-en*

recommend empfehlen *ehmp-FAYL-en*

record player Plattenspieler (*m.*) *PLAHT-en-shpeel-uh*

recordings Aufnahmen (*pl.*) *OWF-naam-en*

records Schallplatten (*pl.*) *SHAHL-plaht-en*

recovery Besserung (*f.*) *BEHSS-ehr-ung*

red rot *roht*

reduce ermäßigen *ehr-MAYSS-ig-en*

reduced (low) nicotine nikotinarm *nik-koh-TEEN-ahrm*

reduced rate Preisermäßigung (f.) *PREYESS-ehr-mayss-ig-ung*
reduction Ermäßigung (f.) *ehr-MAYSS-ig-ung*
register (hotel) sich eintragen *zikh EYEN-traag-en*
registered letter Einschreibebrief (m.) *EYEN-shreyeb-ehbreef*
regular (gas) normal *nor-MAAL*
reincarnation Seelenwanderung (f.) *ZAYL-en-vahn-dehr-ung*
relatives Verwandte (pl.) *fehr-VAHNT-eh*
religion Religion (f.) *reh-lig-YOHN*
religious service Gottesdienst (m.) *GOT-ehs-deenst*
remain bleiben *BLEYEB-en*
remove entfernen *ehnt-FEHRN-en*
rent mieten *MEET-en*
rent Miete (f.) *MEET-eh*
repair reparieren *reh-pah-REER-en*
repeat wiederholen *VEED-uh-hohl-en*
replace ersetzen *ehr-ZETS-en*
republic Republik (f.) *reh-poob-LEEK*
request bitten *BIT-en*
request Bitte (f.) *BIT-eh*
rescue retten *RET-en*
reserve reservieren *reh-zehr-VEER-en*
responsibility Verantwortung (f.) *fehr-AHNT-vort-ung*
rest Ruhe (f.) *ROO-eh*
restaurant Restaurant (n.) *res-tow-RAHNT*
rest rooms Toiletten (pl.) *toy-LET-en*
return zurückbringen *tsoo-REWK-bring-en*, zurückkommen *tsoo-REWK-kom-en*, zurücksenden *tsoo-REWK-zent-en*
revelation Offenbarung (f.) *off-en-BAAR-ung*
ribs Rippen (pl.) *RIP-en*
rich reich *reyekh*
ride fahren *FAAR-en*; **ride a horse** reiten *REYET-en*
ridiculous lächerlich *LEHKH-ehr-likh*
right richtig *RIKHT-ikh*; **to the right** rechts *rehkhts*
right away gleich *gleyekh*
ring Ring (m.) *ring*
rip reißen *REYESS-en*
ripe reif *reyef*
rise Aufstieg (m.) *OWF-shteek*
river Fluss (m.) *fluss*
road Straße (f.) *SHTRASS-eh*
road maps Straßenkarten (pl.) *SHTRASS-en-kaart-en*; **road signs indicated** beschildert *beh-SHILD-ehrt*
roast braten *BRAAT-en*
role Rolle (f.) *ROL-eh*
roll rollen *ROL-en*
rolls Brötchen (pl.) *BRERT-khen*, Wecken (pl.) *VEHK-en*, Semmeln (pl.) *ZEHM-eln*
roof Dach (n.) *dahkh*
rook (chess) Turm (m.) *turm*
room Zimmer (n.) *TSIM-uh*, Saal (m.) *zaal*, Stube (f.) *SHTOOB-eh*
room reservation service Zimmernachweis (m.) *TSIM-uh-nahkh-veyess*
room service Zimmerbedienung (f.) *TSIM-uh-beh-deen-ung*
rose Rose (f.) *ROHZ-eh*
rotten faul *fowl*, verfault *fehr-FOWLT*
round rund *runt*
round-trip ticket Rückfahrkarte (f.) *REWK-faar-kaart-eh*
row Reihe (f.) *REYE-eh*
royal königlich *KERN-ikh-likh*

ruby Rubin (*m.*) *roob-EEN*
rug Teppich (*m.*) *TEHP-ikh*
ruins Ruinen (*pl.*) *roo-EEN-en*
ruler Lineal (*n.*) *lee-nay-AAL*
run laufen *LOWF-en*
Russia Russland (*n.*) *RUSS-lahnt*

S

sad traurig *TROW-rikh*
safe sicher *ZIKH-uh*
safe (box) Tresor (*m.*) *treh-ZOHR*
sale Verkauf (*m.*) *fehr-KOWF*, Ausverkauf (*m.*) *OWSS-fehr-kowf*, Schlussverkauf (*m.*) *SHLUSS-fehr-kowf*
salesgirl Verkäuferin (*f.*) *fehr-KOYF-ehr-in*
sales tax Umsatzsteuer (*f.*) *UM-zahts-shtoy-uh*
salt Salz (*n.*) *zahlts*
salve Salbe (*f.*) *ZAALB-eh*
(the) same (der, die, das) selbe (*dehr, dee, dahs*) *ZEHLB-eh*
sanitary napkins Damenbinden (*pl.*) *DAAM-en-bind-en*
sapphires Saphire (*pl.*) *zah-FEER-eh*
Saturday Samstag (*m.*) *ZAHMS-taak*
saucer Untertasse (*f.*) *UNT-uh-tahss-eh*
sausage Wurst (*f.*) *voorst*
save (money) sparen *SHPAAR-en*; **(rescue)** retten *REHT-en*
say sagen *ZAAG-en*
saying Spruch (*m.*) *shprookh*
scalp skalpieren *skahl-PEER-en*
scarf Halstuch (*n.*) *HAHLSS-tookh*
schedule (of events) Veranstaltungskalender (*m.*) *fehr-AHN-shtahlt-ungs-kah-lend-uh*

scissors Schere (*f.*) *SHAY-reh*
Scotland Schottland (*n.*) *SHOT-lahnt*
scrambled eggs Rühreier (*pl.*) *REWR-eye-eh*
screw Schraube (*f.*) *SHROWB-eh*
sea Meer (*n.*) *mayr*
seasickness Seekrankheit (*f.*) *ZAY-krahnk-heyet*
seashore Strand (*m.*) *shtrahnt*
season Jahreszeit (*f.*) *YAAR-es-tseyet*, Saison (*f.*) *seh-ZONG*
seasoning Würze (*f.*) *VEWRTS-eh*
seat Platz (*m.*) *plahts*, Sitz (*m.*) *zits*
secretary Sekretärin (*f.*) *zeh-kreh-TAYR-in*, Sekretär (*m.*) *zeh-kreh-TAYR*
see sehen *ZAY-en*
see again wiedersehen *VEED-uh-zay-en*
seem scheinen *SHEYEN-en*
select (choose) aussuchen *OWSS-zookh-en*
selection Auswahl (*f.*) *OWSS-vaal*
self-service Selbstbedienung (*f.*) *ZEHLPST-beh-deen-ung*
sell verkaufen *fehr-KOWF-en*
semiprecious stones Halbedelsteine (*pl.*) *HAHLP-ayd-el-shteyen-eh*
send senden *ZEND-en*, schicken *SHIK-en*
sentimental schmalzig *SHMAHLTS-ikh*
serious ernst *ehrnst*
serve servieren *zehr-VEER-en*
service Bedienung (*f.*) *beh-DEEN-ung*
sew nähen *NAY-en*
shade, shadow Schatten (*m.*) *SHAHT-en*
shall sollen *ZOL-en*, soll *zol*, wollen *VOL-en*, will *vil*, werden *VAYRD-en*, wird *veert*

shave rasieren *rah-ZEER-en*
she, her sie *zee*
shepherd Schäfer (*m.*) *SHAYF-uh*
shine putzen *PUTS-en*, polieren *po-LEER-en*
ship Schiff (*n.*) *shif*
shipment Sendung (*f.*) *ZEND-ung*
shipping charges Versandkosten (*pl.*) *fehr-ZAHNT-kost-en*
shirt Hemd (*m.*) *hehmt*
shoe Schuh (*m.*) *shoo*
shoelaces Schnürsenkel (*pl.*) *SHNEWR-zehnk-el*
shoe store Schuhgeschäft (*n.*) *SHOO-geh-shehft*
shoot schießen *SHEESS-en*
shop einkaufen *EYEN-kowf-en*
shopping bag Tragetasche (*f.*) *TRAAG-eh-tahsh-eh*
shopping center Einkaufszentrum (*n.*) *EYEN-kowfs-tsehnt-rum*
short kurz *kurts*
shorts (briefs) kurze Unterhosen (*pl.*) *KURTS-eh UN-tehr-hohz-en*
should soll *zol*, sollen *ZOL-en*, sollte(n) *ZOLT(en)*
shoulder Schulter (*f.*) *SHULT-uh*
shove schieben *SHEEB-en*
show zeigen *TSEYEG-en*
show window Schaufenster (*n.*) *SHOW-fehnst-eh*
shower (bath) Dusche (*f.*) *DOOSH-eh*
shower, communal Etagendusche (*f.*) *ay-TAAZH-en-doosh-eh*
shuffle (cards) mischen *MISH-en*
sick krank *krahnk*
sickness Krankheit (*f.*) *KRAHNK-heyet*
side Seite (*f.*) *ZEYET-eh*

sideburns Koteletten (*pl.*) *ko-teh-LET-en*
sign Schild (*n.*) *shilt*
sign unterschreiben *UNT-uh-shreyeb-en*
silence Ruhe (*f.*) *ROO-eh*
(be) silent schweigen *SHVEYEG-en*
Silesia Schlesien (*n.*) *SHLAYZ-ee-en*
silk Seide (*f.*) *ZEYED-eh*
silver Silber (*m.*) *ZILB-uh*
silver plate versilbert *fehr-ZILB-ehrt*
similar ähnlich *AYN-likh*
sin Sünde (*f.*) *ZEWND-eh*
since seit *zeyet*
sing singen *ZING-en*
singers Sänger (*pl.*) *ZEHNG-uh*
single einzeln *EYENTS-ehln*, einfach *EYEN-fahkh*; **unmarried** ledig *LAYD-ikh*
single room Einzelzimmer (*n.*) *EYEN-tsehl-tsim-uh*
sit sitzen *ZITS-en*
sit down sich setzen *zikh ZEHTS-en*
size Größe (*f.*) *GRERSS-eh*, Nummer (*f.*) *NUM-uh*
skates Schlittschuhe (*m.*) *SHLIT-shoo-eh*
skating rink (ice) Eisbahn (*f.*) *EYESS-baan*
ski Schi (*m.*) *shee*
ski lift Schilift (*m.*) *SHEE-lift*
skim milk Magermilch (*f.*) *MAAG-uh-milkh*
skin Haut (*f.*) *howt*
skirt Rock (*m.*) *rok*
sled Schlitten (*m.*) *SHLIT-en*
sleep schlafen *SHLAAF-en*
sleeping car (1st-class) Schlafwagen (*m.*) *SHLAAF-vaagen*; **(2nd-class)** Liegewagen (*m.*) *LEEG-eh-vaag-en*
sleeping pills Schlaftabletten (*pl.*) *SHLAAF-tah-blet-en*

sleeves Ärmel (*pl.*) *EHRM-el*
slides Dias (*pl.*) *DEE-ahss*
slip Unterrock (*m.*) *UNT-uh-rok*
slippers Hausschuhe (*pl.*) *HOWSS-shoo-eh*
slow langsam *LAHNG-zaam*
small klein *kleyen*
small change Kleingeld (*n.*) *KLEYEN-gelt*
smile lächeln *LEHKH-eln*
smoke rauchen *ROWKH-en*
smoked geräuchert *geh-ROYKH-ehrt*
smoking section Raucher (*pl.*) *ROWKH-uh*
snack Imbiss (*m.*) *IM-biss*
snails Schnecken (*pl.*) *SHNEHK-en*
snow Schnee (*m.*) *shnay*
snuff Schnupftabak (*m.*) *SHNUPF-taa-bahk*
soap Seife (*f.*) *ZEYEF-eh*
society Gesellschaft (*f.*) *geh-ZEL-shahft*
socks Socken (*pl*) *ZOK-en*
soft weich *veyekh*
soft-boiled weichgekocht *VEYEKH-geh-kokkt*
sold out ausverkauft *OWSS-fehr-kowft*
some einige *EYEN-ig-eh*
somebody jemand *YAY-mahnt*
something etwas *EHT-vaas*
son Sohn (*m.*) *zohn*
song Lied (*n.*) *leet*
soon bald *bahlt*
sorrow Leid (*n.*) *leyet*
soul Seele (*f.*) *ZAYL-eh*
soup Suppe (*f.*) *ZUP-eh*
sour sauer *ZOW-uh*
south Süd (*m.*) *zewt*
souvenir Souvenir (*n.*) *soo-veh-NEER*, Andenken (*n.*) *AHN-dehnk-en*
spa Kurort (*m.*) *KOOR-ort*
spades (cards) Pik (*n.*) *peek*
Spain Spanien (*n.*) *SHPAAN-yen*

spare part Ersatzteil (*m.*) *ehr-ZAHTS-teyel*
sparkling water Sprudelwasser (*n.*) *SHPROOD-el-vahss-uh*
sparkling wine Schaumwein (*m.*) *SHOWM-veyen*
spark plugs Zündkerzen (*pl.*) *TSEWNT-kehrts-en*
speak sprechen *SHPREHKH-en*; **speaking (on the telephone)** am Apparat *ahm ah-pah-RAAT*
special besonders *beh-ZOND-ehrs*
special delivery letter Eilbrief (*m.*) *EYEL-breef*
specialist (medical) Facharzt (*m.*) *FAHKH-ahrtst*
special sale item Sonderangebot (*n.*) *ZOND-ehr-ahn-geh-boht*
spend (money) ausgeben *OWSS-gayb-en*; **(time)** verbringen *fehr-BRING-en*
spend the night übernachten *EWB-uh-nahkht-en*
spices Gewürze (*pl.*) *geh-VEWRTS-eh*
spire Kirchturm (*m.*) *KIRKH-turm*
spirits Geister (*pl.*) *GEYEST-uh*
spiritual geistlich *GEYEST-likh*
splendid herrlich *HEHR-likh*
spoiled verfault *fehr-FOWLT*
spoon Löffel (*m.*) *LERF-el*
sport Sport (*m.*) *shport*
spring (season) Frühling (*m.*) *FREW-ling*; **(mechanical)** Feder (*f.*) *FAYD-uh*; **(water)** Quelle (*f.*) *KVEL-eh*
stadium Stadion (*n.*) *SHTAAD-ee-ohn*
stainless (steel) rostfrei *ROST-freye*
stamp (*verb*) stempeln *SHTEHMP-eln*

stamp (postage) Briefmarke (f.) *BREEF-mahrk-eh*

stamp dealer Briefmarken-händler (m.) *BREEF-mahrk-en-hehnt-luh*

stand stehen *SHTAY-en*

start anfangen *AHN-fahng-en*, starten *SHTAHRT-en*

statue Statue (f.) *SHTAAT-oo-eh*

stay bleiben *BLEYEB-en*

stay Aufenthalt (m.) *OWF-ent-hahlt*

steamer Dampfer (m.) *DAHMPF-uh*

stewed geschmort *geh-SHMORT*

stewed fruit Kompott (n.) *kom-POT*

still noch *nokh*

stock Lager (n.) *LAAG-uh*

stockings Strümpfe (pl.) *SHTREWMPF-eh*

stolen gestohlen *geh-SHTOHL-en*

stomach Magen (m.) *MAAG-en*

store Laden (m.) *LAAD-en*

story (tale) Geschichte (f.) *geh-SHIKHT-eh*; **(floor)** Stock (m.) *shtok*

stop halten *HAHLT-en*

straight ahead geradeaus *geh-RAAD-eh-ows*

strawberry Erdbeere (f.) *EHRT-bayr-eh*

stream Strom (m.) *shtrohm*

street Straße (f.) *SHTRAASS-eh*

streetcar Straßenbahn (f.) *SHTRAASS-en-baan*

striking auffallend *OWF-fahl-ent*

string Schnur (f.) *shnoor*

strong stark *shtahrk*

stuck verklemmt *fehr-KLEHMT*

student Student (m.) *shtoo-DEHNT*

stupid dumm *dum*

styptic pencil Blutstiller (m.) *BLOOT-shtil-uh*

style Art (f.) *ahrt*

Styria Steiermark (f.) *SHTEYE-uh-maark*

sublime hehr *hayr*

substitute Ersatz (m.) *ehr-ZAHTS*

suffer leiden *LEYED-en*

sugar Zucker (m.) *TSUK-uh*

suit (man's) Anzug (m.) *AHN-tsook*; **(woman's)** Kostüm (n.) *kos-TEWM*

suitable passend *PAHSS-ent*

suitcase Koffer (m.) *KOF-uh*

summer Sommer (m.) *ZOM-uh*

sun Sonne (f.) *ZON-eh*

sunburn Sonnenbrand (m.) *ZON-en-brahnt*

Sunday Sonntag (m.) *ZON-taak*

sunglasses Sonnenbrille (f.) *ZON-en-bril-eh*

sunny sonnig *ZON-ikh*

supplement (surcharge) Zuschlag (m.) *TSOO-shlaak*

suppositories Zäpfchen (pl.) *TSEHPF-khen*

surfboard Surfbrett (n.) *surf-breht*

sweater Pullover (m.) *pul-OHV-uh*

Sweden Schweden (n.) *SHVAYD-en*

sweetheart Schatz (m.) *shahts*

sweets Süßigkeiten (pl.) *ZEWSS-ikh-keyet-en*

swim schwimmen *SHVIM-en*

swimming pool Schwimmbad (n.) *SHVIM-baat*

Switzerland Schweiz (f.) *shveyets*

synagogue Synagoge (f.) *zewn-ah-GOHG-eh*

T

table Tisch (*m.*) *tish*

tailor Schneider (*m.*) *SHNEYED-uh*

take nehmen *NAYM-en*

take time (last) dauern *DOW-ehrn*

talcum powder Talkumpuder (*m.*) *TAHL-kum-pood-uh*

tame zahm *tsaam*

tape Klebestreifen (*m.*) *KLAYB-eh-shtreyef-en*

tape recorder Tonbandgerät (*n.*) *TOHN-bahnt-geh-rayt*

tart Torte (*f.*) *TORT-eh*

taste schmecken *SHMEK-en*

tax Steuer (*f.*) *SHTOY-uh*

tax exempt steuerfrei *SHTOY-uh-freye*

taxi Taxi (*n.*) *TAHK-see*

taxi driver Taxifahrer (*m.*) *TAHK-see-faar-uh*

tea Tee (*m.*) *tay*

teach lehren *LAYR-en*

teacher Lehrer (*m.*) *LAYR-uh*, Lehrerin (*f.*) *LAYR-uh-rin*

telegram Telegramm (*n.*) *tay-leh-GRAHM*

telephone Telefon (*n.*) *tay-leh-FOHN*, Fernsprecher (*m.*) *FEHRN-shprehkh-uh*

telephone telefonieren *tay-leh-foh-NEER-en*, anrufen *AHN-roof-en*

telephone booth Telefonzelle (*f.*) *tay-leh-FOHN-tsehl-eh*

telephone directory Telefonbuch (*n.*) *tay-leh-FOHN-bookh*

television set Fernseher (*m.*) *FEHRN-zay-uh*

temple Tempel (*m.*) *TEHMP-el*

temporarily provisorisch *pro-vi-ZOHR-ish*, zeitweilig *TSEYET-voyel-ikh*,

tender zart *tsahrt*

tennis court Tennisplatz (*m.*) *TEHN-iss-plahts*

tennis racket Tennisschläger (*m.*) *TEHN-iss-shlayg-uh*

tent Zelt (*n.*) *tsehlt*

terrible schrecklich *SHREHK-likh*

than als *ahls*

thank danken *DAHNK-en*

thanks Dank (*m.*) *dahnk*

that das, dass *dahs*

the der *dehr*, die *dee*, das *dahs*

theater Theater (*n.*) *tay-AAT-uh*

there da *daa*, dort *dort*

therefore also *AHL-zoh*

there is (are) es gibt *ehs gipt*

thermal bath Thermalbad (*n.*) *tehr-MAAL-baat*

thermometer Thermometer (*n.*) *tehr-mo-MAYT-uh*

they sie *zee*

thick dick *dik*

thin dünn *dewn*

thing Ding (*n.*) *ding*

think denken *DEHNK-en*, glauben *GLOWB-en*

thirst Durst (*m.*) *durst*

thirsty durstig *DURST-ikh*

this dies *dees*

throat Hals (*m.*) *hahlss*

through durch *durkh*

through traffic Durchgangsverkehr (*m.*) *DURKH-gahngs-fehr-kayr*

thumbtacks Reitßzwecken (*pl.*) *REYESS-tsvek-en*

Thursday Donnerstag (*m.*) *DON-ehrs-taak*

tiara Tiara (*f.*) *tee-AAR-ah*

ticket (Fahr)karte (*f.*) *(FAAR) kaart-eh*

tie Krawatte (*f.*) *krah-VAHT-eh*

tie binden *BIND-en*

tie pin Krawattennadel (*m.*) *krah-VAHT-en-naad-el*

time Zeit (*f.*) *tseyet*, Uhrzeit (*f.*) *OOR-tseyet*, Mal (*n.*) *maal*

tip Trinkgeld (*n.*) *TRINK-gehlt*

tire Reifen (*m.*) *REYEF-en*

tired müde *MEWD-eh*

tissues (paper) Papiertücher (*pl.*) *paa-PEER-tewkh-uh*

title Titel (*m.*) *TEET-el*

to zu, nach *tsoo, nahkh*

tobacco Tabak (*m.*) *TAH-bahk*

tobacco shop Tabakladen (*m.*) *TAH -bahk laad-en*

today heute *HOYT-eh*

toe Zehe (*f.*) *TSAY-eh*

toilet Toilette (*f.*) *toy-LET-eh*

toilet paper Toilettenpapier (*n.*) *toy-LET-en-pah-peer*

tomorrow morgen *MORG-en*

tongue Zunge (*f.*) *TSUNG-eh*

tonight heute Nacht *HOYT-eh nahkht*

tonsils Mandeln (*pl.*) *MAHND-eln*

too zu *tsoo*

tool Werkzeug (*n.*) *VEHRK-tsoyg*

tooth Zahn (*m.*) *tsaan*

toothache Zahnschmerzen (*pl.*) *TSAAN-shmehrts-en*

toothbrush Zahnbürste (*f.*) *TSAAN-bewrst-eh*

topazes Topase (*pl.*) *toh-PAAZ-eh*

touch berühren *beh-REWR-en*

touch up auffrischen *OWF-frish-en*

tough zäh *tsay*

tourism Fremdenverkehr (*m.*) *FREMD-en-fehr-kayr*

tourist Tourist (*m.*) *too-RIST*

tourist attractions Sehenswürdigkeiten (*pl.*) *ZAY-ens-vewrd-ikh-keyet-en*

towel Tuch (*n.*) *tookh*

tower Turm (*m.*) *turm*

town Stadt (*f.*) *shtaht*

tow truck Abschleppwagen (*m.*) *AHP-shlehp-vaag-en*

To your health! Zum Wohl! *tsum vohl*

toys Spielwaren (*pl.*) *SHPEEL-vaar-en*

track (railroad) Gleis (*m.*) *gleyess*

traffic Verkehr (*m.*) *fehr-KAYR*

traffic jam Stau (*m.*) *shtow*

traffic light Ampel (*f.*) *AHMP-el*

tragedy Tragödie (*f.*) *trah-GERD-yeh*, Trauerspiel (*n.*) *TROW-uh-shpeel*

trailer Wohnwagen (*m.*) *VOHN-vaag-en*

train Zug (*m.*) *tsook*

tranquilizer Beruhigungs-mittel (*n.*) *beh-ROO-ig-ungs-mit-el*

translate übersetzen *ewb-uh-ZETS-en*

transmit (money) überweisen *ewb-uh-VEYEZ-en*

travel reisen *REYEZ-en*, fahren *FAAR-en*

travel bureau Reisebüro (*n.*) *REYEZ-eh-bewr-oh*

travelers' check Reisescheck (*m.*) *REYEZ-eh-shehk*

treasure Schatz (*m.*) *shahts*

treat behandeln *beh-HAHND-eln*

tree Baum (*m.*) *bowm*

trim stutzen *SHTUTS-en*

trinkets Nippsachen (*pl.*) *NIP-zahkh-en*

trip Reise (*f.*) *REYEZ-eh*, Fahrt (*f.*) *faart*

truck Lastkraftwagen (LKW) (*m.*) *LAHST-krahft-vaag-en (el-kaa-vay)*

true wahr *vaar*

trump (card) Trumpf (*m.*) *trumpf*

truth Wahrheit (*f.*) *VAAR-heyet*

try versuchen *fehr-ZOOKH-en*

try on anprobieren *AHN-proh-beer-en*

Tuesday Dienstag (*m.*)
DEENS-taak

turn drehen *DRAY-en*, wenden
VEHND-en

turn off (road) abbiegen
AHP-beeg-en

turquoises Türkise (*pl.*) *tewr-KEEZ-eh*

twilight Dämmerung (*f.*)
DEHM-ehr-ung

type Sorte (*f.*) *ZORT-en*

typewriter Schreibmaschine
(*f.*) *SHREYEP-mah-sheen-eh*

Tyrolean hat *Tirolerhut* (*m.*)
ti-ROHL-uh-hoot

U

ulcer Geschwür (*n.*) *geh-SHVEWR*

undershirt Unterhemd (*n.*)
UNT-uh-hemt

understand verstehen *fehr-SHTAY-en*

underwear Unterwäsche (*f.*)
UNT-uh-veh-sheh

unforgettable unvergesslich
un-fehr-GEHSS-likh

unfortunately leider *LEYED-uh*

uniform Uniform (*f.*) *UN-ee-form*

(the) United States (die)
Vereinigten Staaten (*pl.*)
*(dee) fehr-EYEN-ikht-en
SHTAAT-en*

universe Weltall (*n.*) *VELT-ahl*

university Universität (*f.*) *u-nee-vehr-zi-TAYT*

until bis *bis*

up oben *OHB-en*

upset stomach
Magenverstimmung (*f.*)
MAAG-en-fehr-shtim-ung

urgent dringend *DRING-ehnt*

use benutzen *beh-NUTS-en*

useful nützlich *NEWTS-likh*

V

vacation Ferien (*pl.*) *FEHR-yen*

valid gültig *GEWLT-ikh*

valley Tal (*n.*) *taal*

valuable wertvoll *vehrt-fol*

value-added tax Mehrwert-steuer (*f.*) *MAYR-vehrt-shtoy-uh*

venerate verehren *fehr-AYR-en*

venereal disease Geschlechts-krankheit (*f.*) *geh-SHLEHKHTS-krahnh-heyet*

ventilator Lüfter (*m.*)
LEWFT-uh

verification Überprüfung (*f.*)
EWB-uh-prewf-ung

verify prüfen *PREWF-en*, kon-trollieren *kon-troh-LEER-en*

very sehr *zayr*

veterinarian Tierarzt (*m.*)
TEER-ahrtst

via über *EWB-uh*

victory Sieg (*m.*) *zeek*

Vienna Wien (*n.*) *veen*

view Blick (*m.*) *blik*, Aussicht
(*f.*) *OWSS-zikht*

vigor Kraft (*f.*) *krahft*

village Dorf (*n.*) *dorf*

vineyard Weinberg (*m.*)
VEYEN-behrk

violin Geige (*f.*) *GEYEG-eh*,
Violine (*f.*) *vee-o-LEEN-eh*

visit besuchen *beh-ZOOKH-en*,
besichtigen *beh-ZIKHT-ig-en*

vitamins Vitamine (*pl.*) *vi-tah-MEEN-eh*

voice Stimme (*f.*) *SHTIM-eh*

voltage Stromspannung (*f.*)
SHTROHM-shpahn-ung

vomit brechen *BREHKH-en*

W

wait warten *VAART-en*

waiter Kellner (*m.*) *KELN-eh*

waiting room Wartesaal (*m.*)
VAART-uh-zaal

wake wecken *VEHK-en*
walk gehen *GAY-en*
walk Spaziergang (*m.*) *shpah-TSEER-gahng*
wall Wand (*f.*) *vahnt*
wallet Geldtasche (*f.*) *GEHLT-tahsh-eh*
waltz Walzer (*m.*) *VAHLTS-uh*
want mag *mahk*, mögen *MERG-en*, will *vil*, wollen *VOL-en*
was war *vahr*; (**passive**) wurde *VURD-eh*
wash waschen *VAHSH-en*
wash and wear bügelfrei *BEWG-el-freye*
washbasin Waschbecken (*n.*) *VAHSH-behk-en*
wastebasket Papierkorb (*m.*) *pah-PEER-korp*
watch Uhr (*f.*) *oor*
watchmaker Uhrmacher (*m.*) *OOR-mahkh-uh*
watch out aufpassen *OWF-pahss-en*
water Wasser (*n.*) *VAHSS-uh*
wave Welle (*f.*) *VEL-eh*
way Weg (*m.*) *vayk*
we wir *veer*
weak schwach *shvahkh*
wear tragen *TRAAG-en*
weather Wetter (*n.*) *VEHT-uh*
wedding Hochzeit (*f.*) *HOKH-tseyet*
wedding ring Ehering (*m.*) *AY-eh-ring*
Wednesday Mittwoch (*m.*) *MIT-vokh*
week Woche (*f.*) *VOKH-eh*
weigh wiegen *VEEG-en*
weight Gewicht (*n.*) *geh-VIKHT*
well done (meat) gut durchgebraten *goot DURKH-geh-braat-en*
well-known bekannt *beh-KAHNT*
(the) West Westen (*m.*) *VEHST-en*

wet nass *nahss*
what was *vahs*
when wenn *vehn*, wann *vahn*
where wo *voh*
where to wohin *VOH-hin*
whether ob *op*
which welche *vehlkh*
whipped cream Schlagsahne (*f.*) *SHLAAK-zanneh*
white weiß *veyess*
who wer *vayr*
whole ganz *gahnts*
wife Frau (*f.*) *frow*
wig Perücke (*f.*) *peh-REWK-eh*
wild toll *tol*
will werden *VAYRD-en*, wird *veert*
win gewinnen *geh-VIN-en*
wind Wind (*m.*) *vint*
winder (watch) Kronenaufzug (*m.*) *KROHN-en-owf-tsook*
window Fenster (*n.*) *FEHNST-uh*; (**ticket, stamp, etc.**) Schalter (*m.*) *SHAHLT-uh*
window seat Fensterplatz (*m.*) *FEHNST-uh-plahts*
windshield Windschutzscheibe *VINT-shuts-sheyeb-eh*
windy windig *VIND-ikh*
wine Wein (*m.*) *veyen*
wine shop Weinhandlung (*f.*) *VEYEN-hahnt-lung*
wine tavern Weinstube (*f.*) *VEYEN-shtoob-eh*
wing Flügel (*m.*) *FLEWG-el*
winter Winter (*m.*) *VINT-uh*
wish wünschen *VEWNSH-en*
witch Hexe (*f.*) *HEHKS-eh*
with mit *mit*
without ohne *OHN-eh*
woman Frau (*f.*) *frow*
wonderful wunderbar *VUND-uh-baar*
wood Holz (*n.*) *holts*
woods Wald (*m.*) *vahlt*
wool Wolle (*f.*) *VOL-eh*
word Wort (*n.*) *vort*

work arbeiten *AHR-beyet-en*,
funktionieren *funk-tsyoh-*
NEER-en
work Arbeit (*f.*) *AHR-beyet*
worth wert *vayrt*
worth the money preiswert
PREYESS-vayrt
would würde *VEWRD-eh*
would like möchte *MERKHT-*
eh
wound Wunde (*f.*) *VUND-eh*
wrap einpacken *EYEN-pahk-eh*
wreath Kranz (*m.*) *krahnts*
wrist Handgelenk (*m.*)
HAHNT-geh-lehnk
wristwatch Armbanduhr (*f.*)
AHRM-bahnt-oor
write schreiben *SHREYEB-en*
writer Schriftsteller (*m.*)
SHRIFT-shtehl-uh
writing pad Schreibblock
(*m.*) *SHREYEP-blok*

wrong falsch *fahlsh*

Y

yearning Sehnsucht (*f.*)
ZAYN-zukht
yellow gelb *gehlp*
yesterday gestern *GEHST-*
ehrn
you Sie *zee*, Ihnen *EEN-en*
young jung *yung*
youth hostel Jugendherberge
(*f.*) *YOOG-ehnt-hehr-behrg-eh*

Z

zip code Postleitzahl (*f.*)
POST-leyet-tsaal
zoo Zoo (*m.*) *tsoh*, Tierpark
(*m.*) *TEER-pahrk*

GERMAN-ENGLISH DICTIONARY

A

Aachen (*n.*)   Aix-la Chapelle
Abend (*m.*)   evening
Abendessen (*n.*)   dinner
Abendgarderobe (*f.*)   evening dress
Abendkleid (*n.*)   evening gown
Abenteuer (*n.*)   adventure
aber   but
Abfahrt (*f.*)   departure
Abflug (*m.*)   departure by plane
abheben   cut (cards)
Abreise (*f.*)   departure
abreisen   check out (depart)
Abszess (*m.*)   abscess
Abteil (*n.*)   compartment
Achtung (*f.*)   attention
Afrika (*n.*)   Africa
Aktentasche (*f.*)   briefcase
Alkohol (*m.*)   alcohol
Allee (*f.*)   avenue
allein   alone
alles   everything
Alter (*n.*)   age
Amethyst (*m.*)   amethyst
ändern   alter
Änderungen (*pl.*)   alterations
Anfall (*m.*)   attack
anfangen   begin, start
Angeln (*n.*)   fishing
Angelschein (*m.*)   fishing license
Angst (*f.*)   fear
Angst haben   fear, be afraid
ankommen   arrive
Ankunft (*f.*)   arrival
annehmen   accept
anschauen   behold, look at

anschließen   connect
Antiquitäten (*pl.*)   antiques
Antiseptikum (*n.*)   antiseptic
Antwort (*f.*)   answer
antworten   answer
Apotheke (*f.*)   drugstore, pharmacy
Apparat (*m.*)   appliance
Äquivalent (*n.*)   equivalent
Argentinien (*n.*)   Argentina
Arm (*m.*)   arm
Armband (*n.*)   bracelet
Arzt (*m.*)   doctor
As (*n.*)   ace
Aschenbecher (*m.*)   ashtray
Asien (*n.*)   Asia
Atem (*m.*)   breath
atmen   breathe
außer   except
auch   also
aufpassen   be careful
auf Wiederschauen   good-bye
auf Wiedersehen   good-bye
Aufzug (*m.*)   elevator
Auge (*n.*)   eye
Augenbrauenstift (*m.*)   eyebrow pencil
aus   from
Ausfahrt (*f.*)   exit road; excursion
Ausflug (*m.*)   excursion
Ausgabe (*f.*)   edition
Ausgang (*m.*)   exit
ausgezeichnet   excellent
Ausländer   foreigner
Ausrüstung (*f.*)   equipment
aussteigen   get off (a vehicle)
Australien (*n.*)   Australia
auswechseln   exchange
Auto (*n.*)   automobile, car
automatisch   automatic
Autor (*m.*)   author

B

Bach (*m.*)   brook
backen   bake
Bäckerei (*f.*)   bakery
Bad (*n.*)   bathroom, bath
Badeanzug (*n.*)   bathing suit
baden   bathe
Bäder (*pl.*)   baths
Badewanne (*f.*)   bathtub
Ballett (*n.*)   ballet
Bank (*f.*)   bank
Bargeld (*n.*)   cash
Bart (*m.*)   beard
Batterie (*f.*)   battery
Bauer (*m.*)   farmer
Bauernhof (*m.*)   farm
Baumwolle (*f.*)   cotton
Bayern (*n.*)   Bavaria
Becher (*m.*)   goblet
befehlen   command
befreien   free
beginnen   begin
begleiten   accompany
behalten   contain
bei   at, alongside
beißen   bite
Bekleidtingsgeschäft
   clothing store
bekommen   get, obtain
belegt   filled up (hotels)
Beleuchtung (*f.*)   auto lights
Belgien (*n.*)   Belgium
Benehmen (*n.*)   behavior
Benzin (*n.*)   gas
bequemlich   comfortable
berechtigt   entitled
Bernstein (*m.*)   amber
berühmt   famous
beschädigen   damage
besetzt   busy (telephone)
besonders   especially
besser   better
besteigen   get on (vehicle, ship)
Betrag (*m.*)   amount
Bett (*n.*)   bed
Bier (*n.*)   beer
Biergarten (*m.*)   beer garden

Bierkrug (*m.*)   beer stein
billig   cheap
bin   am
bitten   ask
Blase (*f.*)   blister
Blasmusik (*f.*)   brass-band
   music
blau   blue
bläulich   bluish
Blinddarmentzündung
   appendicitis
blond   blond
Blume (*f.*)   flower
Bluse (*f.*)   blouse
Blut (*n.*)   blood
bluten   bleed
Blutstein (*m.*)   hematite
Blutwurst (*f.*)   blood sausage
Bohne (*f.*)   bean
Boot (*n.*)   boat
Botanischer Garten (*m.*)
   botanical garden
Brandwunde (*f.*)   burn
Brasilien (*n.*)   Brazil
Brat-   fried
Bratpfanne (*f.*)   frying pan
braun   brown
Braunschweig (*n.*)   Brunswick
brechen   break
Bremsen (*pl.*)   brakes
brennen   burn
Brille (*f.*)   eyeglasses
bringen   bring
Brocken (*pl.*)   crumbs
Bronzen (*pl.*)   bronzes
Brosche (*f.*)   brooch
Brot (*n.*)   bread
Bruch (*m.*)   fracture
Brücke (*f.*)   bridge
Brunnen (*m.*)   fountain
Brust (*f.*)   breast
Buch (*n.*)   book
Buchhandlung (*f.*)   bookstore
Büchse (*f.*)   can
Büchsenöffner (*m.*)   can
   opener
Bundesrepublik (*n.*)   Federal
   Republic

Burg (*f.*) fortress, castle
Bürger (*m.*) citizen
Bürste (*f.*) brush
Bus (*m.*) bus
Bushaltestelle (*f.*) bus stop
Büstenhalter (*m.*) brassiere
Butter (*f.*) butter

C

Campingplatz (*m.*) camping site
chemische Reinigung (*f.*) dry cleaning
China (*n.*) China

D

Dame (*f.*) checkers; queen (cards, chess)
Damensalon (*m.*) beauty parlor
Dänemark (*n.*) Denmark
Decke (*f.*) blanket
decken cover
defekt defective
Delikatessengeschäft (*n.*) delicatessen
denn for
Desodorans (*n.*) deodorant
deutsch German
Deutschland (*n.*) Germany
Diabetiker (*m.*) diabetic
Diamant (*m.*) diamond
dick fat
direkt direct
dirigieren conduct
Diskothek (*f.*) discotheque
Dom (*m.*) cathedral
Doppelbett (*n.*) double bed
Doppelzimmer (*n.*) double room
Dose (*f.*) can
Dosis (*f.*) dosage
dreckig dirty
Drogerie (*f.*) drugstore
Drusen (*pl.*) glands

dunkel dark
dutch by, through
Durchfall (*m.*) diarrhea
durchwählen dial direct
Dutzend (*n.*) dozen

E

echt genuine
Ecke (*f.*) corner
Eier (*pl.*) eggs
Eile (*f.*) haste
ein(e) a, an
Einfahrt (*f.*) highway entrance
Eingang (*m.*) entrance
einlösen cash
eins one (number)
einsteigen get into (a vehicle)
Einsteigen! All aboard!
eintreffen arrive
Eintritt (*m.*) admission, entrance
Eis (*n.*) ice, ice cream
Eisenwarenhandlung (*f.*) hardware store
ekelhaft disgusting
elegant elegant
Ellbogen (*m.*) elbow
Ende (*n.*) end
Engel (*m.*) angel
England (*n.*) England
englischsprachig English-speaking
entdecken discover
Ente (*f.*) duck
entschuldigen excuse
entwickeln develop
er he
Erde (*f.*) earth
Erkältung (*f.*) (a) cold
erklären explain
erlaubt allowed
erst first
Erwachsene (*pl.*) adults
erwarten expect
essbar edible
Essbesteck (*n.*) cutlery

essen eat
Essen (*n.*) food
Esszimmer (*n.*) dining room
Etage (*f.*) floor
Europa (*n.*) Europe
ewig eternal
Exemplar (*n.*) copy
exotisch exotic
Express (*m.*) express
extra extra

F

fabelhaft fantastic
Fähre (*f.*) ferry
fahren drive
Fahrer (*m.*) chauffeur
Fahrrad (*n.*) bicycle
fallen fall
fällig due
falsch false
Familie (*f.*) family
fangen catch
Farbe (*f.*) color
Farbspülung (*f.*) color rinse
Farbtabelle (*f.*) color chart
Faser (*f.*) fiber
Fassung (*f.*) frame (eyeglasses)
feiern celebrate
Feile (*f.*) file
fein fine
Feinkost (*f.*) gourmet foods
Feinschmecker (*m.*) gourmet
Feld (*n.*) field
Fernschnellzug (*m.*) express
Ferse (*f.*) heel
fertig finished
Fest (*n.*) festival
Festspiel (*n.*) festival
    performance
feststellen determine
Festung (*f.*) fortress
Fett (*n.*) fat
Feuer (*n.*) fire
Feuerstein (*m.*) flint
Feuerzeug (*n.*) cigarette
    lighter
Fieber (*m.*) fever

Film (*m.*) film
Filter (*m.*) filter
finden find
Finger (*m.*) finger
Fisch (*m.*) fish
Flasche (*f.*) bottle
Fledermaus (*f.*) bat
Fleischer (*m.*) butcher
fliegen fly
fließen flow
Flohmarkt (*m.*) flea market
Flug (*m.*) flight
Flughafen (*m.*) airport
Flugzeug (*n.*) airplane
Form (*f.*) form
Format (*n.*) format
fort away
fortsetzen continue
fragen ask
Franken (*n.*) Franconia
Frankreich (*n.*) France
französisch French
französisches Bett (*n.*)
    double bed
Frauenarzt (*m.*) gynecologist
frei free
Freitag (*m.*) Friday
fremd foreign
Fremdenheim (*n.*) guest
    house
Freund (*m.*) friend
Freundin (*f.*) friend
freundlich friendly
Friedhof (*m.*) cemetery
frieren freeze
frisch fresh
Friseur (*m.*) barber
Frisur (*f.*) hairdo
Frost (*m.*) frost
frösteln be chilled
Frucht (*f.*) fruit
früh early
Frühstück (*n.*) breakfast
Frühstückszimmer (*n.*)
    breakfast room
fühlen feel
führen have in stock, carry,
    lead, guide

Führerschein (*m.*) driver's license
Führung (*f.*) guided tour
füllen fill
Füllung (*f.*) filling
funktionieren (to) function
für for
Fuß (*m.*) foot
Fußball (*m.*) football
Fußpuder (*m.*) foot powder
Futter (*n.*) animal fodder

G

Gabel (*f.*) fork
Gans (*f.*) goose
Garage (*f.*) garage
Garderobe (*f.*) checkroom
Gärten (*pl.*) gardens
Gärtner (*m.*) gardener
geben give
Gebiss (*n.*) dentures
gebrochen broken
Gebühr (*f.*) commission, charge
Gefahr (*f.*) danger
gefährlich dangerous
gefroren frozen
gegen against
Gegend (*f.*) area
gegrillt grilled
gehen go
gekocht boiled
genießen enjoy
genug enough
Gepäck (*n.*) baggage
Gepäckaufbewahrung (*f.*) baggage checkroom
Gerät (*n.*) appliance
gern gladly
Geschäft (*n.*) business
geschäftlich commercial
Geschäftsreise (*f.*) business trip
Geschenk (*n.*) gift
geschlossen closed
Gesicht (*n.*) face
Gesichtsmaske (*f.*) face pack

Gespräch (*n.*) conversation
gesund healthy
Gesundheit (*f.*) health
Getränk (*n.*) drink
Gewohnheit (*f.*) habit
Glaube (*m.*) faith
glauben believe
Glocke (*f.*) bell
glücklich happy
glühen glow
Gnade (*f.*) grace
gnädig gracious
Gold (*n.*) gold
Golfplatz (*pl.*) golf course
Golfschläger (*pl.*) golf clubs
Gott (*m.*) god
Götter (*pl.*) gods
göttlich divine
Graf (*m.*) count (title)
Gräfin (*f.*) countess
Grammatik (*f.*) grammar
Gräte (*f.*) fishbone
grau gray
Grenze (*f.*) frontier
Griechenland (*n.*) Greece
Grippe (*f.*) flu
groß big
Großbritannien (*n.*) Great Britain
größer bigger
grün green
Grünanlagen (*pl.*) formal gardens, park
grünlich greenish
grüßen greet
günstig favorable
Gürtel (*m.*) belt
gut good
Güte (*f.*) goodness

H

Haar (*n.*) hair
Haarspray (*m.*) hair spray
Haartrockner (*m.*) hair dryer
Haarwasser (*n.*) hair tonic
haben have

Hackfleisch (*n.*) chopped meat
Hafenanlagen (*pl.*) docks
Hafenrundfahrt (*f.*) boat tour of the harbor
Haftschalen (*pl.*) contact lenses
halb half
Halbpension (*f.*) half-board
Hälfte (*f.*) (a) half
Halle (*f.*) hall
Hand (*f.*) hand
Handel (*m.*) commerce
handgemalt hand painted
Handgepäck (*n.*) carry-on luggage
handgeschnitzt hand carved
Händler (*m.*) dealer
Handschuhe (*pl.*) gloves
Handspiegel (*m.*) hand mirror
hängen hang
hart hard
hattgekocht hard-boiled
hat has
hatte had
Heftpflaster (*n.*) adhesive tape
Heide (*f.*) heath
heilen heal
heiter cheerful
Heizapparat (*m.*) heater
Heizung (*f.*) heat
Herbst (*m.*) autumn
Herz (*n.*) heart
herzkrank suffering from heart trouble
herzlich cordial
Heuschnupfen (*m.*) hay fever
Himmel (*m.*) heaven
hinten behind
Hitze (*f.*) heat
Hochglanz (*m.*) glossy finish
Hof (*m.*) courtyard
holen get (fetch)
hören hear
Hörnchen (*pl.*) croissants
Hotelpage (*m.*) bellhop

Hubschrauber (*m.*) helicopter
Huhn (*n.*) chicken
Hühneraugenpflaster (*pl.*) corn plasters
Hund (*m.*) dog
Hündin (*f.*) dog (bitch)
husten cough
Hustenbonbons (*pl.*) cough drops
Hut (*m.*) hat

I

immer always

J

jed- every
jeder everyone

K

Kabine (*f.*) cabin
Kaffee (*m.*) coffee
Kaffeehaus (*n.*) coffeehouse
kahl bald
Kaiser (*m.*) emperor
kalt cold
Kalter Aufschnitt (*m.*) cold cuts
Kamera (*f.*) camera
Kamm (*m.*) comb
kämmen comb
Kammermusik (*f.*) chamber music
Kanada (*n.*) Canada
Kanal (*m.*) canal
kann can (be able)
kaputt broken
Karat (*n.*) carat
Karo (*n.*) diamonds (cards)
Karte (*f.*) card
Kartenkunststücke (*pl.*) card tricks
Käse (*m.*) cheese
Kasse (*f.*) cashier's desk

Kassette (*f.*) cassette
kastanienbraun auburn
Kater (*m.*) hangover
Kathedrale (*f.*) cathedral
katholisch Catholic
Katze (*f.*) cat
kauen chew
kaufen buy
Kautabak (*m.*) chewing tobacco
Kegelbahn (*f.*) bowling alley
kegeln bowl
Kekse (*pl.*) cookies
Kerze (*f.*) candle
Kette (*f.*) chain
Kind (*n.*) child
Kino (*n.*) cinema
Kipfel (*pl.*) croissants
Kirche (*f.*) church
Klasse (*f.*) class
klassische Musik (*f.*) classical music
Kleid (*n.*) dress
Kleider (*pl.*) clothes
Kleiderbügel (*pl.*) clothes hangers
Kleidungsstücke (*pl.*) clothes
Kleingeld (*n.*) change
Klimaanlage (*f.*) air conditioner
Kloss (*m.*) dumpling
Kloster (*n.*) abbey, monastery
Knöchel (*m.*) ankle
Knochen (*m.*) bone
Knopf (*m.*) button
Knoten (*m.*) hair bun
Koch (*m.*) cook
kochen to cook
Köchin (*f.*) cook
Kölnisch Wasser (*n.*) cologne
Komfort (*m.*) comfort
Komödie (*f.*) comedy
Konfekt (*n.*) candy
Königin (*f.*) queen
können be able
könnte(n) could
Kontaktlinsen (*pl.*) contact lenses

Konto (*n.*) account
kontrollieren check
Konzert (*n.*) concert
Kopf (*m.*) head
Kopfschmerzen (*pl.*) headache
Körper (*m.*) body
Kosmetiksalon (*m.*) beauty salon
Kosten (*pl.*) expenses
kosten cost
kostenlos free
Krampf (*m.*) cramp
Krankenwagen (*m.*) ambulance
Kreislauf (*m.*) circulation
Kreuz (*n.*) clubs (cards)
Krone (*f.*) crown
Kuchen (*m.*) cake
Kuckucksuhr (*f.*) cuckoo clock
kühl cool
Kunst (*f.*) art
Kunsteisbahn (*f.*) artificial skating rink
Künstler (*m.*) artist
Künstlerviertel (*n.*) artists' quarter
künstlich artificial
Kupfer (*n.*) copper
Kürschner (*m.*) furrier

L

Land (*n.*) country
Läufer (*m.*) bishop (chess)
Lebensgefahr (*f.*) danger
Lebensmittelgeschäft grocery store
lecker delicious
leer empty
leicht easy
Leim (*m.*) glue
Lidschatten (*m.*) eye shadow
Lidstift (*m.*) eyeliner
Liftjunge (*m.*) elevator operator
Locken (*pl.*) curls
Luft (*f.*) air

luftgekühlt   air-conditioned
Lustspiel (*n.*)   comedy

M

Mädchen (*n.*)   girl
Magentabletten (*pl.*)   antacid
Mandeln (*pl.*)   almonds
Manschettenknöpfe (*pl.*)   cuff links
Mantel (*m.*)   coat
Märchen (*n.*)   fairy tale
Marke (*f.*)   brand
Mehl (*n.*)   flour
Metzger (*m.*)   butcher
mit Luftpost (*f.*)   by airmail
Mixer (*m.*)   blender
Möbel (*pl.*)   furniture
munter   cheerful
Mütze (*f.*)   cap

N

nach   after
Nachmittag (*m.*)   afternoon
Nachtisch (*m.*)   dessert
nah   near
noch einmal   once more
Notausgang (*m.*)   emergency exit
Notfall (*m.*)   emergency

O

Obst (*n.*)   fruit
Ohr (*n.*)   ear
Ohrentropfen (*pl.*)   ear drops
Ohrring (*m.*)   earring
Osten (*m.*)   east
Österreich (*n.*)   Austria

P

Panne (*f.*)   mechanical breakdown
passen   fit
Pelze (*pl.*)   furs

Pension (*f.*)   boardinghouse
Pflicht (*f.*)   duty
Ponyfrisur (*f.*)   bangs
Porzellan (*n.*)   china
postlagernd   general delivery
praktisch   convenient
Prost!   Cheers!
prüfen   check
Puppe (*f.*)   doll

R

Radiergummi (*m.*)   eraser
Rahmen (*m.*)   frame
Rasse (*f.*)   breed
raten   advise
Rathaus (*n.*)   city hall
rechnen   calculate
Rechnung (*f.*)   bill
Reformhaus (*n.*)   health-food store
Reich (*n.*)   empire
rein   clean
reinigen   clean
Reinigungscreme (*f.*)   cleansing cream
Reiseführer (*m.*)   guidebook
reparieren   fix
R-Gespräch (*n.*)   collect call
Richtung (*f.*)   direction
Rindfleisch (*n.*)   beef
Rommé (*n.*)   gin rummy
Rücken (*m.*)   back
Rückenschmerzen (*pl.*)   backache
rufen   call

S

Sahne (*f.*)   cream
sammeln   collect
sauber   clean
Schach (*n.*)   chess
schachmatt   checkmate
schaden   damage
Schadenersatz (*m.*)   compensation

schädlich harmful
Schauspieler (*m.*) actor
Schauspielerin (*f.*) actress
Scheck (*m.*) check
Scheine (*pl.*) bills (currency)
scheußlich awful
schick chic (elegant)
Schlafzimmer (*n.*) bedroom
schlagen beat
schlecht bad
schließen close
Schloss (*n.*) castle
Schlosshotel (*n.*) castle hotel
Schlossverkauf (*m.*) final sale
schmutzig dirty
Schnaps (*m.*) spirits, gin
schneiden cut
Schnitzereien (*pl.*) carvings
Schokolade (*f.*) chocolate
schon already
schön beautiful
Schönheit (*f.*) beauty
Schuld (*f.*) guilt
Schüssel (*f.*) bowl
schwarz black
schwer difficult
schwindlig dizzy
Seilbahn (*f.*) cable-car railway
sein be
Sekt (*m.*) champagne
selbst even
Sessel (*m.*) armchair
sich umsehen browse
sind are
Smaragde (*pl.*) emeralds
Speck (*m.*) bacon
Speise (*f.*) food
Speisesaal (*m.*) dining room
Speisewagen (*m.*) dining car
Spiegeleier (*pl.*) fried eggs
Spiel (*n.*) game
Spielkasino (*n.*) gambling casino
Spirituosen (*pl.*) spirits (alcohol)
Spurrillen (*pl.*) grooves (in road)

Stadt (*f.*) city
Stadtmitte (*f.*) city center
Stadtrundfahrt bus tour of the city
Stange (*f.*) carton
starker Verkehr (*m.*) heavy traffic
steigen climb
Steinschlag (*m.*) failing rocks
Stich (*m.*) engraving
Stickereien (*pl.*) embroidered articles
Stiefel (*pl.*) boots
stören disturb
Stuhl (*m.*) chair

T

Tabelle (*f.*) chart
Tag (*m.*) day
tanken get gas
Tankstelle (*f.*) gas station
Tanz (*m.*) dance
tanzen dance
Tanzschuhe (*pl.*) dancing shoes
Tasse (*f.*) cup
Tat (*f.*) deed
tauchen dive
teuer expensive
tief deep
Tier (*n.*) animal
Tochter (*f.*) daughter
Toilette (*f.*) toilet
tragen carry
Traum (*m.*) dream
träumerisch dreamy
trinkbar drinkable
trinken drink
Trinkwasser (*n.*) drinking water
trocken dry
Tropfen (*pl.*) drops
trotz despite
tun do
Tür (*f.*) door
Turnhalle (*f.*) gymnasium
Tüte (*f.*) bag

U

überall everywhere
um around
Umleitung (*f.*) detour
Umschlag (*m.*) envelope
umsteigen change (trains, etc.)
um wieviel Uhr? at what time
unbedingt absolutely
und and
unfall (*m.*) accident
ungefähr approximately
unten down

V

Ventilator (*m.*) fan
Verabredung (*f.*) appointment
Verbandkasten (*m.*) first-aid kit
Verbandzeug (*n.*) bandages
verbinden connect
verboten forbidden
Verein (*m.*) association
Vergaser (*m.*) carburetor
vergessen forget
vergleichen compare
Vergnügungspark (*m.*) amusement park
vergoldet gold plated
vergrößern enlarge
Vergrößerung (*f.*) enlargement
Verhütungsmittel (*n.*) contraceptive
verlangen demand
Verlobungsring (*m.*) engagement ring
Vermögen (*n.*) fortune
verrenkt dislocated
Verspätung (*f.*) delay
Verstärker (*pl.*) amplifiers
verstopft clogged
Verstopfung (*f.*) constipation
verückt crazy

verzeihen forgive
Vogel (*m.*) bird
Volkslieder (*pl.*) folk songs
Volksmusik (*f.*) folk music
Volkstänze (*pl.*) folk dances
voll full
Vollverpflegung (*f.*) full room and board
von by, from
Vorhänge (*pl.*) curtains
Vorsicht (*f.*) caution;
  Vorsicht! Careful!
Vorspeise (*f.*) appetizer
Vorwahlnummer (*f.*) area code

W

wachsen grow
Wagen (*m.*) car
wählen dial, select
wahnsinnig crazy
Wald (*m.*) forest
Warenhaus (*n.*) department store
Wechselkurs (*m.*) exchange (rate of)
wechseln change
weg away
wegwerfbar disposable
weil because
weit far
weiter further
Weltallbürger (*m.*) citizen of the cosmos
Weltbürger (*m.*) citizen of the world
werden become, will
wieder again
Wild (*n.*) (wild) game
Windeln (*pl.*) diapers
Windungen (*pl.*) curves
wird becomes
Woche (*f.*) week
Wohnung (*f.*) apartment
wollen want
Wörterbuch (*n.*) dictionary

Z

zäh tough
zählen count
zahlen pay
Zahnarzt (*m.*) dentist
Zahnermatz (*m.*) false teeth
Zahnfleisch (*n.*) gums
Zahnradbahn (*f.*) cogwheel railroad
zart tender
zeichnen draw
Zeichnung (*f.*) drawing
zeigen show
Zentrum (*n.*) downtown, city center
Zigarette (*f.*) cigarette
Zigarettenspitze (*f.*) cigarette holder
Zigarre (*f.*) cigar
Zigeuner (*m.*) Gypsy
Zimmermädchen (*n.*) chambermaid
Zmorge (*n.*) breakfast (Swiss)
Zoll (*m.*) customs
Zolibeamte (*m.*) customs official
zollfrei duty-free
zornig angry
zu at, closed, to
Zuckerkrankheit (*f.*) diabetes
zumachen close
zurück back
zurückbringen bring back
Zusammenbruch (*m.*) breakdown
zusätzlich extra
zweisprachig bilingual

INDEX

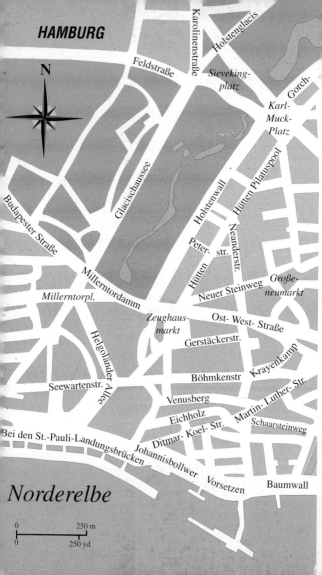